Teaching African American Religions

AMERICAN ACADEMY OF RELIGION

TEACHING RELIGIOUS STUDIES SERIES

SERIES EDITOR
Susan Henking, Hobart and William Smith Colleges

A Publication Series of
The American Academy of Religion
and
Oxford University Press

TEACHING LEVI-STRAUSS
Edited by Hans H. Penner

TEACHING ISLAM
Edited by Brannon M. Wheeler

TEACHING FREUD
Edited by Diane Jonte-Pace

TEACHING DURKHEIM
Edited by Terry F. Godlove, Jr.

TEACHING AFRICAN AMERICAN RELIGIONS
Edited by Carolyn M. Jones and Theodore Louis Trost

AMERICAN ACADEMY OF RELIGION

Teaching African American Religions

EDITED BY

CAROLYN M. JONES

THEODORE LOUIS TROST

OXFORD

UNIVERSITY PRESS

2005

OXFORD
UNIVERSITY PRESS

Oxford University Press, Inc., publishes works that further
Oxford University's objective of excellence
in research, scholarship, and education.

Oxford   New York
Auckland   Cape Town   Dar es Salaam   Hong Kong   Karachi
Kuala Lumpur   Madrid   Melbourne   Mexico City   Nairobi
New Delhi   Shanghai   Taipei   Toronto

With offices in
Argentina   Austria   Brazil   Chile   Czech Republic   France   Greece
Guatemala   Hungary   Italy   Japan   Poland   Portugal   Singapore
South Korea   Switzerland   Thailand   Turkey   Ukraine   Vietnam

Copyright © 2005 by The American Academy of Religion

Published by Oxford University Press, Inc.
198 Madison Avenue, New York, New York 10016

www.oup.com

Oxford is a registered trademark of Oxford University Press

Library of Congress Cataloging-in-Publication Data
Teaching African American religions / edited by Carolyn M. Jones and Theodore Louis Trost.
    p. cm.—(AAR teaching religious studies)
Includes bibliographical references and index.
ISBN-13 978-0-19-516797-9; 978-0-19-516798-6 (pbk.)
ISBN 0-19-516797-X; 0-19-516798-8 (pbk.)
    1. African Americans—Religion—Study and teaching.   I. Jones, Carolyn M.   II. Trost,
Theodore Louis, 1954–   III. Series.
BR563 .N4T389 2005
277.3'0089'96073—dc22   2004020815

9 8 7 6 5 4 3 2 1
Printed in the United States of America
on acid-free paper

Acknowledgments

We would like to offer thanks to the many people whose vision and action made this project possible.

We are grateful to Barbara DeConcini, executive director of the American Academy of Religion (AAR), and to the American Academy of Religion for their support of the teaching workshops of which "Mining the Motherlode of African American Religious Traditions" was a part. Ours was the only workshop that was national in its membership, and Dr. DeConcini and the AAR made that happen. We would also like to thank Edward Gray, director of academic relations for the AAR, who was the liaison for and who so kindly facilitated the first staff meeting in Atlanta. Thanks also to Will Coleman and Caleb, both of whom played a key role in forging a bond among the staff: Emilie Townes, A. G. Miller, Joan Martin, Carolyn Medine, and Will Coleman.

Many, deep, sincere, and heartfelt thanks to Katie G. Cannon, whose vision shaped the workshop, and to Emilie Townes, whose leadership and deep care made it happen.

We would like to thank Susan Henking, editor of the teaching series for the American Academy of Religion for encouraging us to produce the book, and her and Cynthia Read at Oxford University Press for their support (and their patience) during the process.

Our thanks go to Raymond Williams, former director, to Lucinda Huffaker, current director, and to the staff of the Wabash Center for Teaching and Learning in Theology and Religion for funding the grant that has allowed us to produce this book. The Lilly Endowment, Inc., has been our supporter throughout our work, first in its funding of the AAR workshops and then through its continuing relationship with the Wabash Center.

We are grateful to Bernadette McNary-Zak who wrote and rewrote the grant that allowed us to come together and work and to Edwin Aponte for being the "money guy" and a gracious host in our two meetings at Perkins School of Theology, Southern Methodist University.

Many institutions welcomed us warmly, hospitably, and enthusiastically, including Columbia Theological Seminary in Atlanta, Georgia; Union Theological Seminary in New York; and the Perkins School of Theology at Southern Methodist University in Dallas, Texas. Thank you.

Finally, thanks and reverence to the ancestors who clearly wanted us to meet, to work together, and to form and remain community. *Ashe!!*

Contents

Contributors

Edwin David Aponte is Associate Professor of Christianity and Culture at Perkins School of Theology at Southern Methodist University in Dallas, Texas. His research interests include Latino/a religions, African American religions, and North American religious history. He is the coauthor of *Introducing Latino/a Theologies* with Miguel A. De La Torre; together they are also the editors of *A Handbook of Latina/o Theologies*, forthcoming in 2005.

Linda L. Barnes is Assistant Professor at Boston University School of Medicine, where she directs the Boston Healing Landscape Project (an institute for the study of religions, medicines, and healing, with a focus on African Diaspora communities) and teaches medical students, residents, and faculty. A medical anthropologist and scholar of religious studies, she is coeditor, with Susan Sered, of *Religion and Healing in America* (2004) and with Ines Talamantez of *Teaching Religion and Healing* (forthcoming). She is also the author of *Needles, Herbs, Gods, and Ghosts: China, Healing, and the West to 1848* (2005).

Will "Esuyemi" Coleman is cofounder and codirector of the Black Kabbalah Institute, a nonsectarian organization designed to teach and apply principles of the Kabbalah (Hebrew mysticism) for the enrichment of African American spiritual and psychological health. He is also cofounder and CEO/president of the BT Forum, Inc., a theological think tank and corporation of intellectuals focusing on research, writing, and consultation on matters pertaining to African

American religious life. Currently, he is collaborating on a major project called "Black Kabbalah: Darkness and Creation."

Peter R. Gathje is Associate Professor of Religion and Philosophy and Chair of the Religion and Philosophy Department at Christian Brothers University. Dr. Gathje's most recent publication is *A Work of Hospitality: The Open Door Reader* (2002). His current research and teaching interests include religious dimensions of nonviolent social change, Christian ethics, and state violence, particularly the death penalty and war.

Nancy A. Hardesty is Professor of Religion at Clemson University, Clemson, South Carolina. Her most recent book is *Faith Cure: Divine Healing in the Holiness and Pentecostal Movements* (2003). She has published several books on women in American evangelicalism. Her teaching interests include world religions, New Testament, religion in the United States, Christian traditions, and African American religions.

Mary Jane Horton is Assistant Professor of Philosophy/Religious Studies at Cuyahoga Community College, Cleveland, Ohio. She also serves as Program Coordinator for Philosophy, Humanities, and Religious Studies. Her current areas of interest include developing pedagogy to engage students in the study of religion via web-based courses and using community resources for experiential learning.

Carolyn M. Jones is Associate Professor of Religion and African American Studies at the University of Georgia. She has written extensively on Toni Morrison's work, and also on Southern religions and literatures. Her most recent article, coauthored with John Randolph LeBlanc, is "Space/Place and Home: Prefiguring Contemporary Political and Religious Discourse in Albert Camus' *The Plague*" in *Contemporary Political Theory* (2003).

Bernadette McNary-Zak is Assistant Professor of Religious Studies at Rhodes College in Memphis, Tennessee. Her research is centered in early Christianity with a focus on popular and monastic piety in the period of late antiquity. She is also interested in pedagogical issues related to teaching in religious studies.

Stephanie Y. Mitchem is chair of the Department of Religious Studies at the University of Detroit Mercy and teaches classes in African American religions and liberation theologies. She emphasizes the religious lives of black women in her work with womanist theology. In her research, Mitchem explores the rich religious contexts and cultural meanings of African Americans, while critiquing the social injustices structured into American society. She is the author of *Introducing Womanist Theology* (2002) and *Tapping Power: African American Women, Spirituality and Healing* (2004).

Moses N. Moore, Jr., is Associate Professor of American and African American Religious History in the Religious Studies Department at Arizona State University. His research is focused on social and political manifestations of Black religious thought. He is currently completing biographies of Edward W. Blyden and Henry H. Proctor.

Yolanda Y. Smith is Assistant Professor of Christian Education at Yale University Divinity School. Her teaching and research interests include: Christian education in the African American experience, the role of the arts in Christian education, and multicultural approaches to education in the church. She is the author of *Reclaiming the Spirituals: New Possibilities for African American Christian Education* (2004).

Emilie M. Townes is the Carolyn Williams Beaird Professor of Christian Ethics at Union Theological Seminary in New York City. She directed the Mining the Motherlode of African American Religious Life project. She is editor of two essay collections, *A Troubling in My Soul: Womanist Perspectives on Evil and Suffering* (1993) and *Embracing the Spirit: Womanist Perspectives on Hope, Salvation, and Transformation* (1997). She is the author of *In a Blaze of Glory: Womanist Spirituality as Social Witness* (1995); and *Breaking the Fine Rain of Death: African American Health Issues and a Womanist Ethic of Care* (1998). She is currently focusing on two areas of research. The first is the interrelationship between culture and evil. The second is women and health in the African Diaspora with particular attention to Brazil and the United States.

Theodore Louis Trost is Associate Professor in Religious Studies and New College at the University of Alabama, Tuscaloosa. He is the author of *Douglas Horton and the Ecumenical Impulse in American Religious History* (2002). His teaching and research interests lie in the areas of American religious history, popular culture (music and film), and the Bible. He is also the founding member of the musical group called Thaddaeus Quince and the New Originals; their third album is *The Wrest* (2004).

Ralph C. Watkins holds the Doctor of Ministry Degree from Pittsburgh Theological Seminary and a Ph.D. in sociology from the University of Pittsburgh. He is a sociology professor at Augusta State University; he also serves as the Director of Ministry Development at Beulah Grove Baptist Church. Dr. Watkins is an active scholar with a long list of publications and conference presentations. His syndicated column "Black in the City" can be read in over thirty-two black weekly newspapers throughout the Southeast. He is the author of the book *I Ain't Afraid to Speak My Mind* (2003) and a contributor to the book *Noise and Spirit: The Religious Sensibilities of Rap Music* (2003), edited by Anthony Pinn.

Daphne C. Wiggins is the Associate Pastor and Coordinator of Congregational Ministries at Union Baptist Church, in Durham, North Carolina. Most recently she was the Assistant Professor of Congregational Studies at the Divinity School at Duke University. She has also served on the faculty of the Religion Department at Texas Christian University. Her research areas are women clergy, gender and congregations, and the Black Church. She is the author of *Righteous Content: Black Women's Perspectives of Church and Faith* (2004).

Teaching African American Religions

Introduction: Mining the Motherlode of African American Religious Experience

Carolyn M. Jones and Theodore Louis Trost

If you have a gold mine, then there's a point in the gold mine where you have the richest part. And that's called the motherlode. That's . . . the concentrated essence of the spirit of the people . . . black people at our most powerful point in terms of community and peoplehood.

—Bernice Johnson Reagon

Bernice Johnson Reagon's statement from the award-winning *Eyes on the Prize* television series *locates* this collection of essays, a collection that emerged from a teaching workshop called "Mining the Motherlode of African American Religious Experience" and cosponsored by the American Academy of Religion and the Lilly Endowment.[1] The image of the motherlode suggests a deep and sustaining vein of power, of Africanism, beneath the African American religious surface. This rich vein nurtures African American life. It includes more than the readily recognizable retentions from the African past, though such retentions make up a part of the resource. The "motherlode," in a more complex mode, points to a way of being—for the writers in this volume, a "religious" way: one that resonates at the depths of New World African Diaspora experience.

This notion of "motherlode" rehabilitates and reappropriates images of landscape, location, and space. The landscape of the Americas has always been an imagined space. While that landscape became a colonized place, the African presence in the landscape influenced its transformation into place.[2] The often unauthorized modes of being, the indigenous orientation that Africans brought with them, came to expression in this new place (under masks, in secret, and in transgressive modulations) as dispossessed Africans created their identities as African Americans.

African Americans are exiles, as Edward Said constructs that term: citizens of two homes—doubly located, with double consciousness.[3] Mining the motherlode comes to mean, therefore, paying honor to the two homes, to two places of origin: seeing the links between them and bridging the gaps that obscure the links. Such an activity involves two key themes of this volume: memory and history. Our mining is not meant to violate the motherlode, or to strip it of resources, but to *mind* what it teaches us. This is to claim a particular kind of attention and relation to the motherlode that is life-affirming, centered, reciprocal, and spirit-filled. Our mining is a form of resistance. We argue that African American experience is not at all a matter of dislocation and marginality. Africans in the New World have always been meaning makers. Simply put, the master narrative is wrong when it claims that African Americans have no motherlode; that they have no place or practices of their own; that "the African" suffered complete erasure in the crucible of slavery.

Our work is to carry this interpretation into scholarship and, in this instance, into the classroom. The classroom is located on a border, in a contact zone. If African American identity involves double consciousness, the classroom involves multiple modes of being. Such a space requires renewed attention to methodology in teaching and for innovative thought about the meaning of the teacher and the student as agents in the classroom space in this postmodern and postcolonial world. Both the classroom and our methods, therefore, are explorative—sometimes bold and sometimes tentative. We hope that these essays not only will suggest approaches to teaching African American religions specifically but also will serve as a "for instance" for teachers of religions in general. We realize that those reading the volume will search its particular parts for their needs, but there is, we want to claim, a wholeness here, wholeness that has emerged from several years of ongoing reflection and conversation in our community of teacher-learner-scholars. What we hope to demonstrate here is a way of educating students through the lens of the African American experience.

African American religions entered into the academy later than other subjects in the discipline of religious studies. Some of the important scholars of African American religions writing today (indeed, some of the voices in this volume) are groundbreakers who are still laying the foundation and marking out the boundaries of the subject. As they do so, they engage new borders of scholarship and nuances of meaning. We attempt here the same kind of work. Borders and zones, therefore, are a consistent metaphor in this volume.

The notion of borders emerged first in Latino studies, in the work of Gloria

Anzaldua.[4] The concept began to inform postmodern and postcolonial studies and entered the theory of education through such thinkers as Henry Giroux. The notion of borders as spaces of interaction, as contact zones, is articulated in the work of Mary Louise Pratt.[5] Both of these authors are embraced and engaged in 'part I, "The Classroom as Contact Zone." We see the contact zone's complexity at work as well in the work of part II, "Challenges to the Textual Canon and the Regnant History," which infuses the "accepted" histories and other content we teach with the "discredited" knowledge of experiencing subjects. The contact zone is expressly evident in the teaching-oriented essays of part III, "Decoding and other Modes of Analysis." Will Coleman's performative piece on "tribal talk" provides the transition to the third, more praxis-oriented, part of the work, *enacting*, as it were, the classroom as contact zone. Characteristic of the emphases in the last section is Ralph Watkins's reflection upon the process of turning the classroom into a contact zone, alive with imagined and forgotten pasts.

Contact and conflict are, therefore, important issues to consider when approaching the work we do here. The borders between racial and ethnic persons (between, as it is usually constructed in the United States, black and white), between students and professors, between scholars and their institutions, and between scholars, institutions, and society are all present in the study of African American religions and, therefore, in these discussions. These are difficult and explosive sites. These borders are, in one sense, in "place," as Michel de Certeau defines place: sites of already determined definitions. As de Certeau suggests: "The law of 'proper' rules in the place; the elements taken into consideration are beside one another, each situated in its own 'proper' and distinct location, a location it defines."[6] Place, therefore, suggests that which is fixed in terms of institution and order. As teachers, we are bound to place, as such. We are located in institutions with their own senses of rightness, and we are bounded by disciplinary constraints and by what is recognized as "religion." There are "facts" that we want our students to know. In short, we want to do justice to a field of study. The necessity to teach "in place" is one we honor.

In teaching African American religions, however, we face the problem of "space." African American religions engage in syncretism and, thereby, challenge accepted definitions of traditions. As such, they create spaces

> composed of intersections of mobile elements. . . . Space occurs as the effect produced by the operations that orient it, situate it, temporize it, and make it function in a polyvalent unity of conflictual programs or contractual proximities.[7]

Spaces are not fixed and defined but are zones of interaction—thus, our use of the term *contact zones*. There are a variety of such zones that overlap in the practice of African American religion, and some are more volatile than others.

We, therefore, cannot focus on the Black Church tradition, for example, as the sole locus of African American religious experience; moreover, when we do focus on that experience, we must recognize and be just to its complexity. The essays locate African American religions in many contested spaces, within traditions and at the meeting places of traditions, but also outside traditions, in unexpected places—particularly in art. Indeed, story is one significant element of these essays. In these areas of contact, conflict, and, sometimes, confluence, three issues emerge, for us, as significant: authority and authenticity; essentialism and the tools necessary for teaching; and what it means to teach for transformation, which returns us to the problem of authenticity.

Throughout the essays, the question of who has the "right" to think and to speak about African American religions underlies our discussion. The issue is in the foreground in the essay of Nancy Hardesty, who puts forward most strongly the question of who has the educational background, the capacity, and the correct race—in short, the authentic voice—to teach a course in African American religions. Hardesty asks: What credentials, both academic and personal, count?

Such a question makes us face the issue of essentialism. The challenge in teaching African American religions is to avoid creating an exotic "other" that can be understood in only specific ways. We all recognize that in teaching religions we essentialize; the Christianity or Islam or Buddhism that we present in the classroom is, generally speaking, an overly structured and sanitized version of the religion. We resist such "neatness" in these essays. One feature of our community is that, as these essays were coming together, many of us were in transitions. We were dealing with familiar and with new classrooms simultaneously. This matter is confronted, in particular, in the essays by Yolanda Smith, Bernadette McNary-Zak, and Daphne Wiggins. What worked in one place, these writers found, did not work in another, both methodologically and in terms of content. Our own transitions suggested to us that we cannot "finish" the subject matter and the methodology for teaching the African American religious experience. It is ever-evolving, as are we.

The subject itself—and indeed, we would argue, teaching in the twenty-first-century classroom—requires, therefore, a larger "toolkit." Such a toolkit must include interdisciplinary and perhaps multidisciplinary approaches. It must also emphasize the material: the body; artifacts; movement. The work of Yolanda Smith, Bernadette McNary-Zack, and Ralph Watkins suggests this broad approach. The "banking" method of teaching and learning may give students the necessary "facts," but we ask for more. The reader will find in the essays of Moses Moore, Peter Gathje, and Nancy Hardesty, for example, critical attention devoted to theoretical models and the contents of particular texts. Doing justice to the "facts," however, is one part of our larger goal: to teach, as we hope to, for transformation.

Before we turn to transformation, let us say here that our orientation means that, while we discuss a variety of approaches to and contents of African American religious experiences, we in no way promise "coverage." That is to say, there is no chapter on "The Nation of Islam" or "African American Pentecostals"—though the essays by Carolyn Jones and Ralph Watkins, among others, and some of Will Coleman's improvisations touch upon these matters. This volume is less a comprehensive survey of identifiable "topics" and more a concentrated meditation on the moment of exchange in the classroom, the teaching and learning moment. It is our hope and our conviction that these "examples" are applicable to a wide variety of contents and contexts. To be sure, we suggest content, resources, and approaches, but we want to suggest, as well, that the methods by which one might incorporate these materials will be improvisational, situation-dependent, and that mere transplantation will not produce a particular result.

Facing this complexity, that of our and our readers' orientations, lets us turn to the question of teaching for transformation. This issue of transformation is a tricky one. It poses the questions: What do we think our students are now? What do we want them to become? And, who are we that we think we can or should change them? In other words, we have to ask: "transformation into what and for what end?" James A. Banks argues that

> transformative teaching and learning is characterized by a curriculum organized around powerful ideas, highly interactive teaching strategies, active student involvement, and activities that require students to participate in personal, social and civic actions to make their classrooms, schools, and communities more . . . just.[8]

This work is done in context and in community. These essays feature a variety of contexts in varied communities. Our students are not "one thing," and the authors work hard not to essentialize them. From Mary Jane Horton's location in a community college in the North to Stephanie Mitchem's and Peter Gathje's locations in schools affiliated with particular religious traditions, to Yolanda Smith's and Edwin Aponte's locations in the seminary, to Bernadette McNary-Zak's location in a liberal arts college, to Ted Trost's, Moses Moore's, and Carolyn M. Jones's locations in large public universities (with Trost and Jones in the South and Moore in the West), our educational contexts are extremely diverse.

Our multiple locations, we hope, will lead our readers to see that teaching approaches must be tailored to the particularities of the students in our classrooms. We face diversity in each class we teach, in relation to age, experience, race and ethnicity, and gender. Therefore, our essays offer and open a variety of approaches and possibilities, such as Linda Barnes's work in a hospital setting on healing or Edwin Aponte's use of Latino theologies to look at African

American religions or Stephanie Mitchem's program to initiate ethnic racial students into the power relationships of the university and to develop home-grown intellectuals.

This reality, that of the contact zone and of the need to meet it creatively yet soundly, returns us to the issue of authenticity. As Charles Taylor has described it in *The Ethics of Authenticity* and in *Varieties of Religion Today: William James Revisited,* our age reveres the construct of the Enlightenment-Romantic individual.[9] Taylor asks how we can move from selves centered on the ideal of self-fulfillment to what we might call a more communally responsible notion of self.[10]

The responsible self is one who can understand, as Taylor puts it, that the *manner* of my action (my orientation to the original expressive self) does not necessitate that the *matter* of my action be totally self-referential.[11] We can look to and for something beyond the self, can see ourselves as and act as part of a larger order.[12] The question in teaching for transformation is not how can we replicate ourselves in our students like Austin Powers's "Mini-Me," but how can we harness the creative energy of our students and direct it. It is the question of how education can move all of us beyond an isolated sense of self and a stultifying sense of fragmentation (a sense that individuals can have no effect) and break the sense that we are isolated individuals in a lonely crowd. We ask: how can we educate toward the realization that freedom is not an impossibility?[13]

Our essays offer a variety of responses. The differences meet in one concern: that we empower our students to become self-motivated learners and, thereby, thoughtful and effective ethical agents. The transformation we seek is not one of mere tolerance for diversity. Rather, we hope that in this increasingly complex world our students will be immersed consciously in an experience of difference in our classrooms; and we hope that the benefits of this experience will move beyond that classroom. Their critical engagement in this particular, bounded (safe and even loving) contact zone can generate a sense that our identities are not atomistic but relational—and that (as Edwin Aponte and other authors suggest) they always have been. Such recognition generates agency in the students' own learning processes and opens the possibility of becoming lifelong learners. The teacher, in such a situation, is authority. That we do not deny. We are masters of the facts. But the teacher is also a loving guide. So we want students to develop their original selves within safe, but fluid, boundaries and take those selves into the world.

African American religions have always represented another "way": the way out of no way, as Daphne Wiggins shows us. Charles Taylor points to the adversarial nature of our culture, an orientation that undercuts compromise, and to the fragmenting nature of advocacy politics that makes issues that require sacrifice difficult to address.[14] He points to a contemporary inability to identify with community and to generate effective action. African American identity, born in a crucible that was a terrible contact zone, nevertheless improvised a mode of being that (while we recognize the unrecognized and unvoiced sufferings of the silent and the devastation of those who could not make it, who were murdered, lost, and forgotten) was more than mere survival. It was a balance of the exceptional individual finding the necessarily communal so all could be active in achieving the goal of freedom. African American religion has played a large role in that process. Like all forms of religion, it has done damage through compromise and control. But it also (and, we might argue, more often) has offered a model for dignity, thriving, transformation, and change, for individuality and community.

It is that energy for change, that hope—indeed that power—that we want to bring to the classroom. We hope the reader gets a sense of it in our work together. This work takes place in an environment of learning that is complex. It includes other colleagues and our students; the classroom and the institution; the person and the world. This book is for those who remain students, for the life-long learners interested in investigating and applying pedagogical processes that make us smarter and wiser and that open us to the world. This is a book by students of African American religion who are, at the same time, teachers of it, and we hope our readers are—or become—the same.

NOTES

1. Bernice Johnson Reagon, interviewed in "No Easy Walk (1961–1963)," in *Eyes on the Prize*, narrated by Julian Bond, written by Steve Fayer, and directed by Henry Hampton, 1987; VHS Blackside Productions and Pacific Arts Video, 1992.

2. Michel de Certeau, *Practice of Everyday Life* (Berkeley: University of California Press, 1988).

3. For example, at the end of *Culture and Imperialism* (New York: Vintage Books, 1994), 336: "No one today is purely one thing." Said goes on to argue that such a double or multiple location calls for a new kind of thought: one that is difficult, concrete, sympathetic, and contrapuntal.

4. Gloria Anzaldua, *Borderlands/LaFrontera: The New Mestiza* (California: Aunt Lute Books, 1999).

5. Mary Louise Pratt, *Imperial Eyes: Travel Writing and Transculturation* (New York: Routledge, 1992).

6. de Certeau, *Practice of Everyday Life*, 117.

7. Ibid.

8. James A. Banks, "The Historical Reconstruction of Knowledge about Race: Implications for Transformative Teaching," *Educational Researcher* 24 (March 1995): 22.

9. Charles Taylor, *The Ethics of Authenticity* (Cambridge: Harvard University Press, 1991), and Charles Taylor, *Varieties of Religion Today: William James Revisited* (Cambridge: Harvard University Press, 2004).

10. Taylor, *Ethics of Authenticity*, 60.

11. Ibid., 81.

12. Ibid., 84.

13. Ibid., 110, 99. Taylor, *Varieties*, 88.

14. Ibid., 114, 116.

PART I

The Classroom as Contact Zone

I

Teaching in the Contact Zone: The African American Religions Course in the Large Public University

Carolyn M. Jones

Teaching African American Religion in a large (32,000–35,000 student) public university presents specific challenges. At the University of Georgia, the African American Religion course is one option for fulfilling the diversity requirement of the Franklin College of Arts and Sciences. In teaching this course, I have found the usual dis-ease when race is a focus in the South. This discomfort manifests itself as anger, confusion, and indifference. Anger and confusion are easier to address than indifference, which is my real enemy.

The classroom, in a course like African American Religion, is what Mary Louise Pratt calls a contact zone.[1] In such a space, we encounter those who have been "other," but we also encounter what has been made in such a space: culture itself and our own presuppositions, understandings, and misunderstandings about culture. To examine the problematics of the contact zone, I will first describe the African American Religion course as I most recently taught it. Second, I will look at the issues involved when a classroom becomes a contact zone. My way of working through those issues and tensions is to employ the methods of my discipline, Arts, Literature, and Religion. A focus on art as both religious and political lets me present freedom as a matter of style. That idea centers my teaching of Islam in America. In the third section, I will discuss my use of David Remnick's biography of Muhammed Ali, *King of the World*, and of America in the Civil Rights era as a vehicle for approaching

the significance of the Nation of Islam. Finally, building on the spiritual journey of Muhammed Ali, I want to turn to the central issue—for me—in teaching religion, whether it is African American Religion or not: transformation.

Description and Focus of the Course

I focus the course in African American Religion on autobiography and biography. The historical text is Gayraud S. Wilmore's *Black Religion and Black
Radicalism: An Interpretation of the Religious History of African Americans*.[2] We
read: Frederick Douglass's *Narrative*[3] to study slavery and the classical slave
narrative; Pauli Murray's *The Autobiography of a Black Activist, Feminist, Lawyer,
Priest, and Poet*[4] to look at Christian spiritual autobiography; Karen McCarthy
Brown's *Mama Lola*[5] to conclude the discussion of African traditional religion
(and, specifically, African American women and religion); David Remnick's
biography of Muhammed Ali, *King of the World*[6] to examine the Nation of Islam
(and constructions of black masculinity); and "The Life of Omar Ibn Said"[7]
from *The Multilingual Anthology of American Literature*, to revisit the slave narrative and to look at traditional Islam in America. We also read Martin Luther
King's "My Pilgrimage to Nonviolence," from *Stride Toward Freedom*.[8] In addition, we listen to music: spirituals, gospel, blues, and, provided by the students, rap and hiphop.

My questions, given that my area of specialty is Arts, Literature, and Religion, are two. First, how have African Americans utilized and transformed
the traditions they brought with them and those they encountered in order to
articulate identity, both individual and communal? And second, how does artistic expression—particularly in narrative and music—play a role in this transformation? To take art seriously, I contend, lets any person participate in how
African American peoples work subversively within culture, how African
Americans change existing forms and create new forms to express an identity
that embraces freedom.

I require a variety of graded assignments. Variety is key for this course. It
meets a diversity requirement and attracts many different kinds of students.
The numerous graded assignments allow me to assess effectively the diversity
of students—from athletes to religion majors—in the class. I give two examinations, and the students have the option either to write a five-page paper (on
either *Mama Lola* or *King of the World*) or to give a class presentation. The paper
option developed because of the too-large size of the class and because doing
a presentation frightened many students, particularly the white students—
though many later gave presentations.

Unspoken fears filled the first days. Indeed, on the first day of class one
of my best students—an older white male who is a religion major—said to me
on his way out of class, that he would "*never* speak in this class."

Classroom as Contact Zone

My student's reaction—though he ended up speaking a lot and thoughtfully—defined the tensions in the classroom. The "contact zone" is the situation created by colonialism and slavery and "their aftermaths as they are lived out across the globe today."[9] Contact zones are "social spaces where disparate cultures meet, clash and grapple with each other, often in highly symmetrical relations of domination and subordination"; they are the spaces "in which peoples geographically and historically separated come into contact with each other and establish ongoing relations, usually involving conditions of coercion, racial inequality, and intractable conflict."[10] In the contact zone, relationship and conflict create—I would argue, an unrecognized and, though unconsciously lived out and consciously resisted—hybridity. This interface leads to a change in mind and in culture, as improvisation becomes part of outright resistance as well as masking. Pratt's emphasis on the interactive and improvisational dimensions of encounter suggests that the postcolonial and postslavery world is a shared culture.

Ashis Nandy, in *The Intimate Enemy*, further articulates the notion that colonialism is a shared culture and also a psychological state. First, it includes codes that both the rulers and the ruled can share. The main function of these codes is to alter the original cultural priorities on both sides and bring to the center of the colonial culture already existing subcultures previously recessive or subordinate in the two confronting cultures. Second, the culture of colonialism presumes a particular style of managing dissent. As Nandy puts it, "particularly strong is the inner resistance to recognizing the ultimate violence which colonialism does to its victims, namely that it creates a culture in which the ruled are constantly tempted to fight their rulers within the psychological limits set by the latter."[11] The university, which is (ideally though rarely actually) a microcosm of the larger society and which, therefore, operates under its terms, becomes, as Henry Giroux puts it, a "terrain of contestation."[12] As Stephanie Mitchem observes in "Border Disputes," utilizing Giroux's notions of borders as the sites of this contest, we, as teachers, both articulate the meaning of and lead students to and across borders. One of my goals is to reveal the intimate levels on which contact/contest occur at these borders and to offer alternative modalities for articulating dissent. If it works, by the end of the course we are a cooperative community, not a competitive and hostile group of individuals.

So much is hidden in America, perhaps particularly in the South—out of fear and under politeness. These habits of concealment have a cost. To conceal the true meaning of the "other" who is part of the self is to conceal from the self an "inner primordial experience and a definition of the human mode of being which includes richness and variety."[13] The modes by which masks are momentarily lifted—in sports and in entertainment, primarily—may actually remask what is deeply at stake in human interactions: what attitudes are deeply held and almost unshakeable in us as we go about interacting with each other daily. These preconceptions, ideas, fears, and "unspeakable things unspoken," to quote Toni Morrison, come forward when we are forced to speak, to discuss situations of colonialism, issues of race and gender, and politics in the charged location in the classroom.

Whether they know it or not—and the aim of the course for me is that they come to know it—the students are practicing habits of concealment even as they are working through the history, emotions, structures, and ideologies of the past in order to begin to work out a future. Georgia is uniquely situated in this regard. Founded as a slave-free colony, the settling population quickly believed that it could not survive and thrive without slave labor, and slavery was introduced. Georgia was and is a center for African American life and thought. Atlanta, after emancipation, became the face of the New South, and in Atlanta, during Reconstruction, Booker T. Washington, at the Atlanta Exposition, and W.E.B. DuBois articulated solutions to the "Negro problem." Georgia has the sad distinction of being the state in which the most people were lynched. It is also the state from which came Martin Luther King, Jr. (My students knew very little about him. Many white students view him as either an agitator or as a hero only for black people, and the African American students, many of whom describe themselves as "militant," know nothing about the complexities of nonviolent resistance and come to class with a view of King as passive.) Atlanta was one center of the modern civil rights movement and, now, is home to a diverse population and to a variety of religious communities and is governed largely by African Americans. For example, the current and former mayors are African American, as are many of the key city officials. All this, compounded by Atlanta's definition as the New New South, "The City Too Busy To Hate," inviting great diversity, and by Atlanta's contentious location in relation to white, rural Georgia, my students live out daily and unconsciously.

What they take for granted is: first, a dominance of whiteness on campus and in their everyday lives, actually and ideologically, and, second, a Christian—largely Protestant—view of the world. Both contribute to classroom dynamics, which, as Lynn Weber Cannon rightly points out, are "structured by inequalities of power among the participants."[14] Given these inequalities, there are hot spots everywhere, and systemic problems are the most difficult to address because most of my postmodern students view their positions in the world in very individual ways. When they acknowledge the workings of systems and their own participation in them, they see systems either as sources of conspiracy—an "X Files" world—or as benign.

How, then, does one begin to negotiate this contact zone? Cannon argues that a positive outcome in the classroom is most likely to be achieved when "(1) people of similar statuses (2) work together toward a shared goal (3) for collective gain (4) with institutional support."[15] I would add, with Giroux, that the classroom is also a place that produces knowledge—deciding what knowledge is of most worth and, with that decision, presupposing and presenting a vision of the future, setting a direction and organizing student energy toward that moral vision.[16] As Giroux argues, a *transformative* (a term to which I will return) pedagogy has particular goals:

> Such a pedagogy transcends the dichotomy of elite and popular culture by defining itself through a project of educating students to feel compassion for the suffering of others, to engage in a continual analysis of their own conditions of existence, to construct loyalties that engage the meaning and importance of public life, and to believe that they can make a difference, that they can act from a position of collective strength to alter existing configurations of power. Such a pedagogy is predicated on a notion of learned hope, forged amidst the realization of risks, and steeped in a commitment to transforming public culture and life: it stresses the historical and transformative in its practice.[17]

This is my ideal vision. How do I—the footsoldier in a sometimes wavering institutional support for diversity and one who does not even pretend that she, as a black woman, comes to this material value neutral—bring about the conditions to make it so?

I am not an openly confrontational, Socratic teacher. My method is, rather, one of community building. I begin, unlike Cannon, with the recognition that power is uneven in our culture and in the classroom—and that it will remain so. I offer a space of hospitality, as Jacques Derrida has begun to articulate hospitality. As host, I have final power, but my goal is to welcome, make comfortable, and empower students at the safe space of my table, within my own, consciously recognized, exercise of power.[18] Acknowledging my power, I equalize status, as much as I can, in the classroom. This means that we move toward a spirit of negotiation that allows each voice to have validity—particularly within situations of conflict. We do have, whether we like it or not, an already agreed-on language. It is a language of Western democracy in which we participate, a language of citizenship, one that includes such terms as "freedom" and "equality." I articulate early and often that the African American experience has been, in part, about seeking full participation in these structures, even as African American understandings of these structures change them.

We also have a common language of religion that must be as open to critique as the language of democracy because African Americans did not accept wholesale what they were thrust into. In the South, this language is the Protestant ethic, though my classroom will include a few Jewish, Catholic, and Muslim students as well. Making a critique of religion is harder for students than making one of American politics. When we can agree upon the terms of critique, discourse begins. That agreement to disagree, the process of questioning and reforming deeply held beliefs, is ongoing, but at about one month into the course, we can question formulations like: "Suffering is always positive because it leads to a better afterlife; therefore, passive and silent endurance is a positive virtue for oppressed peoples." In the future, I would like to be more conscious and intentional about articulating a ground for conversation, but I—partly, anyway—want the students to develop their own ground. That comes, to some degree, from letting myself become a kind of target, by startling students, making them angry, and provoking them (usually unintentionally) with my ideas.

What this process does is decenter and recenter—or, in my Religion and Literature sense, destory and restory.[19] This is a ritual process, and I explain this to the class. Students come to the class with many emotions and opinions. The Euro-American students are often fearful and resentful. The African American students, in the majority for one of the few times in their college careers, are delighted. The choice of seats, in my last class, suggested this. The Euro-American students tended to sit at the edges and toward the back; the African American students occupied the center and the front. The experience is very different for these two groups.

As Llyn De Danaan suggests in "Center to Margin: Dynamics in a Global Classroom," Euro-American students are used to being subject.[20] They are used to looking at the "other" as object, from a position of privilege—with, as Pratt puts it, "imperial eyes [that] passively look out and possess."[21] They are uncomfortable with studying what they think does not involve them. A good example is an experience I had in a Religion and Literature course in which we studied Toni Morrison's *Song of Solomon*. One day when I asked a question about what makes Pilate, a central female character in the novel, distinct, one student said, irritably, "That damned earring." We had to have a conversation, of course, about appropriate language and respect, but the issue was deeper. Morrison's voice does not put white people in the forefront—or even *in* most of her works—in any way. The student felt excluded, and she did not see what this book "had to do with her."

Euro-American students resist this kind of disorientation, this loss of discursive control of the center. They respond in many ways. They may act out. One particularly effective (and annoying) strategy is to see everything as funny. This response makes sense, given our Fox and Warner Brothers culture. We are used to seeing black people as funny. They may also pity the "other."[22] Some claim themselves as victim—they may either feel blamed or they may overidentify—or as oppressed. One of my most difficult tasks, for example, is to keep the discussion of Du Bois and the double consciousness focused on black people in late nineteenth-century/early twentieth-century America. All my students want to claim and thereby universalize the double consciousness, and one student became more and more angry when I would not let her do so. While it may be ultimately true that all modern people have a double consciousness, to start from that vantage point undercuts looking at this particular historical moment for black people who were under the stress of a failed Reconstruction. According to Da Danaan, students employ other strategies. They may discount what they hear both from the professor and from other students or go outside the structure of the classroom and complain to departmental heads and deans.[23] They complain of ambiguity, seek "closure," and wish to redefine the agenda.[24] Lynn Cannon argues that, in the classroom, the privileged often try to dominate the discussion.[25] My experience is that they sometimes dominate by silence, by refusing to participate.

African American students also feel disoriented. From the early sense of being the center—believing, as one student told me, "I know all this"—they realize that they do not know this material as well as they thought, if at all. Some students want to be the authoritative voice; others desire simply to take the class. A different kind of acting out may occur, one that is also about exercising power: responding derisively or critically to white students when they do venture to speak, for example.

This leads as well to anger—from all. I do have some rules about anger: No name-calling or abuse, no yelling and belittling. Terms must be clarified, not just flung out as "truth." They can be tough with each other—and they are—but they must be fair. Finally, after years of teaching, I have decided to let the anger—when appropriately expressed—come out, to hear it and acknowledge it, not try to stop it, though it still upsets me and can unsettle a class. I try to stress that anger is valid, that it is perhaps the starting-point of change, but not good enough as a final emotion and position for an intellectual.

What I try to do—and I admit that I am a teacher who stumbles and struggles with every class—is to help them to read the world as "the other" in order to get what Giroux calls "a view from elsewhere."[26] The common ground for my students is religion. Religion is our subject, but a definition of religion that many students have not considered. I focus on African American religion not as experience of God in church but as multifaceted/faced social force for resistance, change, and identity and community formation and solidarity. Most of my students are Christian, usually Baptist, Pentecostal, or Methodist. Their definition of religion is extremely individual. It involves their personal relationship with Christ who saves them. Almost all of them are startled by African traditional religions and the Nation of Islam, which are the foci of the course along with Christianity.

I link religion to social construction to defamiliarize it. I try to complicate the recitation of the horrors of the slave trade and slavery by discussing the world it made—what Charles H. Long calls the new *arche*, initiated in colonialism.[27] With colonialism, new possibilities of thought were opened in the mind; new modes of thinking about the body developed; and new economic structures opened up the world. Long, using Marx, argues that in commercial exchange, we represent ourselves by objects, an idea with which my cell phone–toting, new car–driving, stylishly dressed students are familiar. The object, I suggest, becomes not only the contractual but also the spiritual. The symbol of exchange takes the place of contact between real human beings. Acknowledging this, I argue, we come to understand the language of the spirit in new ways. Conversion becomes a term of transaction as well as one of religious change. The new *arche* "emphasizes the notion of progress; [translates] the meaning of novelty and otherness into the calculus of color."[28]

In commercial exchange as in ritual, values are set. Religious change comes about as a result of the conquests and of slavery and as a result of resistance to both. What also developed were ways of masking on both sides—a reality we must acknowledge—as in the case of, for example, African traditional religions. For example, Long argues, in "Perspectives for a Study of African-American Religion in the United States," that biblical imagery plays a role in African American representation, but, he continues, "to move from this fact to any simplistic notion of blacks as slaves or former slaves converted to Christianity would, I think, miss several important religious meanings. The Biblical imagery was used because it was at hand; it was adapted to and invested with the experience of the slave."[29] The adoption and adapting of the metaphors at hand mask how the conquered retain and perpetuate their beliefs while practicing them under other guises. This idea is difficult for students who are devout. When we watched, for example, *Carnival of the Spirit,* one of my devout black students wrote on his question card that the priestess interviewed was clearly misguided and that he would pray for her soul.

On all levels, then, I am confronting self- and community definition, asking what is of value and what/where is freedom. For African Americans and others who were the objects of exchange indicating value and who lost land and self-definition, the questions of freedom and value are enhanced. How does one who is objectified gain value in this new *arche,* both in the self and in the "majority" culture?

One answer—my answer—has been art, and art is, most of the time, my way to my students, and it defines transformation for me. Art, particularly music, is one mode in which black people dominate in our culture, and all my students accept that, to greater or lesser degrees. Art is the one act that students are willing not only to participate in but also to try to mimic. To repeat, to copy, as John Randolph LeBlanc and I argue in an unpublished essay, "Space/Place and Home: Political and Religious Discourse in Albert Camus's *The Plague,*" is a way to come to know:

> In religion—for example, in the repetition of word and action in liturgy—and in politics—for example, in the repetition of word and action in the taking of oaths or in various other forms of political

participation—we often narrate and enact what we do not fully understand. Doing so, we come, gradually, to a deeper understanding of identity and of community.

Art, therefore, becomes our meeting place. Once I introduce the spirituals, the volunteers for presentations come, hesitantly, forward. I play them spirituals, blues, and jazz; they play for me gospel (traditional and modern), rap, and hiphop. I let them define what this music means in the terms of the course. Gradually, they come to see, as Paul Gilroy argues in *The Black Atlantic*, that slaves, whose lives were rigidly disciplined, were often allowed artistic expression, within limits; therefore, we cannot and should not think of African American art apart from African American political action.[30] The artistic was one space in which black people were able to transform their present realities and to create "*an-other* reality," one, Charles Long insists, that is on the level of the "religious consciousness"[31] and that is what I emphasize. This lets them (re)turn to the autobiographies and biographies in a different way, to see them as art, as a process of self-fashioning, within a culture that has particular historical, political, and social limitations and implications.

The notion of the self as a work of art is the transition to my presentation of the Nation of Islam. For that section, we focus on the figure of Muhammed Ali and his artistic self-fashioning through the combination of sports, a major motif of African America life, and religion.

Nation of Islam: Muhammed Ali, Spiritual Journey, and the Constructions of African American Masculinity

David Remnick's *King of the World: Muhammed Ali and the Rise of an American Hero*, offers a way to look at the intersection of politics, society, history, and art in the life of one man practicing African American Islam in the 1940s–1960s civil rights era in America. We begin the discussion of the Nation of Islam with a discussion of Islam in the slave population of America, using, for example, Albert J. Raboteau's *Slave Religion: The "Invisible Institution" in the Antebellum South*.[32] Raboteau and others remind us that slaves who were Muslims presented a particular modality to the slave system. They were often literate, able to read and to write a language of which their owners had no knowledge. This unique situation explains what we see, for example, in the slave narrative of Omar Ibn Said, who, at his master's request, makes an apologetic for slavery but who, at the same time, makes a subversive criticism of his owners through his citation of the Koran, affirming the power of Allah over any human master.[33]

Having established the presence of Islam in the slave population, we begin the discussion of the Nation of Islam with Hans A. Baer and Merrill Singer's description of "messianic-nationalist sects" *in African American Religion in the Twentieth Century: Varieties of Protest and Accommodation.*[34] That text allows us to make a distinction between "traditional" Islam and Elijah Muhammed's Nation of Islam. We, next, turn to Ali. Remnick's Pulitzer Prize–winning biography and social history functions in the class in many ways. It is a beautifully written history of the origins and concerns of the modern civil rights era and of the origin and place of the Nation of Islam in it. Equally important, it also focuses on sports, one art form (I argue) in which African Americans have expressed themselves and have gained cultural currency. Students experience a society that creates commodities quickly. They are part of and experience the reality in which "colonization = thingification," as Aime Caesare puts it.[35] What I want them to come to see is that, while artistic form may be appropriated and controlled, the creative act of the artist remains free; therefore, the aim must be to make the self into a work of art. Ali, whose particular poetic and powerful black masculine style was both titillating and frightening to America, is such a figure, and the Nation of Islam is part of his transformation.

Throughout the course, I return, again and again, to G.W.F. Hegel's master/slave dichotomy. Hegel argues that the slave, though the slave is, finally, superior, becomes a slave because he or she is unwilling to fight. For Hegel, civilization is "made" in the *agon.* In contest, a civilization's worth is proven. The same is true, for Hegel, for individual human beings. Those who will fight are free.

In the course, we have already seen this statement tested. The most powerful example is that of Frederick Douglass's fight with Covey, the slave-breaker. In his standing up, a central motif of humanity and of manhood, and in his refusal to be beaten, Douglass becomes a paradigm of freedom. Violence seems like the only response to oppression, if we agree with Hegel's terms and if we read Douglass literally. In the course, however, Martin Luther King's nonviolence seems to offer another response to Hegel. The question that comes to the fore is: what part does violence play in the quest for liberation?

Boxing opens a way for us to discuss the question of whether violence is a liberatory force. The boxing ring is a sacred space, bounded and controlled. The space between two boxers is the proving ground, a kind of battlefield. It can be understood as the space in which the defeat of the enemy is total. In early bare-knuckle boxing, for example, matches could go on for forty, fifty, even a hundred rounds. The arena is also an ideologically charged space. I remind the students of the power and stature of Joe Louis in the African American community and for white American culture. His defeat of Max Schmelling on June 22, 1938, was a cultural victory. Franklin Roosevelt told Louis, "We need muscles like yours to beat Germany," and Louis's defeat of Schmelling was considered a defeat for Germany. Boxers as warriors carry a code of honor, and the match becomes a test of honor and of courage. The match is constructed as a battle between good and evil.

Joyce Carol Oates in *On Boxing* ties the ring to the cosmos and the fight to identity:

> Boxers are there to establish an absolute experience, a public accounting of the outermost limits of their beings; they will know, as few of us can know ourselves, what physical and psychic power they possess—of how much, or how little, they are capable. To enter the ring near-naked and to risk one's life is to make of one's audience voyeurs of a kind: boxing is so intimate. It is to ease out of sanity's consciousness and into another, difficult to name. It is to risk, and sometimes to realize, the agony of which agon (Greek, "contest") is the root.[36]

Oates compares the boxing ring to an altar but argues that it is an altar to mankind's ongoing aggression, a space of pain. Writers have been attracted to

> the sport's systematic cultivation of pain in the interest of project, a life goal: the willing transposing of the sensation we know as pain (physical, psychological, and emotional) into its polar opposite. If this is masochism—and I doubt that it is, or that it is simply—it is also intelligence, cunning, strategy. It is an act of consummate self-determination—the constant reestablishment of one's being. To not only accept, but to actually invite what most sane creatures avoid—pain, humiliation, loss, chaos—is to experience the present moment as already, in a sense past. *Here* and *now*, are but part of the design of *there* and *then*; pain now but control, and therefore triumph later.[37]

Such a pure vision of action—although we recognize in Oates's passage that American aggression, ironically, is worked out by its oppressed: those on whom it has been already exercised—is complicated by the social problems in America and by notions of African American character. For Remnick, Ali is a symbol of both action and complication. He is both one who molds his age and is, at the same time, a reflection of it: "I had to prove you could be a new kind of black man," Ali said; "I had to show that to the world."[38]

Remnick sets Ali in relief with Sonny Liston and Floyd Patterson to show the difficulty of such a project of self-construction. Sonny Liston is culturally defined as the "Bad Negro": as Caliban and Bigger Thomas, as a gorilla or jungle cat.[39] He is Mafia-connected; therefore, his immense power is always in service to another. He was motivated by a desire to be worthy,[40] but, to American culture, which needed him to be the "bad nigger," he never was. Floyd Patterson, in contrast, is the "Good Negro," a race man, supported by white America and "good" black people, and motivated by his shame and pride. The match between these men was a media event. Such notable writers as

Norman Mailer weighed in, making their match a morality play.[41] Both were commodified and made into things: objects of the desiring American gaze and prooftexts for/of African American character.

Ali positions himself outside the good/bad dichotomy, and the Nation of Islam helps him to do so. He gains, through this repositioning, a power spiritualized political voice. Remnick argues that

> [Clay] had quietly forsaken the image of the unthreatening black fighter established by Joe Louis and then imitated by Jersey Joe Walcott and Floyd Patterson and dozens of others. Clay was declaring that he would not fit any stereotypes, he would not follow any standard set ofbehavior. And while Liston had also declared his independence from convention (through sheer don't-give-a-shit truculence), Clay's message was political. He, and not Jimmy Cannon or the NAACP, would define his blackness, his religion, his history. He was a vocal member of an American fringe group, and America would soon be hearing about it.[42]

Ali had advantages that neither Liston nor Patterson had. He was born middle class, for example, and far from being one who was silent and constructed, Ali was, from the beginning, a voice, articulating his own self. What the Nation gave Ali was a perspective for critique of what he could be turned into and a purity of lifestyle that was compatible with his own sense. The Nation's message of black superiority, its alternative mythology, and, particularly, its definitions of manhood[43] intersected with Ali's developing sense of self.

The arena of battle shifted when Clay converted and became Ali. In this transition, he is involved with the major figures in the Nation's modern history. He is a devotee to and, it seems, sometimes a pawn of Elijah Muhammed, and he, first, embraces the friendship and guidance of and then rejects Malcolm X. Remnick is careful and skillful as he describes these men and their impact on America and on the image of Ali. When Ali was slated to fight Floyd Patterson, for example, the American nation was on Patterson's side. Religion became the focus of the battle. Patterson said, " 'The image of a Black Muslim as the world heavy-weight champion disgraces the sport and the nation.' "[44] Ali, as the "other"—black, beautiful, religiously "other," and vocal—continued to force America to face itself, particularly in his refusal to go to Vietnam and his going to prison for that decision. Ali's religion—his ethical stance—cost him a period of his life, much money, and, for a short time, his title.

Underneath the flash and bravado that is Ali, Remnick paints the picture of an increasingly devout man. In a sense, Cassius Clay is becoming the work of art that is Muhammed Ali throughout his life, and we see that spiritual journey, with its victories and defeats, that self-sculpting with its beauty and its mistakes. At the end of the work, Remnick shows us Ali now, a man fragile but fully himself and at peace with Allah. The once-reviled Ali is, to my students' generation, a cultural hero: he lit the Olympic flame; he is the subject of a song by the Fugees; and he is the beloved elder. That he was not always so, and that religion played such a key role in his confrontation with America, amazes my students. At the end of the book, Remnick speaks with Ali, who tells him: "One day you wake up and its Judgment Day. I don't worry about disease. Don't worry about anything. Allah will protect me. He always does." He has said this many times.[45] Ali continues, " 'You don't own nothing. You're just a trustee in this life.' "[46] Remnick leaves us with the image of Ali going into the house to make his afternoon prayers.

The autobiographies in the course present to us individuals engaging their particular historical and social moment and practicing and thinking through religion as a tool for transformation. Remnick's, connecting sports, religion, and social history, is one that students like—a lot. It helps them to see religion as more than individual practice; they see religion as a power that permeates all of human life, bringing about change. They can reexamine the issue of violence, assessing when it is destructive and when it is revolutionary and transformative. The issue of transformation is one with which I began and is where I want to end.

Teaching Religion Period: Classroom as Transformative Space

Practicing religion is an action that has ontological and social implications. As the practitioner changes, fashions a religious identity, he or she, potentially, changes the world—in small and large ways. My desire, as a teacher, is that the classroom becomes a place of transformation. I have struggled, however, with the idea of "transformation." What is that? Do I really want to be responsible for creating an "experience" in the classroom? If that "experience" is to bring about transformation, of what kind? What is transformation for or toward? To what ends are we transformed? For African Americans, transformation has involved the deepest and most traditional definition of spirituality: that what the "self" experiences is reinvested in the community to move it toward a goal: freedom. That transformation happens at the crossroads, to use a blues metaphor—a crossroads between the divine and the human, between the public and the private, between history and memory, between "majority" culture and "minority" culture, and between "self" and "other." At this crossroads, choices are made that inform not just what a "self" will be but, perhaps, what the lives of others will become. These choices, religion reminds us, are made in relation not just to the self and the human "other" but also in relation to a power that transforms us even as we move in the world changing it. African American life—including, particularly, religious life—has involved a responsibility to others. The "saving" of self, while perhaps important, is of little real meaning if it does not move outward to participate in a larger reality.

Henry Giroux dreams of democracy, a pedagogy that encourages our students to "author"[47] their own voices—what I have called self-fashioning—and, through that authority, to remake society. He must, I think, be dreaming with that great twentieth-century dreamer, Martin Luther King, Jr., whose "I Have A Dream" speech is the exemplar of how personal force becomes effective public, social, and religious criticism. One life can change the world; one voice can make the prophetic cry for justice. My desire is to help students see that, to contribute to moving students toward responsible, informed, and articulate authorship of self and society, so that they do not have to depend on others to think for them. King's dream was the American dream, made whole—just— and possible for all; I share that dream. Indeed, there are times I see my life as a small manifestation King's and others' hopes.

The wholeness King dreamed—which for the individual is transformation into full identity and for the society is the transformation into a just order— can happen only through participation. One of King's calls in the speech is "Go back,"[48] and, I would add, teach the world. Do all my students "get it" and will they all do it? No. But that's okay. Teaching, finally, may be no more than lighting a match or a torch in a dark room. The sudden light blinds some, and they turn away. A course as a single point of light cannot and does not illuminate the whole, but perhaps makes possible the first clear look at what is right around us. That first look, in the classroom that is contact zone, is at the neighbor—to paraphrase Dietrich Bonhoeffer, the nearest thou at hand. Perhaps there are those who, looking into the face of the other and seeing that face, perhaps clearly, for the first time, who being seen and acknowledged there, will, with a comrade or alone, pick up the torch and light another. That is my hope.

NOTES

1. Mary Louis Pratt, *Imperial Eyes: Travel Writing and Transculturation* (New York: Routledge, 1992).

2. Gayraud S. Wilmore, *Black Religion and Black Radicalism: An Interpretation of the Religious History of African Americans* (Maryknoll, NY: Orbis Books, 1998).

3. Frederick Douglass, *Narrative of the Life of Frederick Douglass, An American Slave* (New York: Penguin Books, 1982).

4. Pauli Murray, *The Autobiography of a Black Activist, Feminist, Lawyer, Priest, and Poet* (Knoxville: University of Tennessee Press, 1989).

5. Karen McCarthy Brown, *Mama Lola: A Vodou Priestess in Brooklyn* (Berkeley: University of California Press, 2001).

6. David Remnick, *King of the World: Muhammed Ali and the Rise of an American Hero* (New York: Random House, 1998).

7. Ala Alryyes, trans., "The Life of Omar Ibn Said," in *The Multilingual Anthology of American Literature*, Marc Shell and Werner Sollars, eds. (New York: New York University Press, 2000), 63–93.

8. Martin Luther King, Jr., *Stride Toward Freedom* (San Francisco: Harper and Row, 1958).

9. Pratt, *Imperial Eyes*, 4.

10. Ibid., 4, 6.

11. Ashis Nandy, *The Intimate Enemy: Loss and Recovery of Self under Colonialism* (Delhi: Oxford University Press, 1988), 3.

12. Henry A. Giroux, "Liberal Arts Education and the Struggle for Public Life: Dreaming about Democracy," in *The Politics of Liberal Education*, Darryl J. Gless and Barbara Hernstein Smith, eds. (Durham, N.C.: Duke University Press, 1992), 120.

13. Charles H. Long, *Significations: Signs, Symbols, and Images in the Interpretation of Religion* (Philadelphia: Fortress Press, 1986), 138.

14. Lynn Weber Canon, "Fostering Positive Race, Class, and Gender Dynamics in the Classroom," *Women's Studies Quarterly* 18, 2 (1990): 126.

15. Ibid., 127.

16. Giroux, "Liberal Arts Education," 121.

17. Ibid., 130.

18. John D. Caputo, ed., *Deconstruction in a Nutshell: A Conversation with Jacques Derrida* (New York: Fordham University Press, 1997), 110.

19. Walter T. Davis, *Shattered Dream: America's Search for Its Soul* (Valley Forge, PA: Trinity Press International, 1994), xi.

20. Lyn DeDanaan, "Center to Margin: Dynamics in a Global Classroom," *Women's Studies Quarterly* 18, 12 (1990): 125–136.

21. Pratt, *Imperial Eyes*, 7.

22. DeDanaan, "Center to Margin," 136.

23. Ibid., 141–143.

24. Ibid., 140.

25. Cannon, "Fostering," 129.

26. Giroux, "Liberal Arts Education," 136.

27. Long, *Significations*, 107.

28. Ibid., 107.

29. Ibid., 179.

30. Paul Gilroy, *The Black Atlantic: Modernity and Double Consciousness* (Cambridge: Harvard University Press, 1993), 56–57.

31. Long, *Significations*, 177.

32. Albert J. Raboteau, *Slave Religion: The "Invisible Institution" in the Antebellum South* (New York: Oxford University Press, 1980), 46–47.

33. Alryyes, trans., "Life of Omar Ibn Said," 63–93.

34. Hans A. Baer and Merrill Singer, *African American Religion in the Twentieth Century: Varieties of Protest and Accommodation* (Knoxville: University of Tennessee Press, 1992), 111–113.

35. Aime Cesaire, "Discourse on Colonialism," in *Colonial Discourse and Post-Colonial Theory*, Laura Chrisman and Patrick Williams, eds. (New York: Columbia University Press, 1994), 177.

36. Joyce Carol Oates, *On Boxing*. (New York: HarperCollins, 2002), 8.

37. Ibid., 26, 28.

38. David Remnick, *King of the World: Muhammed Ali and the Rise of an American Hero* (New York: Random House, 1998), xiii.

39. Ibid., 21.

40. Ibid., 34.

41. Ibid., 23.

42. Ibid., 207.

43. Ibid., 129.

44. Ibid., 275.

45. Ibid., 306.

46. Ibid., 306.

47. Giroux, "Liberal Arts Education," 137.

48. Martin Luther King, Jr., "I Have A Dream," in *The Essential Writings and Speeches of Martin Luther King, Jr.*, James M. Washington, ed. (San Francisco: HarperCollins, 1991), 219.

REFERENCES

Alryyes, Ala, trans. "The Life of Omar Ibn Said." In *The Multilingual Anthology of American Literature*, Marc Shell and Werner Sollors, eds., 63–93. New York: New York University Press, 2000.

Baer, Hans A., and Merrill Singer. *African American Religion in the Twentieth-Century: Varieties of Protest and Accommodation*. Knoxville: University of Tennessee Press, 1992.

Brown, Karen McCarthy. *Mama Lola: A Vodou Priestess in Brooklyn*. Berkeley: University of California Press, 2001.

Cannon, Lynn Weber. "Fostering Positive Race, Class, and Gender Dynamics in the Classroom." *Women's Studies Quarterly* 18, 12 (1990): 126–134.

Caputo, John D., ed. *Deconstruction in a Nutshell: A Conversation with Jacques Derrida*. New York: Fordham University Press, 1997.

Cesaire, Aime. "Discourse on Colonialism." In *Colonial Discourse and Post-Colonial Theory*, Laura Chrisman and Patrick Williams, eds., 172–180. New York: Columbia University Press, 1994.

Davis, Walter T. *Shattered Dream: America's Search for Its Soul*. Valley Forge, PA: Trinity Press International, 1994.

Douglass, Frederick. *Narrative of the Life of Frederick Douglass, An American Slave*. New York: Penguin Books, 1982.

DeDanaan, Llyn. "Center to Margin: Dynamics in a Global Classroom." *Women's Studies Quarterly* 18, 12 (1990): 135–144.

Gilroy, Paul. *The Black Atlantic: Modernity and Double Consciousness*. Cambridge: Harvard University Press, 1993.

Giroux, Henry A. "Liberal Arts Education and the Struggle for Public Life: Dreaming about Democracy." In *The Politics of Liberal Education*, Darryl J. Gless and Barbara Herrnstein Smith, eds. Durham, N.C.: Duke University Press, 1992.

Jones, Carolyn M., and John Randolph LeBlanc. "Space/Place and Home: Political and Religious Discourse in Albert Camus's *The Plague*." Unpublished paper.

King, Martin Luther, Jr. *Stride Toward Freedom*. San Francisco: Harper and Row, 1958.

———. "I Have a Dream." In *The Essential Writings and Speeches of Martin Luther King, Jr.*, James M. Washington, ed., 217–220. San Francisco: HarperCollins, 1991.

Long, Charles H. *Significations*. Philadelphia: Fortress Press, 1986.

Murray, Pauli. *The Autobiography of a Black Activist, Feminist, Lawyer, Priest, and Poet*. Knoxville: University of Tennessee Press, 1989.

Nandy, Ashis. *The Intimate Enemy: Loss and Recovery of Self under Colonialism*. New Delhi: Oxford University Press, 1988.

Oates, Joyce, Carol. *On Boxing*. New York: HarperCollins, 2002.

Raboteau, Albert J. *Slave Religion: The "Invisible Institution" in the Antebellum South*. New York: Oxford University Press, 1980.

Remnick, David. *King of the World: Muhammed Ali and the Rise of an American Hero*. New York: Random House, 1998.

Wilmore, Gayraud S. *Black Religion and Black Radicalism: An Interpretation of the Religious History of African Americans*. Maryknoll, NY: Orbis Books, 1998.

2

On the Plantation

Nancy A. Hardesty

My university was originally a plantation, Fort Hill. John C. Calhoun (1782–1850), vice president (1825–32) and defender of slavery in the Senate (1832–43, 1845–50), left the house and the land to his daughter, Anna Maria Calhoun, who died in 1875. Her husband, Thomas Green Clemson, willed it to the state in 1888 for a "high seminary of learning." The state already had a liberal arts university, the University of South Carolina in Columbia, and so Clemson was to be an agricultural and engineering college. It opened July 6, 1893, as a land-grant college and an all-male military academy.

The first (white) women were admitted in the spring of 1955. The first African American student was Harvey B. Gantt. In 1965 he received a B.A. in architecture, with honors. He has since become the mayor of Charlotte, North Carolina, and candidate for the United States Senate. He married Lucinda Brawley, the first African American woman to enroll at Clemson.[1]

In a state where approximately 30 percent of the population is black, only about 8 percent of the university's 17,000 students are (out of 12,000 to 14,000 undergraduates and about 5,000 graduate students). Several reasons might be given for this. First, Clemson is rural and somewhat isolated in the Upstate, the foothills of the Appalachian Mountains. The University of South Carolina in Columbia, the state capital, has between 15 and 20 percent African American students. The Midlands and Low Country do have a significantly higher percentage of African Americans in the population than does the Upstate. Second, the state has a number of public and private historic black colleges, for example, South Carolina State University and Claflin University (Methodist) in Orangeburg; Allen College (African Methodist Episcopal) and Benedict College (Baptist) in Columbia; Morris College (Baptist) in Sumter; and Vorhees College (Episcopal) in Denmark, South Carolina. Third, Clemson has provided few academic resources to African American students. There is only a minor in African American studies, currently housed in the History Department. In my Department of Philosophy and Religion, only two people (traditionally a Christian and a Jew) teach religion courses. We have offered a major in philosophy but only a minor in religion. Among the twelve faculty members of my department, I am currently the only woman, and there are no people of color in full-time positions (a Chinese man hired to teach Chinese language has more recently offered courses in comparative philosophy and the religions of China). The head of African American studies, a black male, is the only person of color among the twenty-one members of the History Department.

Origins of My Course

A few years ago the director of African American studies appealed to our department to consider developing a course in African American religion. Since I am the person who regularly teaches courses titled "World Religions" and "Christian Tradition," and my dissertation included the topic of abolition, I assumed the task was mine. Shortly thereafter I saw an announcement for the American Academy of Religion Lilly Teaching Fellowships in "Mining the Motherlode of African American Religious Life." It presented the perfect opportunity to get the training I needed to develop and offer such a course. I applied and was delighted to be accepted. Creating a course became my project.

As a Euro-American I had tried to include references to African American religions in my courses, but I was well aware that my own undergraduate and graduate education had been seriously lacking in this regard. Neither my Christian liberal arts college nor my graduate school had offered courses in African American studies at the time of my enrollment.

Since participating in the seminar, I have twice offered a basic course titled "African American Religion,"[2] in the fall of 1999 and the fall of 2001. The 300-level course is open to all students without prerequisite. Most students take religion classes for general education humanities or elective credit. We do have a number of religion minors, and we now offer a philosophy major with an emphasis area in religious studies, so some students take courses to fulfill the requirements of these programs. In 1999 I had only seven brave students who completed the course: five black, two white. In 2001 I had twenty-eight students: twenty-three black and five white. The course has become a regular addition to the curriculum and will continue to be offered every other year in regular rotation.

A Historical Approach

Given my own training in the History of Christianity at the University of Chicago Divinity School, I favor a historical approach. I also have a master's degree in journalism, which accentuates my focus on facts rather than theories and theologies. I tend to see "religion" in terms of religious communities, their practices and their histories. Although I am a committed Christian feminist, I usually do not focus on religious activities for social justice, but I do strive for a balance of male and female authors and subjects. And despite expectations to the contrary from some in the university and surrounding community, I assumed from the beginning that I would go beyond Protestant Christianity to include a variety of religious traditions in this particular course.

Thus I have searched for a helpful set of textbooks. The first year I used Gayraud S. Wilmore's *Black Religion and Black Radicalism* and Anthony B. Pinn's *Varieties of African American Religious Experience*.[3] Although updated, I found that Wilmore's book (suffused, as it is, with the consciousness of the civil rights era) lacked the historical perspective that I wanted to convey. Even though Pinn's excellent book was far more detailed about Vodon and Santeria than either I or my students could handle, I have retained it because I have found nothing better. He also has chapters on Islam and black humanism. In 2001 I also used Albert J. Raboteau's *African-American Religion* and Cheryl J. Sanders's *Saints in Exile: The Holiness-Pentecostal Experience in African American Religion and Culture*.[4] Raboteau's book is lively and well illustrated and takes a historical approach. The only drawback is that it seems to be more on a high school rather than college level. The paperback version, recently published by Oxford University Press under the title *Canaan Land*, is much less expensive but also has just a handful of pictures in the middle. Sanders's book fills in material on the Holiness and Pentecostal traditions, which interest me, and she adds material on the history of music in the Black Church, which is a real plus.

The search for the ideal text is an eternal quest in many classes. Especially in courses I teach every other year, I seem to adopt new texts each time. In addition to the usual criteria—how many books will the students read? are the books in paperback so that the total cost is within reason?—I want to tell the story of African American religions historically in this course. I want to focus on the different religious communities—their founding, major developments, major leaders: their unique "flavor."

In addition to Raboteau, Juan Williams and Quinton Dixie give a good, well-illustrated historical overview in *This Far by Faith: Stories from the African American Religious Experience*; their book is now in paperback.[5] The book is a companion volume to a Public Broadcasting System television series, so one could show clips from the series. It is focused around individuals such as

Denmark Vesey and Bishop Henry McNeal Turner. It also contains a strong section on Pentecostalism. Both Raboteau and Williams and Dixie offer material on Islamic slaves.

Anthony B. Pinn and Anne H. Pinn have authored *The Fortress Introduction to Black Church History*. It offers chapters in depth on Methodists, Baptists, Pentecostals, and liberation thought. It has a few pictures and small but welcome portraits of major leaders. The Pinns' approach is most congenial with my own, so I definitely will use their book, along with others, in the future.

For those who wish to emphasize social justice, Andrew Billingsley has written *Mighty Like a River: The Black Church and Social Reform*, also now in paperback.[6] Focusing primarily on Southern churches, Billingsley begins by talking about the antebellum church and then has chapters on such topics as "the male youth crisis," HIV/AIDS, and the rise of womanist theology. The book is based on a survey of nearly a thousand black churches concerning their programs. Billingsley gives an excellent overview of the strong role so many Christian churches have played in black communities across the country. This is a book I also might well use in the future. I am still looking for books that might focus just on Islam in the African American community or offer a more general overview of African and Afro-Caribbean religions in the United States.

Course Content

Most students who sign up for religion courses already have some knowledge of, and a solid interest in, the subject matter. However, interesting them in an exploration of the history of the institutions with which they are familiar is sometimes a harder sell. Although about one-third of Clemson's students are from out of state, I felt that one of the relevancies of this particular course was the potential for local and regional connections, so I have tried to stress those.

I began the course with a lecture and handout on early Christianity in North Africa in order to help students see that Christianity is not just a European religion. We then talked about the Middle Passage and the religions that slaves brought with them to the new world. Three-quarters of all slaves entered the United States through the port of Charleston, South Carolina. We noted the differences between slaves' conditions in the southern United States and those in the Caribbean and Latin America. This led into explorations of African tribal religions (Yoruba, Fon, Kongo, etc.) and the development of Vodun, Santeria, and Candomble, with readings from Pinn's book. Raboteau added to this with his good discussion of Islamic slaves. Allan D. Austin, in *African Muslims in Antebellum America*, has documented more than seventy-five Muslim slaves, most of them in North and South Carolina and Georgia.[7]

Next we began a survey of the historical development of black Christianity, predominately Protestant. The oldest black congregation in the country is usually said to be the Silver Bluff Baptist Church, Silver Bluff, South Carolina, less than a hundred miles down the Savannah River from the Clemson campus.[8] We also discussed the "invisible institution," slave resistance and rebellions (e.g., Denmark Vesey's revolt in Charleston), and the large numbers of slaves who were originally members of white-controlled southern Episcopal, Methodist, and Baptist churches.

We looked at the 1816 founding of the African Methodist Episcopal Church by Richard Allen and the free blacks in Philadelphia, as well as the beginning of the African Methodist Episcopal Zion Church by James Varick in New York City. In the period following the Civil War, we detailed the growth of independent black denominations in the South, including the Colored (now Christian) Methodist Church and the National Baptist conventions.

My own wider research interests have concentrated recently on the Holiness and Pentecostal movements, and so we explored the Holiness movement of Amanda Berry Smith, Charles Price Jones, and Charles Harrison Mason. We noted William Seymour's inauguration of Pentecostalism on Azusa Street in Los Angeles in 1906, and its development in Bishop Mason's Church of God in Christ as well as the "oneness" or "Jesus only" Pentecostalism of G. T. Haywood's Pentecostal Assemblies of the World.

In the twentieth century we looked at the black nationalism of Marcus Garvey and the rise of Rastafarianism. We traced the development of Noble Drew Ali's Moorish Science Temple, and Nation of Islam from Master Fard and Elijah Muhammad, through Malcolm X, Wallace Deen Muhammad, and Louis Farrakhan—which brought us back to the attraction of traditional Islam among African Americans in the United States. We concluded the semester with discussion of the roles of religious institutions in the Civil Rights and Black Power movements, along with the development of black and womanist theologies.

Church Visits

My teaching style is rather traditional, based in lecture and discussion. Students are evaluated on the basis of their knowledge of assigned readings as evidenced in class discussions and on periodic examinations. For the other component of their evaluation students had a choice. They could either research and write a fifteen- to twenty-page paper, or they could visit four different predominately African American religious institutions and write a three- to four-page reaction paper for each visit. Most students chose the visit option. Students were asked to observe the architectural elements of the worship space, the music, the structure of the service, the composition of the leadership, the use of scriptures, the race and class of the congregation, the administration of sacraments, and so on. For Euro-American students, this was an intimidating assignment, but even for African American students it often meant leaving their familiar comfort zones and venturing into unfamiliar religious settings.

Within Clemson and neighboring towns, students had opportunities to visit a rather formal A.M.E. church led by a woman; lively Baptist churches; a House of Prayer for All People (founded in the 1930s by Bishop "Sweet Daddy" Grace); a biracial Assembly of God that bills itself as the "extreme church"; and a small Seventh-day Adventist congregation. In Greenville, about thirty miles away, students visited a very fast-growing, multiracial, independent charismatic church called Redemption World Outreach. There is also a historically black Reformed Episcopal Church and St. Anthony of Padua Roman Catholic Church. A newly formed mosque in Clemson and a more established one in Greenville attract African American members, as well as a core of Muslim graduate students and immigrants. Students from other areas of the state and country were able to visit the black nationalist Shrine of the Black Madonna in Atlanta and a historic black Episcopal church in Charleston.

These visits provoked innumerable questions and comparisons, particularly on days when the reaction papers were due. Why do many of these churches have more than one offering and ask people to bring their contributions up to the front? Why do some women dress all in white? Why are people in some groups so demonstrative—dancing in the aisles, weeping, shouting, speaking in tongues, falling to the floor? Why are some services so long while others are much shorter? There really are black Catholics and Episcopalians? Why do some churches have pipe organs and others prefer guitars and drums? The exchange was not only between black and white students but also among African American students of different religious, regional, and social backgrounds as well. It often gave black students the opportunity to be the authorities and to teach me and their fellow students about various aspects of black religious life. It gave white students and their teacher experiences of being in the minority and culturally marginalized. The assignment allowed all students to experience firsthand some of the religious diversity covered in the reading material. It also gave them the opportunity and impetus to ask different questions than those posed by the textbooks and instructor.

Teaching African American Religion as a Euro-American

The first time I taught the course, I was very tentative and hesitant. Much of the material was new to me; I was still learning myself (and, of course, I still am). The Wilmore book was organized somewhat historically but left large gaps for me to fill. The Pinn book was far more detailed than either I or my students could digest. While I had previously had the two white students in class, I knew only one of the black students and that from outside class. For the first several weeks we all walked on eggshells around each other. The small class was both a plus and a minus. Since I was still feeling my way, having fewer students was easier to cope with. I could get to know each one more personally. However, with so few, the absence of one or two changed the classroom dynamics dramatically, especially since the class contained few talkative individuals. Eventually the class did develop a good rapport and learning environment.

The second time through, with the class considerably larger, I had a very solid core of both black and white students who had taken courses with me before. In fact, a core group of the African American students had formed a critical mass in my New Testament class the previous semester. This immediately laid a foundation of trust and camaraderie in the classroom into which other students could buy. One of those from the New Testament class was an African American woman of my age who was a staff member in another department. She sometimes served as an intermediary within the classroom, and at other times gently and lovingly challenged me in ways that were helpful and as younger students were reluctant to do. Within the class, several subgroups also formed, especially as students banded together to do their church visits. Several of the students were enrolled in another class of mine that met earlier in the day. These multiple ties provided a strong web of relationships and a community of trust in the classroom.

Several additional topics beyond my stated curriculum provoked major class discussions. In both semesters, at student instigation, we spent a whole period discussing the Prince Hall Masons, a black fraternal group in which many ministers have been active but about which some religious groups feel ambivalence because of its rituals, religious symbolism, and vows of secrecy. Students seemed to be fascinated by the group, perhaps because Greek fraternities and sororities are strong on campus. And at least one student in each class was both knowledgeable about the group and willing to share information. One day in the first class we simply laid aside the day's curriculum to share feelings about the suicide of an African American athlete on campus. September 11, 2001, occurred during the second class, so time was spent sorting out our feelings about that and talking about the many faces of Islam.

Teaching African American religions as a Euro-American has difficulties beyond mastering the material and establishing rapport with the students. My specialization is in American evangelical Christianity. However, I regularly teach world religions. Nobody has ever questioned whether I should be teaching Hinduism or Buddhism, even though I have never been to India or had a graduate course in Asian religions. Yet there seems to be an undercurrent of questioning: how can this white woman teach black religion?

This issue has emerged in several guises. After the director of African American studies asked our department chair if such a course could be developed and even came to a departmental meeting to request that our (all-white) faculty develop courses suitable for inclusion in the African American

studies minor, when my course came up for approval before the college curriculum committee, the director approached the department chair and asked
who would be teaching the course. My boss replied, "Well, Nancy developed
the course and so she will be teaching it." Apparently the director's assumption
had been that we would propose such a course, get it approved and listed in
the catalog, and then the department would hire a person of color to teach it.
This expectation may have been fueled by the fact that the university did have
a fund at one time specifically to hire black faculty outside of regular departmental channels. My teaching the course was not questioned by the departmental, college, and university curriculum committees, who readily approved
it. But the director never did sign the form to approve the course for inclusion
in the African American studies minor. A new director has now done so.

At some point during each semester in which I have taught the course the
director made a point of telling me that a local pastor or pastors (unnamed)
were "surprised" that I was teaching the course and that I was including non-
Christian religions in the curriculum. He assured me that he had defended
my scholarship and my academic freedom, but I always asked myself: "Why
is he sharing this with me? What is the agenda here?" Part of the tension here
may be between a community assumption that local ministers are best
equipped to teach religion and a general lack of awareness concerning the
academic study of religion in a public university.

While my teaching evaluations in these courses have been uniformly positive, the same undercurrent has appeared in a few comments. What I view as
sharing ownership of the material with the students, all of us sharing learning
and teaching together, they sometimes view as lack of expertise on my part.
And some of it is. Many of them have spent their lives in black Baptist, Methodist, or Pentecostal churches. I have spent my sixty-year church life in other
traditions. But when I, as a Protestant, ask Roman Catholics to share their
experiences, I do not get the same reaction. And as a historian, I do know far
more factually about the history of most black denominations in America than
college students who have only spent the past twenty years in one congregation.
But somehow the racial divide is different, deeper.

Or perhaps it is simply that the hopes and expectations are different. Black
students would simply prefer to have an African American church member
teaching the course, just as evangelical and fundamentalist students would
prefer to have a person of similar persuasion teaching my New Testament
course. I am just not the person to meet those expectations. Many students, at
least at this Southern university, find comfort, meaningful relationships, and
encouragement in campus religious groups. Many, I think, expect to find in
religion classes a similarly nurturing place. They also assume that since the
course material will be somewhat familiar, the course will be less challenging.
Those expectations may also remain unfulfilled.

Black students on our campus certainly do need and deserve more black faculty role models, and I would welcome an African American to our department. But in these times of severe budget constraints, it is doubtful that any new positions will be available in our department. Nor do we employ adjunct faculty. Therefore, for the foreseeable future, I will be teaching the course.

I would encourage other white scholars to teach courses in African American religion as well. For many of us, such courses are a natural fit with our courses in American religion in general. The courses are certainly a valuable addition to the curriculum for both black and white students. Knowledge of African American religions also enriches our teaching in other areas.

Synergy

In addition to developing and teaching the course in African American religion, my participation in "Mining the Motherlode of African American Religious Life" has spilled over into all of my other courses.

In world religions, I have added references to African tribal religions in addition to the Native American and Aboriginal examples I had previously used. Pinn's book, plus presentations by a Yoruba priest and a Vodun priestess, as well as visits to exhibits at the African American and African art museums during the New York City portion of the "Motherlode" project, gave me new understandings of African and Afro-Caribbean religions and firsthand experiences to share with my students. Research for my African American Religion course has given me a much longer historical view of Islam-related religions in the United States, and I have integrated that into my presentations on Islam.

In my New Testament course, I have begun routinely to use the term "North Africa" rather than "Egypt" in discussing the Jewish Diaspora and matters in the early Christian church. I think many Euro-Americans, and perhaps many African Americans as well, tend to picture all of Jewish and Christian history in European terms. Repeated references to "North Africa" remind me at least, and hopefully my students, that Africa was very much a part of the Christian story from before the beginning. And the "Middle East" includes parts of Africa as well as Asia. Jesus and the early followers of the Way were not blue-eyed blonds.

Participating in the Lilly Teaching Workshop has also influenced my research. I have been researching and writing a book about divine healing in the Holiness and early Pentecostal movements. Previously in my writing about Pentecostalism, I had always credited Charles Parham, a white minister in Topeka, Kansas, with the founding of Pentecostalism in 1901, as most historians do. But after participating in this workshop and reading Douglas J. Nelson's dissertation on William Seymour,[9] I have concluded that Seymour has been overlooked and his importance to the movement discounted due to the blatant racism of early reports of the revival and perhaps unrecognized and unacknowledged racism of later white historians, myself included. Thus both in my teaching and in my writing about Pentecostalism, I now begin with Seymour and the 1906 Azusa Street Revival in Los Angeles, for which he was responsible.

Thus, when I taught a senior seminar on religion and health, Seymour's ministry played a prominent part in my discussion of the Christian divine healing movement; so did Sarah Mix, a nineteenth-century woman who was an early practitioner within the Holiness Movement.[10] In that class I also used a book on African ritual by Malidome Some, brought to me in a previous class by one of my African American students. I would not have discovered it on my own, but it turned out to be a perfect beginning for the cross-cultural course. I had previously taught a seminar on the subject with only the African tribal materials in Donald Kinsley's *Health, Healing and Religion: A Cross-Cultural Perspective.*[11]

My own education continued in the fall of 2002 when, in regular rotation, I taught a course titled "Christian Tradition." In the past I have usually tried to cover the topics that I learned in graduate school, that is, European Christianity. This time I deliberately chose *Christianity: A Global History*[12] by David Chidester, who teaches at the University of Cape Town, South Africa. He includes not only solid material on African American religion but also Christianity in Africa, Asia, and Latin America. Rather than highlighting missionary efforts in these places, he focuses on indigenous, independent Christian movements. For students of all colors this problematizes questions of what is "true" Christianity and what are cultural accretions.

Participating in "Mining the Motherlode of African American Religious Life" not only has added another class to my teaching repertoire but also has changed, broadened, and deepened the perspectives with which I approach all of my teaching. Things are also changing here on the plantation. The director of African American Studies has retired, and a new and dynamic leader has been hired. The appointment continues to be housed in the History Department, but the administration is committed to making the program collaborative among all of those teaching related courses throughout the university. The university has already attracted several energetic young black scholars, and their work is paving the way for a new day.

NOTES

1. Harvey B. Gantt was born in Charleston, S.C., in 1943. After graduation from Clemson University, he received a master's degree in city planning, in 1970, from the Massachusetts Institute of Technology Department of Architecture. He founded Gantt Huberman Architects in Charlotte. In 1983 he was elected Charlotte's first black mayor. He twice ran unsuccessfully against Senator Jesse Helms. He has served

as the Martin Luther King Jr. Visiting Professor of Architecture at the Massachusetts Institute of Technology.

2. Discussions within the Lilly Teaching Workshop led to the conclusion that it would be preferable to say "African American Religions," but by this time my course was already in the catalog under the singular.

3. Gayraud S. Wilmore, *Black Religion and Black Radicalism,* 3rd ed. (Maryknoll, NY: Orbis Books, 1998); Anthony B. Pinn, *Varieties of African American Religious Experience* (Minneapolis: Fortress Press, 1998).

4. Albert J. Raboteau, *African-American Religion* (New York: Oxford University Press, 1999); Cheryl J. Sanders, *Saints in Exile: The Holiness-Pentecostal Experience in African American Religion and Culture* (New York: Oxford University Press, 1996).

5. Anne H. Pinn and Anthony B. Pinn, *Fortress Introduction to Black Church History* (Minneapolis: Fortress Press, 2002); Juan Williams and Quinton Dixie, *This Far by Faith: Stories from the African American Religious Experience* (New York: Morrow, 2003).

6. Andrew Billingsley, *Mighty Like a River: The Black Church and Social Reform* (New York: Oxford University Press, 1999; paperback ed. 2003).

7. Allan D. Austin, *African Muslims in Antebellum America: Transatlantic Stories and Spiritual Struggles* (New York: Routledge, 1997); see also Sylviane A. Diouf and Sylviane Kemara, *Servants of Allah: African Muslims Enslaved in the Americas* (New York: New York University Press, 1998).

8. Frank Roberson and George Mosley, "When a Few Gather in My Name," demonstrate religious activity at Silver Bluff in 1750, though the oldest documentation of that activity is from 1773. Silver Bluff's claim is disputed by Springfield Baptist Church in Augusta, Georgia, founded in 1787. First African Baptist Church in Savannah, Georgia, dates its origins to 1783, when Reverend George Liele was baptized, though he did not start the church until 1788. But by most accounts, both Springfield and the church in Savannah owe their origins to leaders from Silver Bluff. See Carly Phillips, "Church Roots Traced Back 252 Years," *Post and Courier* (Charleston), July 17, 2002.

9. Douglas J. Nelson, "For Such a Time as This: The Story of Bishop William J. Seymour and the Azusa Street Revival" (Ph.D. diss., University of Birmingham, England, 1981). White scholars have been very critical of this dissertation, challenging some of Nelson's facts and the conclusions he drew from them. However, I agree with him that the numerous quotations that he cites concerning Seymour's appearance and actions during the revival are incredibly racist. The fact that Parham would not allow Seymour to sit in his Houston classroom with white students and then Parham's subsequent denunciation of Seymour and the Azusa Street meetings are also clearly racist. I also find persuasive Nelson's argument that later historians continued to slight Seymour by portraying Pentecostalism as a movement that sprang into existence seemingly without human assistance. Seymour's humility and spiritual demeanor in the face of attack and criticism only add to his stature. See my *Faith Cure: Divine Healing in the Holiness and Pentecostal Movements* (Peabody, MA: Hendrickson, 2003).

10. Mrs. Edward Mix, *Faith Cures and Answers to Prayer,* with critical introduction by Rosemary D. Gooden (Syracuse, NY: Syracuse University Press, 2002).

11. Malidome Patrice Some, *Ritual: Power, Healing and Community* (New York:

Penguin, 1993); Donald Kinsley, *Health, Healing and Religion: A Cross-Cultural Perspective* (Upper Saddle River, NJ: Prentice Hall, 1996).

12. David Chidester, *Christianity: A Global History* (San Francisco: HarperSanFrancisco, 2000).

REFERENCES

Austin, Allan D. *African Muslims in Antebellum America: Transatlantic Stories and Spiritual Struggles.* New York: Routledge, 1997.

Chidester, David. *Christianity: A Global History.* San Francisco: HarperSanFrancisco, 2000.

Diouf, Sylviane A., and Sylviane Kamara. *Servants of Allah: African Muslims Enslaved in the Americas.* New York: New York University Press, 1998.

Mix, Mrs. Edward. *Faith Cures and Answers to Prayer.* With a critical introduction by Rosemary D. Gooden. Syracuse, NY: Syracuse University Press, 2002.

Nelson, Douglas J. "For Such a Time as This: The Story of Bishop William J. Seymour and the Azusa Street Revival." Ph.D. diss., University of Birmingham, England, 1981.

Pinn, Anne H., and Anthony B. Pinn. *Fortress Introduction to Black Church History.* Minneapolis: Fortress Press, 2002.

Pinn, Anthony B. *Varieties of African American Religious Experience.* Minneapolis: Fortress Press, 1998.

Raboteau, Albert J. *African-American Religion.* New York: Oxford University Press, 1999.

Sanders, Cheryl J. *Saints in Exile: The Holiness-Pentecostal Experience in African American Religion and Culture.* New York: Oxford University Press, 1996.

Williams, Juan, and Quinton Dixie. *This Far by Faith: Stories from the African American Religious Experience.* New York: Morrow, 2003.

Wilmore, Gayraud S. *Black Religion and Black Radicalism.* 3rd ed. Maryknoll, NY: Orbis Books, 1998.

3

Border Disputes: Honoring Our Ancestors, Honoring Ourselves

Stephanie Y. Mitchem

The study of African American religious thought gives students and teachers the opportunity to reenvision scholarship. One way students come to appreciate personal and national histories anew is through the idea of honoring the ancestors. Black students, in particular, come to honor themselves as they learn to recognize the intellectual validity of their own religious experiences; this honoring takes place in a society that regularly diminishes these same experiences. In honoring self and ancestors, all students—black and white—open new channels for dialogue. New paradigms for self, community, and research are inaugurated for most groups of students and are affirmed for me as a black woman. These alternative possibilities sometimes clash with education in the old key, thereby causing border disputes.

Henry Giroux developed the idea of border pedagogy and the notion of educators as border workers. Border pedagogy engages and transgresses, rather than ignores, the issues of culture, history, power, and difference in society and in the classroom. Giroux writes:

> Border pedagogy decenters as it remaps. The terrain of learning becomes inextricably linked to the shifting parameters of place, identity, history, and power. Border pedagogy shifts the emphasis of the knowledge/power relationship away from the limited emphasis on the mapping of domination toward the politically strategic issue of engaging the

ways in which knowledge can be remapped, reterritorialized, and de-centered in the wider interests of rewriting the borders and coordi-nates of an oppositional cultural politics. This is not anabandon-ment of critique as much as it is an extension of its possibilities.[1]

This chapter explores the ideas of honoring ancestors and self in the class-room, along the borders. To begin this exploration, I focus on some aspects of the borders of black lives in the United States. The borders of education be-come the focus in the next section. The idea of honoring ancestors is related to the course I developed, "Womanist Spiritual Autobiography"; and honoring self is discussed in relation to the course "Womanist Theology and Literature."

Life on the Border

The setting of borders and the resultant disputes are ingrained in the history of the United States. While Giroux discusses the meaning of borders as related to culture, history, power, and difference, borders are daily given personal meanings for people of color. African Americans particularly live with an acute awareness of the borders because the boundaries were set to exclude us. At the same time, the borders functioned to maintain the constructions of white-ness, because *they* are not *us*. The borders are sharp around matters of race and compounded with questions of gender and class. But the reality is that the constructions of race in the United States create definitional boundaries that constrain all of us. Each American has personal stories that name or enforce borders, especially around issues of race.

When I was growing up, teen dance programs on television were begin-ning to define American teens' identities while capturing their consumer in-terests. In those days, the programs exclusively featured white teens, as there were no nationally televised black dance programs yet, and certainly no (pub-licized) interracial dancing. My friends and I would gather on Saturday after-noons and watch the gray tones of white kids with bouffant-styled hair. Though there was some racial and ethnic integration in our working-class neighbor-hood, we all tended to socialize in our look-alike groups, especially in our younger years when we were much less mobile. So, on Saturdays we younger children would be watching television and trying to understand why the white people danced differently from the way we did. It was a mystery, even as tele-vision defined a sense of "us and them" in our youthful minds. Where did "they" get their dances? How come there were no black teens on the program that could show them what to do? Why couldn't they keep to the rhythm? Finally, one Saturday, Delores came to the viewing session with a great insight. She had asked my brother why "they" danced like that. "White people," she pronounced gravely "dance to the song's words, not the music." We then spent the next several Saturdays trying to figure out *which* lyrics made up their dance rhythms.

There is humor for me in that memory but also several cold realities. The first is that black people in the United States have learned to develop analytical frames, from childhood onward, in which *we* study *them*. These frames stand us in good stead as we navigate through the alien worlds of classroom, stockroom, and boardroom: worlds that seek to exclude us. Our analyses become part of networking bases from which we develop survival modes: we share information, disclose fears, and develop relationships. In other words, we strengthen black group identification, in spite of the varieties within African American communities. Our determinations of white motivations or intentions are sometimes based on our distance from power and privilege. Our determinations are sometimes just as uninformed as *theirs* are about *us*.

I am of the first generation in my family to complete an advanced degree, an unconsidered possibility in my parents' lives. My parents were the first generation to attend college. Their motivations, I suspect, came from the expectation that college was a guaranteed-moving-up social process for black people. My father did not complete his degree requirements, since a couple of years' attendance was enough for him to land a good job. My mother finally obtained a bachelor's degree as a returning student, since it was a requirement to keep her job. They both took advantage of their college education to land civil service positions. They, like many Americans of their generation, understood safe careers as those from which they could retire after the requisite twenty-five years in a single job. But the world has kept changing, and that scenario is no longer feasible. Some Americans have been able to keep pace with the changes better than others.

As a teenager, when I glimpsed the world of borders in the images of a television screen, my parents and I were excluded by the marks of class, color, and gender. Today, young people cross many of these earlier borders by creating new realities, and thereby becoming part of the social changes. Techno, rap, house parties, and green hair are no longer exclusive to one race or class. However, despite some misleading public relations campaigns to prove that racism is a nonissue or that the glass ceiling is gone, borders created by the dominant society are resilient, perhaps decorated with new wallpaper and paint, but still real. On white college campuses, border issues converge, at best, for discussion and understanding, at worst, for resentment and anger. Students in my classes in Detroit enter with these border issues and their own assortment of experiences in place. Black students continue to confront the alienness of white epistemological frameworks, superbly exemplified by academe. White students bear other preconceptions passed on through their parents, and they view the status quo as beneficial. The white students' expectations of white privilege are affirmed by the structures of the university in many ways, from administrative decisions to class offerings. White students often expect that their views of the world will be reflected in the life of the classroom, which makes the denial of racism a preferred option. Bringing these experiences into my classrooms, black and white students are the primary class participants, each group bearing their own histories of noncommunication. As one point of commonality, both groups of students generally continue, as did my parents' generation, to seek secure jobs through college education.

University of Detroit Mercy is an urban, Catholic college that primarily serves undergraduates. The student population is 35 percent black, 60 percent white, 5 percent other ethnicities. There are significant numbers of commuter students and adult learners who work multiple jobs and care for families. The religious studies courses primarily fulfill core requirements, with a small number of undergraduate majors. When I plan for these classes, I recognize the students' deeper need for an education that prepares them for the world through improved communication, community building, and life choices, informed by analyses of political realities, privilege, and power. The study of African American religious life is an analytical framework that brings all these issues into dialogue: hidden histories, power relationships, national realities, and personal truths all make appearances.

Like many other faculty members, I also do research. As a researcher, my focus has been on womanist thought, which began to develop in the 1970s and really gained wings during the 1980s. Gender became a specific focus for the black women in religious communities who had been excluded from discussions and development of black theology during the 1960s. My own interest in black and women's theologies grew during my time in the seminary in the 1980s when I kept waiting for the portion of any course that affirmed my religious experience. Instead, my experiences were rendered unimportant by my instructors, since we were to think about the *universal*, not particulars. But how could I make connections when I did not fit the universals? Eventually, on my own, I discovered that there were black women thinking about the same things. The books that I found led me to begin doctoral studies.[2] For me, coming to womanist thought in those studies was like coming home. My own growth as a scholar in alien academic territory connected with my personal experiences of neighborhood and family to bring me to a greater appreciation of the students with whom I work.

Coming to the Motherlode

When I began the American Academy of Religion/Lilly Foundation's "Mining the Motherlode" workshop, I had been teaching five years at the college level. I had learned to teach using shared readings with discussions rather than lecture, risking being part of a community of learners through group work, while aiming to build community among students. While there was some success, there were many other considerations, born of my life experiences. Therefore, one of my goals for the workshop was to connect activism to intellectual work, and to make that connection itself becomes part of a social analysis process. As I well knew, the individual learner comes from a given social context and is brought into dialogue with academic canons. Coming from a working-class background, I asked this question: can life experiences be affirmed *through* academia, rather than in spite of it?

I believe that connecting activism and intellectual life, while questioning the roles that experience can play in academe, are necessary for rich scholarship. Contemporary American higher education is rapidly becoming a mass project rather than an elitist realm. Despite anti-affirmative actions that would maintain privilege for the "right" people, colleges scramble to attract students, and most Americans are programmed to expect college degrees. Students still face a world that sends them to school for "a better job" rather than a better world, emphasizing the personal over the communal. Family and the media hold up income as the primary flag of success to which we pledge allegiance. In this mercenary climate, the questions I raise are sharpened. Is the connection of daily wisdom with canonical scholarship even possible? Are we academics in danger of hiding behind abstractions rather than dealing with the mess of human diversity? Practically speaking, can qualitative analysis and synthetic-parallel thinking positively influence the students I encounter? These questions take me into border work.

Prior to the workshop, I often assigned students attendance at community-based events, especially since the Detroit area is so rich in black religious invention—from the Shrine of the Black Madonna to Spiritualist churches.[3] Not satisfied with merely attempting to get the students to experience these churches, I asked how I could lead students to consciously tap into their own wisdom as a source of credible knowledge. I brought my questions into the workshop.

In order to begin addressing these ideas, I structured my fall term classes differently, trying riskier methods. (It was important that I had the collegiality of the workshop membership as a significant source of support.) I became conscious of new questions in the process of this risky work. For instance, in one of the classes, I attempted to get students to select the grade they wished to receive at the course's end. Based on the menu of assignments and attendance requirements, students contracted for their desired grade. By midterm, it was clear that this experiment was a failure. Students had contracted for grades they could not achieve. Most of the students in this class were adults with families and jobs who regularly made decisions and fulfilled commitments. What was disconnected for them in the classroom?

My own questions and life experiences underlined the fact that I needed more information on the students' expectations for their educations. Through local resources, I met with Michael Thomas, the director of a program at a local public college for underachieving African American students. The program aimed to improve the students' grades. Michael Thomas found that student confidence and self-esteem are linked to this process. The results he reported were phenomenal, bringing over half these students to better than passing grades, with many moving into honors levels of study. The key, he reported, was helping the students break the code of higher education. Michael Thomas and Dr. Gwen Pringle developed the "Student Survey on Effective Approaches and Techniques for Teaching African American Students." In order to understand the students I encountered, I adapted their survey for my use.

The survey consisted of two sections. The first gathered student demographics: age, years in school, part- or full-time, and so on. The second asked the following five short-answer questions.

1. What are your academic goals?
2. From your past or current teachers at UDM, indicate what you liked or disliked.
3. What would you like teachers to know to help you reach your goals?
4. What do you believe teachers should know about African American students in order to help them better?
5. Can you think of other suggestions?

I surveyed ninety-nine African American students in one semester throughout the university, and learned much about their determinations of their needs. In response to the first question, identification of academic goals gave indications of students' abilities to make realistic links with what a university education could or could not do for them. The desires for success in an academic setting must be connected with the skills of knowing how the institution works; black students are often excluded, for various reasons, from this awareness. I was also struck by their use of written language. "Bachelor's . . . Degree . . . Master's . . . Honors . . . Top . . . Law School" and most of their majors' names were in capital letters, indicating the importance of these titles as ideals for their lives.

Students primarily focused on self-esteem/respect issues when responding to the third question. Students generally wanted the leadership and mentorship of faculty but sought a mutually respectful relationship. Students' comments often focused on their own life stresses, such as being a working parent, having to work overtime, and so on. Students wanted to be appreciated for their abilities as students: they worked hard and wanted a quality education. One student's words summed this up: "I have dreams, don't disrespect them."

Issues of race surfaced in the survey. One student's statement, "Our race of people are the same as others, do not treat us [differently]," was given context by other statements like "Teachers should know that African American students are just as smart as anyone else." Some students indicated experience of being stereotyped by a teacher; others stressed capabilities or pride of African American students. One remark, "Stop acting as if we're invisible," indicates that some students experienced being treated differently by instructors. A few students' statements in the vein of "I haven't had any problems *yet*" were not hopeful and indicated expectations of problems. Student retention and recruitment are impacted by the way these messages are carried among the network of students. After gathering the survey results, I was able to understand more broadly what some disconnecting factors for the students were, such as their perceptions of how they related to and were treated in the academic setting. I had known from my own experiences, but was able to see more clearly, that lack of role models coupled with few opportunities for mentoring, served to further distance students. So, realizing the role that black religion could play in furthering these academic dialogues, I was ready to begin structuring the course again.

Honoring Our Ancestors

One of the intellectual conflicts many students encounter is society's lack of appreciation for the depth and complexity of African American religious life. To begin with, it is not just American/white religious thought in a different color. But to appreciate this fact, different shades of meaning must be brought into focus—and this can be painful. Explorations by black writers point to this dimension. For instance, Michael Eric Dyson recently utilized cultural studies in the book *I May Not Get There with You: The True Martin Luther King Jr.*[4] With a different and challenging twist, Dyson breaches sacred social territory and analyzes the ways that Martin Luther King's legacy is reduced to a safe cultural icon. Cheryl Townsend Gilkes's book *If It Wasn't for the Women*[5] develops a sociological analysis that reconfigures contemporary understandings of gender role expectations of black men and women while viewing black social and church relations with new eyes. These and other current texts can surely upset students' understandings, which are derived from misleading cultural frameworks. In other words, Dyson, Gilkes, and other scholars impart analyses that counter simplistic, bumper-sticker-size readings of race, class, and gender.

Many undergraduate students of any race, well versed in the popular readings, flounder in my classes when dropped into these academic streams without lifejackets; indeed, they become overwhelmed. A few students are affirmed in the new readings, relieved that their secretly held ideas are not heresy. As with many of my colleagues, I view my task as a teacher to be more than the force-feeding of dry information into the students' heads. The deeper need is to ask students to reconsider their own frameworks of understanding as they encounter ideas that challenge their beliefs. Students also need ways to understand that different religious scholars have diverse goals in their work, and everything written is not doctrine.

In the setting of a white university where black experiences are often excluded from the canons of most disciplines, learning analytical frameworks that focus on black people can initiate new awareness and help students to rethink the categories held by various disciplines. Approaching religion from the perspectives of black people (a rare experience at a white university) assists students in rethinking their lives as scholars. The course "Womanist Spiritual Autobiography" was developed with these issues in mind.[6]

The course overview defines spirituality as a route to begin rethinking self in relation to religious understandings. Spiritual autobiography can point out ways that faith is lived. These personal reflections can become the basis of deeper theological reflection that has meaning to a faith community. Connecting these faith stories with autobiography, an important literary genre for women in general, adds another level to the processes of rethinking self and discipline. The autobiography in the hands of black American women becomes a political tool. Faith is of great importance in most black women's written work, and still serves as a tool to evangelize a particular faith tradition or to advocate for social change. Autobiographical writing by black women from the nineteenth century to the present, along with the students' own faith reflections, is used in this exploration.

One assignment in the course was designed to encourage students to become aware of some of the relationships between personal stories and the wider community. Students were to write a "Journaling" paper that discussed selected aspects of their spiritual autobiographies. (For the instructions and list of questions for this assignment, see appendix 1.) Insights from the students' papers were discussed in small groups, which had been formed the first day of class. The narratives of historic black women helped most students rethink the discipline of history and the richness of cultural exchanges. The spiritual narratives that students shared in their small groups helped many students to regard one another as scholars, to draw from common wisdom, to become a community of learners.

After teaching this course, I felt that students gathered three benefits. First, students began to appreciate that cultural permeability, not the American melting pot, is a better way to describe the relations among cultures. Permeability gave students a framework that helped them to grasp some of the complex cultural developments of black people. Permeability also helped to frame the multifaceted relationships found when studying African American religions. Second, students were able to become a bit more comfortable with ambiguity, a place we often reached with our research efforts. Ambiguity stands in contrast to the idea that scholarship can bring crystal-clear answers. Third, students were invited into a process of self-reflection that opened them to the idea that creative, honest living includes continual questioning.

Honoring Our Selves

African American religious studies brings heightened tensions for black students as classroom discussions raise temperatures and consciousness on a variety of levels. African American religious life and expression encompass the breadth of black life in the United States—political, cultural, economic, sociological, theological, and ethical. Teaching black religion without reference to black experiences and the dilemmas arising from those experiences is not education; rather, it is miseducation.

Miseducation ruins the mind, as Carter G. Woodson pointed out in his 1930 text *The Mis-education of the Negro*. Woodson wrote: "When you control a man's [or a woman's] thinking you do not have to worry about his [or her] actions. You do not have to tell him not to stand here or go yonder. He will find his "'proper' place" and stay in it. You do not need to send him to the back door. He will go without being told. In fact, if there is no back door, he will cut one for his special benefit."[7]

Academe can perpetuate the back door. Academic disciplines, generally, maintain an exclusive canon and thus have been slow to recognize the intellectual validity of the experiences of those designated "Others."[8] African Americans are viewed with suspicion until they prove their worthiness. Such worth is established first by pledging allegiance to the canon and second by minimizing cultural disagreements: it's all right to complain, just not too loudly. These messages are subtle but very well communicated. Minds are controlled.

Therefore, it is not surprising that when a teacher invites black students to incorporate and analyze their own cultural experiences, a crisis is sometimes precipitated. Students start looking for the intellectual back door to which their own experiences have been so often relegated. African American religious thought provides opportunities to reconsider relationships: of students to scholarship and of students to themselves and their communities. Teaching is a bridge that can help connect black students to their own histories and experiences. One implication of these connections is opening new possibilities for scholarship informed by black experience, in other words, their own experiences. White students become connected to stories of an America they never knew existed. Their comfortable patterns of thinking are upended by black folks' concretized experiences. Pedagogical tools to address these concerns for both black and white students' benefits might include folk tales, stories, or literature of black people. In this light, the everyday realities of black people's lives can be viewed as an important basis from which to draw religious meanings. This approach requires a willingness to listen to stories of past and present, which includes the personal stories of teachers and students. Attendant analyses of power relationships become part of the process. Many of the students become colearners in sharply questioning the status quo: Why are things the way they are? How can we change them?

"Womanist Theology and Literature" was a course designed to engage some of these issues. Certainly personal stories were important, and an early draft of *Introducing Womanist Theology*[9] was circulated. The literary texts used in the class drew from black women's autobiographical and fictional works: Billie Holiday, *Lady Sings the Blues*; Octavia Butler, *Parable of the Sower*; and Barbara Neely, *Blanche on the Lam*.[10] This mixture of black women's literature and personal narratives became a rich vein for exploring African American religious thought and American social realities and creating community among students. (For the discussion questions used for this class, see appendix 2.) By the end of the class, I arrived at the understanding that the students' deepest learning had come in their appreciation for the gifts of self and culture.

The conduit for this appreciation was the course objective to explore the power of language. "Language" was understood to include spoken, sung, written, and visual communication. So Billie Holiday's music as well as her autobiography were considered. Expanding the concept of "language," the class also visited an art gallery owned and operated by black women, featuring several African American women's works. The explorations of language included finding ways that black women name the meanings of faith and salvation. Octavia Butler's work presented one stark apocalyptic view that inspired student reflections on the end times. Neely's Blanche is a day worker, a domestic, who responds to her realities even as she carves out other options for herself and her family. This led to discussions of ways that black women name their experiences of the holy, especially reflected in everyday language of praise/prayer words, contemporary gospel music, or everyday greetings, for example, the often-used "Have a blessed day."

Finally, the note of community-building among students was especially strong. Not all students in the class were African American, yet all the students found that tapping into their own experiences became a route to providing links to each other. Students saw themselves in relation to the wider community of city, nation, and world.

Conclusion: At the Border

These classes created a bond between the students as a group and with me as a teacher. Both black and white students stay in touch with me. The responses to the classes varied. Certainly, a few students were just grateful to have the class end. But more often I hear other stories. Some students have let me know of arguments with current teachers and ask for my help to think of constructive strategies to oppose the instructor. Some students seek more material so that they can continue reading topics raised in class. Some students have changed their majors to English or other liberal arts, honoring their own gifts and abilities. Two students in a philosophy class refused to quietly accept that teacher's statement that there was no African philosophy until 1960. Other students continue to find ways to express the importance of their approaches to material and, most important, to tell their own stories and validate the world in which they live. Several students have later brought me their creative writing about their own lives, usually written for English classes. Another student began doing research on her family in the South. These actions blur the concepts of "intellectual," "academic," and "scholarship," as students recognize that their lives have value in academe. Students become border-crossers. Border pedagogy, as Giroux says, has this potential. "Put simply, students must be encouraged to cross ideological and political borders as a way of furthering the limits of their own understanding in a setting that is pedagogically safe and socially nurturing rather than authoritarian and infused with the suffocating smugness of a certain political correctness."[11] The borders are places of opportunity, new frontiers to be mapped. In the past, canonical guards patrolled the borders under the banners of classism, keeping out ideas that did not match the white, male, middle-class world. But such scholarly unity was a lie, as color lines were embedded in the tenets of modernity. Other people lived and thought beyond these constraints.

Studying African American religions can become an opportunity to guide students to the borders. The cultural barriers that I experienced as a child, the social boundaries that my parents knew, are constructed in new ways—unless we transgress those borders. African American religions' complex richness was the key I found to become a border worker or guide, instead of a canonical guard. The discoveries beyond the borders become a community project that can only enrich all our humanity.

APPENDIX I: ASSIGNMENT FOR WOMANIST SPIRITUAL AUTOBIOGRAPHY: WRITING YOUR SPIRITUAL AUTOBIOGRAPHY

The following are only suggested questions, as your own story may take you in different directions. The only questions that you will be asked to discuss in class are marked with an asterisk (*), as they are more general, less personal. No student is required to discuss any portion of her or his autobiography in class. The final statement is marked with [##], and is the basis of the Journaling paper, due at the end of class.

- How do I define God/the Divine One today? How did I define God in my earliest memory?
- What has happened between then and now to shape my belief?

- What is a great spiritual mystery I want answered?
- Am I more comfortable talking about "faith" or "spirituality"? Why?
- What is sacred to me?
- I best pray . . .
- I define prayer as . . .
- Where do I mark the beginning point of my own faith development? Why there? What is the story I tell myself about that point?
- On a faith line (like this one) place the markers that brought you to this point in your faith life: _____X (you are here)
- A symbol of my faith life today would be . . .
- A symbol of my faith journey would be . . . (You can describe or draw it.)
- Continuing the faith line, I hope to see or experience the following markers in my own spiritual future. (Describe the markers.)
  X_____ →
- A symbol of that preferred future is . . .
- What or who have been the important spiritual influences in my life, for good or ill?
- Describe why they are important. What do I discover about those influences?
- Write a letter to one of the people who are important.
- Now, how do I define what I believe in today?

Based on this exploration, I have learned about myself or my beliefs or I hope that . . .

APPENDIX 2: ASSIGNMENT FOR WOMANIST THEOLOGY AND LITERATURE: DISCUSSION QUESTIONS FOR YOUR CONSIDERATION FOR THE NOVELS

Questions for *Lady Sings the Blues:*

- How does she negotiate race? How does she negotiate power?
- How does she negotiate poverty? How does she survive in a hostile work environment?
- Where is her power?
- How, in this autobiography, is black culture "controlled" or "patrolled" by the dominant society?

Questions for *Blanche on the on the Lam:*

- Who is Blanche? (Do you know her or someone like her?)
- Point out the patterns characteristic of: conversation; friendship; familial relationships. What does or doesn't ring true about them?
- Give examples of Blanche's expressions of the "way things are."
- Give examples of Blanche's subversive or survival activities.

Questions for *Parable of the Sower:*

- What makes this science fiction *black?*
- Is there a black *women's* dynamic in the text?
- Is there a reflection on politics? Is Butler's vision of the human community hopeful?
- If this book were a movie, who would star?
- What are the author's aims?
- How is language used? Is it effective in reaching the author's aims?

For each book, consider:

- What is "good"?
- What is life? What is life-giving?
- In this book, who is the human person? The community?
- How do you know?

NOTES

1. Henry A. Giroux, *Border Crossings: Cultural Workers and the Politics of Education* (New York: Routledge, 1992), 30.

2. Toni Morrison, *Sula* (New York: Knopf, 1973), Maya Angelou, *I Know Why the Caged Bird Sings* (New York: Random House, 1970) and Mary Helen Washington's edited volume, *Black Eyed Susans: Classic Stories by and about Black Women* (New York: Anchor Books, 1975) offer fiction that lifts up African American women's lives. Sonia Sanchez, *We a BaddDD People* (Detroit: Broadside Press, 1970) and others use poetry to express black women's ideas. These texts opened the door for me to discover other writers. Note that the publishing dates of the books—1970s—were *before* I had begun master's-level studies.

3. The Shrine of the Black Madonna is a black church movement begun in the early 1970s by the then Reverend Albert Cleage. See Cleage's *Black Christian Nationalism: New Directions for the Black Church* (New York: Morrow, 1972). For an examination of Spiritualist churches, see Hans A Baer, *The Black Spiritual Movement: A Religious Response to Racism* (Knoxville: University of Tennessee Press, 1984), and Claude Jacobs and Andrew Kaslow, *The Spiritual Churches of New Orleans: Origins, Beliefs, and Rituals of an African American Religion* (Knoxville: University of Tennessee Press, 1991).

4. Dyson, *I May Not Get There with You, The True Martin Luther King Jr.* (New York: Free Press, 2000).

5. Gilkes, *If It Wasn't For the Women* (Maryknoll, NY: Orbis Books, 2001).

6. Womanist religious scholarship began to grow in the 1980s. In fine: the womanist approach draws from the religious lives and meanings of black women and from the perspectives of African American women and uses critical ethical analyses to construct theologies that are connected with or lead to activism.

7. Carter G. Woodson, *The Mis-education of the Negro* (Trenton, NJ: Africa World Press, 1990), xiii.

8. Patricia Hill Collins lays out this continuing marginalization of noncanonical ideas and black women in academia in *Fighting Words: Black Women and the Search for Justice* (Minneapolis: University of Minnesota Press, 1998). Note especially chapter 3, "On Race, Gender, and Science: Black Women as Objects and Agents of Sociological Knowledge" and chapter 4, " 'What's Going On?': Black Feminist Thought and the Politics of Postmodernism."

9. The completed text has now been published. See Stephanie Y. Mitchem, *Introducing Womanist Theology* (Maryknoll, NY: Orbis Books, 2002).

10. Billie Holiday with William Duffy, *Lady Sings the Blues* (New York: Penguin Books, 1956); Octavia Butler, *Parable of the Sower* (New York: Warner Books, 1993); and Barbara Neely, *Blanche on the Lam* (New York: Penguin Books, 1993). Special thanks to Carolyn Medine Jones for suggesting the Holiday work.

11. Giroux, *Border Crossings*, 33.

REFERENCES

Angelou, Maya. *I Know Why the Caged Bird Sings*. New York: Random House, 1970.

Baer, Hans A. *The Black Spiritual Movement: A Religious Response to Racism*. Knoxville: University of Tennessee Press, 1984.

Butler, Octavia. *Parable of the Sower*. New York: Warner Books, 1993.

Cleage, Albert. *Black Christian Nationalism: New Directions for the Black Church*. New York: Morrow, 1972.

Collins, Patricia Hill. *Fighting Words: Black Women and the Search for Justice*. Minneapolis: University of Minnesota Press, 1998.

Dyson, Michael Eric. *I May Not Get There with You: The True Martin Luther King Jr.* New York: Free Press, 2000.

Gilkes, Cheryl Townsend. *If It Wasn't For the Women*. Maryknoll, NY: Orbis Books, 2001.

Giroux, Henry A. *Border Crossings: Cultural Workers and the Politics of Education*. New York: Routledge, 1992.

Holiday, Billie, with William Duffy. *Lady Sings the Blues*. New York: Penguin Books, 1956.

Jacobs, Claude, and Andrew Kaslow. *The Spiritual Churches of New Orleans: Origins, Beliefs, and Rituals of an African American Religion*. Knoxville: University of Tennessee Press, 1991.

Mitchem, Stephanie Y. *Introducing Womanist Theology*. Maryknoll, NY: Orbis Books, 2002.

Morrison, Toni. *Sula*. New York: Knopf, 1973.

Neely, Barbara. *Blanche on the Lam*. New York: Penguin Books, 1993.

Sanchez, Sonia. *We a BaddDD People*. Detroit: Broadside Press, 1970.

Washington, Mary Helen, ed. *Black Eyed Susans: Classic Stories by and about Black Women*. New York: Anchor Books, 1975.

Woodson, Carter G. *The Mis-education of the Negro*. Trenton, NJ: Africa World Press, 1990.

4

Incorporating the African American Religious Experience into the Community College Curriculum and Classroom

Mary Jane Horton

I teach at the urban Metropolitan Campus of Cuyahoga Community College, located near downtown Cleveland, Ohio. It is one of 1,171 community colleges nationwide that provide affordable credit courses to over 5 million students. Forty-four percent of all U.S. undergraduates attend community colleges, according to the American Association of Community Colleges. The Cuyahoga Community College urban campus is located in the inner city of Cleveland, between a low-security prison and large multiblock, low-income housing projects, and enrolls about 6,500 of the 24,000 students attending the college. The other two campuses are located in the suburbs and mainly attract students who live in those areas. The majority (58 percent) of the students at the Metropolitan Campus are African American; 28 percent are white; and 12 percent are other races/ethnic groups. The average student age is 30.5; 60 percent of the students are over the age of 24, and 69 percent of the students are female. The majority of students reside in the Cleveland inner-city zip codes, and a third of the students have attended the Cleveland municipal schools.[1] In this chapter, I present several teaching strategies I use to engage African American students in the study of religion and several ways I use African American religions to engage all students in the study of religion.

My classes are rich in religious diversity. In a typical class, I have four or five Roman Catholic students, several African American Baptists of various groups, Hispanic evangelicals, African American Pentecostals, perhaps two Muslims (including African American Muslims and others from the Middle East), a Seventh-Day Adventist, and one Buddhist or Hindu. I have been seeing more African American and Hispanic Pentecostal students from small independent storefront churches of Christian "nondenominational" types—churches that are consistent with the socioeconomic level of the students who live in the zip codes in Cleveland's inner city, where many storefront churches are located. In the past, my students have included Sikhs, Jews, Wiccans, Rastafarians, Jehovah's Witnesses, agnostics, and atheists.

The community college presents unique educational challenges in ethnic diversity as well. Many African American students, for example, are female first-generation college students, who combine full-time college enrollment with a part-time or full-time job and with being a single parent. Among the Asian and Hispanic students, many are recent immigrants from Central America, South America, and Asia. There is also a growing number of students from Russia, Albania, Romania, and other eastern European countries. The student population includes a diverse group of international students from about fifty countries. The English as a Second Language program enrolls about 250 international students and recent immigrants. Although the college sponsors an annual "Diversity Day" celebration, every day seems like diversity day at the Metropolitan campus as the mixture of students makes for a very cosmopolitan atmosphere. This diversity of students is a frequent topic of campus conversation and a source of pride, and most professors tend to use every opportunity to leverage this diversity in classroom discussions. Aside from the international students, who often come from wealthy families, the campus is a microcosm of Cleveland's inner city and reflects the city's racial, ethnic, and economic demographics. Although tuition is only about $70 per semester credit hour, 74 percent of the students receive financial aid, and some participate in welfare-to-work programs.

Like my student population, my own work is diverse. It would be considered nontraditional by many in the academy. In this community college teaching environment, I find myself on the fringes of the field of religious studies, fully aware that the scholarly work is being done by others and that I engage in a work of teaching that is generally looked down on by those in research-oriented academic institutions. As is often the case in community colleges, I have a dual teaching position in philosophy and religious studies. I also teach "Introduction to Humanities" courses. I teach classes in three formats: traditional classroom, televised courses, and web-based courses via the Internet. With a teaching schedule of five courses per semester and ten hours of contractual office hours per week, I have little time for research. I also have additional responsibilities as program coordinator for philosophy, humanities, and religious studies that are administrative in nature. They include scheduling and staffing about seventy sections of ten different courses per year and the recruitment and retention of the adjunct faculty who teach the majority of our classes. I also mentor new adjunct faculty and share my materials and teaching techniques with them.

Addressing the needs of, particularly, the African American students led me to apply to the "Mining the Motherlode" workshop. As program coordinator, I initially noticed a low enrollment of African American students in the religious studies courses and thought that a new course in African American religion would attract more African American students to study religion and revitalize the program. Since I had no expertise in this area, I began attending Ashland Theology Seminary, in the Black Church studies program, and completed a master's degree in theology with a Black Church studies specialization. At Ashland, I learned about African American Christian practices and traditions, both in classes and from my classmates who were ministers and pastors in local African American churches. As a result of the Black Church studies classes, my most striking realization was that African American Christian practices were not just another variation of Christianity but had liberation theology at their core as reflective of social, political, and economic concerns of African Americans. Being an adult student in a new discipline also gave me insights into my role as a teacher, as I thought about the dynamics of the classroom.

Many of these issues were ones upon which I reflected in the workshop. I finalized the structure of the new "African American Religious Experience" course during the Lilly Teaching Workshop. In the workshop, I was exposed to additional varieties of African American religions, including the Black Jews, the Shrine of the Black Madonna, and African religious traditions such as Yoruba practice and Vodun. I incorporated these practices into my courses. Currently, three sections of "African American Religious Experience" are offered each term, and the annual enrollment is about one hundred. Enrollment in other religious studies classes has also increased as a result of this addition to the curriculum. Many students who complete the "African American Religious Experience" class go on to take other religious studies courses.

One effect of the workshop experience has been my incorporation of aspects of African American religious experience in the "Comparative World Religions" course. These additions introduce students to the numerous varieties of African American religious practice that are evident in the greater Cleveland area. These include the Nation of Islam, as well as African American Muslims and others. To help my students engage this material, I have developed classroom exercises that are a direct result of the collegial collaboration and experimentation of the workshop. In general, these exercises generate a vital learning environment with increased student engagement and significant dialogue about racism, classism, and sexism within religious practice. The workshop showed me the interdisciplinary nature of African American religions. I use African American religions to engage African American students, who now have an opportunity to see themselves and their practices—something they generally do not experience in traditional courses. The study of African American religions also provides an intriguing entry point into the study of religion in general. I have found that it also brings engagement from students who know nothing about African American religions.

Given the interdisciplinary nature of African American religions, the variety of practices, and the exuberance of the worship activities, African American religions are particularly well suited to generate excitement and enthusiasm in the religious studies classroom. From the perspective of students from mainline white congregations, African American religions are exotic, mysterious, and intriguing. Given the segregated nature of religious congregations in America, most white students have not seen exuberant African American worship in the music, preaching, and gifts of the Holy Spirit. From a historical perspective, most students are not aware of the specific ways that Christianity was used to justify slavery in the United States. They are quite surprised to hear that slaves were taught by Christian ministers using slave catechisms that contained wording such as: "Question: What did God make you for? The Answer: To make a crop."[2] They are surprised to learn that Malcolm X's rejection of the Christianity as "the white man's religion" was based on these types of historical practices.[3] Both the historic Black Church and the Nation of Islam, with various liberation theologies at their core, reflect the interdisciplinary role of African American religions in addressing the economic, social, cultural, and political needs of African Americans in the United States. Rather than "ghettoize" African American religions in teaching African American students, my approach is to use these exercises to engage all students in the study of religion and to increase their awareness of the varieties of religious expression in their community and the multiple role that they serve for their followers. These exercises create a vital learning environment with classroom engagement and an openness to new traditions.

One aspect of my teaching that is increasingly part of education in all institutions is distance learning. I teach a "tele-course" that includes a videotaped series of lectures and interviews that students watch on their own, three videotaped seminars that I conduct, and several written assignments and essay exams that I structure for the course material. In this tele-course, titled "Beliefs and Believers, Comparative World Religion," I incorporate information on Islam and African Americans, particularly. One approach that I use to engage African American students in the tele-course is a written assignment in which students use Michael Malloy's eight elements of religion—belief system, community, central myths, ritual, ethics, characteristic emotional experiences, material expression, and sacredness—as an analytical tool.[4] They identify these elements in a religion with which they are familiar. They also describe what is misunderstood by "outsiders" about the religion and what they, as "insiders," find to be most and least attractive about their religions. Although it is engaging for most students to identify these elements in their own religions, it is especially engaging for African American students to focus on their own religious practice within an academic framework. They have seen little mention of their religious practices in traditional texts or courses. This is effective as they apply theory to concrete examples from their own experiences. Since they tend to not see themselves in a traditional course, this exercise is one way that they can see themselves and their religious practice within an academic framework; from this experience they learn to be open to the traditions of other religions.

In my "traditional" classroom, I face a variety of issues. In my teaching environment at an urban community college, the classroom is not an elite place but rather it is reflective of the Cleveland urban demographics. Overall, the realities of this setting are that students often have low reading abilities and poor writing skills and occasionally manifest inappropriate behaviors. They have other "obstacles" to learning such as full-time jobs, families, and so on. Virtually every student in my classroom is nontraditional. Many of them are older students, entering a college classroom for the first time.

The primary advantage of teaching older students is that they have a great deal of life experience. I have developed exercises to leverage the students' life experiences for the collective community of learners in the classroom. These exercises are examples of the ways I channel students' life experiences into meaningful interaction in the classroom to engage students in the material and to give them exposure to the varieties of religious practices in the Cleveland area. Generally, I first establish a safe space to foster a community of learners, by honoring their traditions, giving meaningful assignments, and providing an opportunity for discussion. This is important to older students, who want to apply the material to their lives and their work. So whenever possible I present the material in this manner.

In *Teaching to Transgress: Education as the Practice of Freedom,* bell hooks suggests that learning should be exciting. I realized during my time at Ashland that such excitement was not something I had experienced as a student in the undergraduate classroom. It took me twelve boring years to complete my undergraduate business degree. I share with students that my desire for an exciting classroom was driven by my own experiences as a bored, unengaged student. I share that I attended the Cuyahoga Community College Metropolitan Campus as a part-time student as I attempted to balance full-time employment and family obligations. I share that I made a major midlife career change and just completed my master's degree several years ago. As I have been a student most of my adult life, I use selective self-disclosure and share ideas that have helped me to juggle family, full-time employment, and course work. I acknowledge my students as whole persons who are also attending classes. Since virtually all of them are juggling home, work, and family just as I did as a student,

I often give time management and study skills information, including reading tips. I acknowledge the students' multiple obligations in the structure of the class by providing a very detailed syllabus with all required readings, exam dates, and assignments so students can plan their work for the term. In addition, I try to help them identify and remove obstacles to their academic success during the term. For many of them, the main obstacle is writing, so I include a number of short writing assignments and refer students for tutoring, assistance at the writing center, or additional course work when needed. Sometimes essay exams are problematic, so I provide instructions on preparing for an essay exam or dealing with text anxiety.

Some of the specific classroom teaching strategies that I use to engage African American students—and, indeed, all students—in the study of religion and of African American religious experience are described hereafter. As you will note, my exercises attempt not only to teach the content—the "facts" of African American religious experience—but also to engage the students in interrogating their own experiences in relation to what we learn. They become lifelong learners. Developing a community of learners, therefore, is my first task.

Creating a Community of Learners by Establishing "Class Norms"

As the essays that open this volume suggest, the classroom is a contact zone—and it is very much so in my diverse environment. Before attempting to engage students in the study of African American religious experience, a subject that involves the controversial topics of race and religion, I have to establish a classroom atmosphere that is a safe space for the exchange of ideas and for the work of a community of learners. Generally speaking, my students have been trained in the "Jerry Springer Show" model of discussion and conflict resolution. Since I have also observed that students do not listen to each other or respect their classmates, I have taken to heart bell hooks's view that "one of the responsibilities of the teacher is to help create an environment where students learn, that in addition to speaking, it is important to listen respectfully to others."[5]

On the second day of class, I ask students to think about past classes and the types of classroom behaviors that they have found disruptive to their learning. I stress that this is *their* class and that they have the right to identify what is unacceptable to them or what interferes with their learning. For example, cell phones ringing during an exam do not disturb me, but they are disruptive to the students taking an exam. Given the realities of my setting, most students have had bad experiences and are very willing to name these disturbing behaviors. I also stress that the very subject matter of religion is dangerous, as people have killed each other because of religious beliefs for centuries, so ground rules for class discussion are needed for meaningful dialogue. Then, I have students form groups of five to six, with the instructions to take ten minutes to develop the norms or rules that they want in the class for the term. After ten minutes, a representative from each group introduces his or her group members to the class and reads the list of class norms that that group has developed. I write these on the board with a minimal amount of comment, editing or evaluation. Each group's suggestions are recorded until the board is filled with norms.

After all proposed norms are recorded on the board, I ask for suggestions for combining similar ideas, additions, deletions, clarification, and so on. To solicit additional norms, I might ask "What about food in class?" or "What about cell phones?" or "What about children in class?" and will work with the class to develop a norm that is acceptable to the majority. I might ask "What about a student who dominates the class discussion?" "How do we make certain that everyone has a chance to speak?" Students might also suggest norms for the professor such as "begin and end class on time." To affect this, I request that the students give me a five-minute warning at the end of class. After the list is finalized on the board, I again request additions, deletions, and discussion. We continue the discussion until all agree on the list.

Generally students develop norms about cell phones, coming to class prepared, not disturbing others if late, food, children, respecting others' opinions, and profanity. The need to raise one's hand to speak has appeared on every list, as the quiet students remark that that is the only way that they get to contribute.

I begin the next class by distributing a typed list to the students and asking them to verify that the list correctly reflects the discussion. I discuss the notion of shared responsibility for the success of the class and that it is their class and they have the right to decide how it will be run. For the rest of the term, latecomers are given the list of class norms, along with the syllabus, and I stress that these are the class rules that were developed by the students on the second day of class. At the first transgression, I loudly announce: "That is exactly what your fellow students did not want to happen in here. Your classmates were very clear about the fact that such an activity was detrimental to their learning." If students start shouting out answers or engage in side conversations, especially when another student is speaking, I refer to the class norms. They allow me to say: "With so many students that want to speak we really need to use the class norm of raising hands so everyone has a chance to speak and to be heard by others."

Although this class norms exercise may appear to "waste" one hour of valuable class time, it helps to set the foundation on which to build a community of learners and pays huge dividends in saved time during the term in dealing with student behavior issues. I had initially developed the class norms exercise as a classroom management technique, but in the process I had some unintended results. Most of all, it helps students feel engaged in the class on the second day and facilitates a meaningful exchange of ideas in an atmosphere of mutual respect. It structures civil dialogue and an exchange of informed opinions. I still enforce the rules in the classroom, but they are now the students' rules, not mine.

Religious History Reflection, Religious Objects, and "Attending" an African American Pentecostal Service

Once the classroom is a safe space for learning, much can happen there. One way that I involve students in more than a "banking" model of learning is to use material culture that requires that they use their bodies as well as their minds. I also use film, not for information but as experiential learning.

I introduce this religious history exercise by saying that each student comes to class with some experience of religion and that it is an important beginning step for each student to think about his or her past experience with religion. My goal is to leverage their life experiences to foster engagement and excitement in the material. Students are asked to prepare two- to three-sentence responses to a list of questions about their religion traditions, their exposure to other religions, and their experience with religious objects. The exercise includes questions about family religion, the celebration of religious holidays, important rituals, religion objects, exposure to other religions, the family's view of other religions, and the student's current practice. Students who have seen little religious experience in their homes are asked to focus on their exposure to another religion. I stress that all information is confidential and that self-disclosure is always at the student's option. I begin the class discussion of the assignment by asking students what they learned from the assignment. Generally, several students will remark that they realized that they have had little exposure to other religions. Once, a fifty-year-old Puerto Rican–born man said that he realized that he had been frightened as a child in a Latino Pentecostal church by the seemingly uncontrollable fits and dancing of the congregation through the gifts of the Holy Spirit. Then a young African American male responded, "I learned how much I love the Lord." He launched into an exuberant Pentecostal testimony of his love for Jesus. Although a few African American Pentecostals have enrolled in my classes in the past, this was the first time for a very personal testimony in class. I was able to honor his tradition within the context of the class by thanking him for his contribution and emphasizing that the student had provided a good example of Pentecostal exuberance, which we would see later in class. I learned from this experience that I could relate just about any student comment to the course material.

As part of this assignment, I also ask about the students' experiences with religious objects. The Roman Catholic students are usually the first to describe material objects. I then share a few items from my collection of Roman Catholic objects, including holy cards, rosaries, plastic Mary statues, Fatima holy water, and grocery store saint candles, including the Our Lady of Fatima, the Virgin of Guadalupe, and St. Martin De Porres. Non-Hispanic students are intrigued by the fact that I buy the candles in the Goya Hispanic foods section at the grocery store, where they appear above the beans and rice. As I pass them around for students to examine, Roman Catholic students often volunteer to describe their use in devotion. I then introduce the appearance of the Roman Catholic saints in the African American religions of Vodun/Voodou and Santeria and explain the presence of the Catholic saints in these Afro-Cuban religions. Then I incorporate a short lecture on this African American religion and the use of a large variety of material objects. I then ask for examples of material manifestation in other faith traditions. Students provide a wide range of examples since they come from a variety of traditions. I bring religious objects to class at every opportunity and encourage my students to do the same. I also have obtained multiple catalogues from various church supply stores such as Henninger's, and I lend these to students between classes. I also refer students to websites that sell church supplies, such as www.henninger's.com, www.catholicsupply.com, www.st-jude.com, and www.marianland.com, so they can explore these at their leisure. For Protestants, it is like a journey into forbidden, mysterious world. Usually one person will say, "But we have been taught that that is idolatry." Such a statement opens the door to later class discussions of Protestant reformation.

While maintaining confidentiality, I also use the information from the students' religious history reflections to engage them. I consciously try to use examples from their faith traditions in lectures and discussion during the term.

A second way I engage in participatory religious experience is to use film. In my setting, it is not practical to attend a Sunday morning African American Pentecostal worship service as a class field trip because most students have family, work, and church obligations. I have substituted in-class videos for group church visits and now prefer them as pedagogical tools. With videos, I know exactly what the students will see and hear. I can provide explanations and answer questions as they arise, and we can immediately engage in a debriefing discussion. When necessary, I can also replay parts of the video for discussion. With videos, I have found that students are engaged and feel comfortable asking questions. In addition, we avoid the potentially voyeuristic feeling of a site visit. Using video, in just seventy-five minutes it is possible to introduce, view, and discuss excerpts from several Christian evangelical services. Students are still encouraged to visit preapproved churches individually or in small groups and to answer specific questions. For Christian services, they answer questions about the physical space of the church and the rituals that are conducted relative to the sacraments for that Christian group. For other religious sites, which may not include a structured service, the questions are more descriptive, such as who, what, when, why, and how, and three things that the student learned from the site visit.

The video series *Mine Eyes Have Seen the Glory*, hosted by Randall Balmer, contains engaging depictions of the diversity of American evangelical worship.[6] Specifically, Balmer presents several evangelical services, including a white suburban megachurch, an African American Pentecostal church, and a Hispanic Pentecostal church. His commentary is informative and empathetic, as he clearly explains Pentecostal enthusiasm, gifts of the Holy Spirit, testimonies, and other activities shown in the videos. The interviews with the believers and ministers are another engaging advantage of the video over a live service. In addition, the video series, which is available for classroom use, provides live footage and commentary on speaking in tongues, faith healing, television evangelism, and the prosperity gospel.

As an introduction to Pentecostalism, I assign two short articles from *Religions of the United States in Practice*, volume 2: "Lucy Smith and the Pentecostal Worship in Chicago," by Wallace Best, and "Tongues and Healing in the Azusa Street Revival," by Gaston Espinosa.[7] I introduce the video by defining the terms *fundamentalist, charismatic, evangelical* and *Pentecostal*, using Randall Balmer's *Encyclopedia of Evangelicalism*.[8] The video demonstrates these terms. As students watch the video of services, they take notes on the occurrence of these elements in the services: (1) order of service, (2) spontaneity, (3) length of service, (4) audience involvement, (5) dress, and (6) emotionalism/enthusiasm. An identification of these elements serves as a starting point for class discussion. Students unfamiliar with Pentecostal exuberance often, initially, are uncomfortable with the physical manifestations of the gifts of the Holy Spirit in the believers and yet are fascinated to see these religious practices. Balmer's commentary acknowledges this discomfort, and his running commentary provides essential explanations about the depicted activities that would be impossible for me to provide during an onsite visit.

During the discussion of the services, I point out the different approaches to evangelical worship services and stress the distinction that Balmer makes between holding a correct belief and having a religious experience. We discuss the ways that the congregation's theological emphasis affects the style of worship. Sometimes the most instructive comments are from the African American students, who, after seeing the white megachurch service for the first time, are quite appalled. They ask, "How can they call that praying or praising? They are just sitting there. They are not really praising." This provides an opportunity to talk about the differences in worship styles between those churches that focus on holding a right belief versus those that emphasize having a religious experience. My goal is for students not only to experience the variety of Christian evangelical worship but also to understand that differences in theological emphasis such as liberation theology can affect the worship style. Students with little exposure to Christianity especially benefit from this approach, as it permits them to experience a number of Christian worship services and to understand the reasons for the diversity in worship styles. For Christians who are familiar with just one worship style, it permits them to experience a variety of styles outside of their own practice and to be more open to the practices of other traditions.

Written Analysis and Response: Womanist Theology

Many of my students, as I indicated earlier, are African American women. To expose them and the rest of my students to current academic thought about African American women's religious experience, I introduce womanist thought in my classes through a written assignment. This assignment asks students to consider the ramifications of imaging God as a white male. I ask them to respond to Patricia L. Hunter's article "Women's Power—Women's Passion," from A Troubling in My Soul: Womanist Perspectives on Evil and Suffering, in which Hunter addresses misogyny in American society and the historic Black Church. She describes the triple jeopardy of classism, racism, and sexism for African American women and the notion of beauty in popular advertising. She describes current issues for African American women in historic Black Churches, such as the refusal to ordain women, and writes: "the Black Church must be held accountable for the oppression it has leveled against its own women."[9] She also explores the ramifications of patriarchy related to the imaging of God as a white and male for African American women, the historic Black Church, and society as a whole.

I begin with a general handout on feminist and womanist theologies. The instructions and assignment requirements are very detailed, so as to model a proper academic writing style, as most students need help with their writing. The detailed instructions also facilitate tutoring and writing intervention at the college writing center. The specific questions and required format decreases the potential for a student's copying from the internet. The detailed format of questions and responses make it is easier for me to detect internet copying, as this format reveals inconsistencies in narrative voice. In my setting, it is necessary to carefully set out requirements for the format of the paper, including such details as what size margins and fonts to utilize and what footnote style to practice. I also list specific issues that the paper must address, including the steps to take in writing the paper. About a week before the assignment is due, I ask about the students' progress and address the difficulties that some students may be experiencing. I acknowledge the discomfort they may be experiencing, and I stress the importance of following the analysis-and-response format so students become familiar with reading and summarizing an article before responding to its contents.

On the day that the assignment is due, I begin the class discussion by again acknowledging the discomfort that some students may have felt with the assignment. I then ask for reactions to the assignment. Students generally have strong reactions to the article. They range from "I could not relate to this at all" to "What does it have to do with me as a white male?" Some students remark "I never thought of this," or "I certainly could not ask this in church." Some see anger in the article and respond negatively. They are offended by the article and respond that Hunter should start her own church if she is unhappy with her traditional Baptist church. Others agree with her: "This is exactly how it is in my church." With this beginning, African American women often volunteer their own experiences, which generally match Hunter's. I then introduce Hunter's discussion of imaging God as white and male by asking students to list the various groups that were studied during the term and then describe how each group imaged God.

This article provokes a lively discussion about race, religion, and the various "isms" that it addresses. African American women have shared with me privately that they were quite surprised to realize that when they prayed they had been imaging a white God. For some Euro-American males, this is their first encounter with an article in which they are not the central characters, and some find it irrelevant.

The success of this discussion about the imaging of one's God depends heavily on the following of the class norms and the success of developing a community of learners who listen to and respect each other. In this moment, students, like the white males, might disengage or respond disruptively. If the class norms work, their disagreement provides points of engagement. At some level, I make sure, in my classes, that students are always engaged, whether they realize it or not, in the kind of theological reflection that Hunter models, one that involves such ideas as the imaging of God and the issues of racism, sexism, and classism.

Discussing this article is usually the culminating exercise of the class. When all goes well, it is a moment when I experience the joy of watching the transition from the "Jerry Springer Show"–style reaction to the engagement of student scholars who have learned to discuss controversial subjects with analysis and reflection and to listen to each other.

Conclusion

Being in the contact zone involves risks and significant opportunities for engagement for me and for my students. Although it is generally stimulating, it can also be frightening. It requires me to be strategic in my course structure, assignments, and class discussions. It also requires me to spend time explaining to students the reasons that we are doing a particular assignment or exercise. Given that my students are nontraditional, I need a variety of experiential learning techniques with an applied orientation to engage them. To do this, I need to be strategic in my approach to teaching so I can first establish a safe environment, the contact zone. It is here that the exercises permit learning to take place as students engage and encounter the issues. Establishing a contact zone and managing the discussion takes careful planning and coordination. For instance, I use the strategy of the class norms to manage students who just want to hear themselves talk or those who are unable to relate their own experiences to the course material.

Through these exercises, I have been able to facilitate growth and learning in my students, as I can see them become more open to ideas from other faith traditions and more aware of differences in practice. Over the past few years there has been a significant increase in the enrollment in religious studies courses, and some students have expressed interest in starting a religious diversity club that would present campus programming on various religious traditions. In my setting I have had opportunities to use my student's life experience in experiential learning with an applied orientation to their lives and careers. Supporting my pedagogical exercises is my personal commitment to bell hooks's view of "education as the practice of freedom."[10]

My students generally remark that my enthusiasm for the subject matter is contagious and that I really made them work and think in the course. A memorable comment was from a middle-aged African American male student who attended my 8:30 a.m. class after working as an orderly all night at a local hospital. At end of the term, he told me, "I really enjoy the way that you get us to speak about issues like religion and race that most professors would avoid. You show us by your example and then give us an opportunity to talk about these things. You teach us not be afraid to talk about them. You are one bold sister." His comment meant much to me because as a teacher I really want to model freedom.

NOTES

1. Statistics are from *Cuyahoga Community College Enrollment Trends and Student Characteristics, Fall Semester, 2003.* Cuyahoga Community College.

2. Gayraud S. Wilmore, *Black Religion and Black Radicalism: An Interpretation of the Religious History of African-Americans*, 3rd ed. (Maryknoll, NY: Orbis Books, 1998), 47.

3. Ibid, 214.

4. Michael Molloy, *Experiencing the World's Religions: Tradition, Challenge and Change*, 3rd ed. (New York: McGraw-Hill, forthcoming).

5. bell hooks, *Teaching to Transgress: Education as the Practice of Freedom* (New York: Routledge, 1994), 150.

6. See *Mine Eyes Have Seen the Glory*, Gateway Films, Worcester, PA: Vision Video, 1992. Distributed with classroom performance rights by Insight Media, 1-800-233-9910.

7. See Colleen McDannell, ed., *Religions of the United States in Practice*, vol. 2 (Princeton: Princeton University Press, 2001).

8. See Randall Balmer, *Encyclopedia of Evangelicalism* (Louisville, KY: Westminster John Knox Press, 2002).

9. Patricia Hunter, "Women's Power—Women's Passion," in *A Troubling in My Soul: Womanist Perspectives on Evil and Suffering*, Emilie Townes, ed. (Maryknoll: Orbis Books, 1997), 197.

10. hooks, *Teaching to Transgress*, 12.

REFERENCES

Balmer, Randall. *Encyclopedia of Evangelicalism*. Louisville, KY: Westminster John Knox Press, 2002.

———. *Mine Eyes Have Seen the Glory: A Journey into the Evangelical Subculture in America*. New York: Oxford University Press, 2000.

Felder, Cain Hope. *Stony the Road We Trod*. Minneapolis: Augsburg Fortress, 1991.

Hayes, Diana L., and Cyprian Davis, eds. *Taking Down Our Harps: Black Catholics in the United States*. Maryknoll, NY: Orbis Books, 1998.

hooks, bell. *Teaching to Transgress: Education as the Practice of Freedom*. New York: Routledge, 1994.

Hopkins, Dwight N. *Introducing the Black Theology of Liberation*. Maryknoll, NY: Orbis Books, 1999.

Lindley, Susan Hill, ed. *You Have Stept Out of Your Place*. Louisville, KY: Westminster John Knox Press, 1996.

McDannell, Colleen, ed. *Religions of the United States in Practice*. Vol. 2. Princeton: Princeton University Press, 2001.

Pinn, Anne H., and Anthony B. Pinn. *Fortress Introduction to Black Church History*. Minneapolis: Augsburg Fortress Press, 2002.

Pinn, Anthony B. *Varieties of African-American Religious Experience*. Minneapolis: Augsburg Fortress Press, 1998.

Raboteau, Albert J. *African-American Religion*. Oxford: Oxford University Press, 1999.

Townes, Emilie M., ed. *A Troubling in My Soul: Womanist Perspectives on Evil and Suffering*. Maryknol, NY: Orbis Books, 1993.

Turner, Richard Brent. *Islam in the African-American Experience*. 2nd ed. Bloomington: Indiana University Press, 2003.

Williams, Juan. *This Far by Faith: Stories from the African-American Religious Experience*. New York: Morrow, 2003.

Wilmore, Gayraud S. *Black Religion and Black Radicalism: An Interpretation of the Religious History of Afro-American People*. 3rd ed. Maryknoll, NY: Orbis Books, 1998.

5

"I Want to Be Ready!": Teaching Christian Education in the African American Experience

Yolanda Y. Smith

The inspiration for developing the course "Christian Education in the African American Experience" emerged from my ongoing work on developing a new model of Christian education that explores the triple heritage of African Americans (African, African American, and Christian) through the African American spirituals. In this work, the spirituals are identified as embodiments of the triple heritage and as sources for deeper insights into the theology and spirituality of the African American church. Characteristics of the spirituals such as the call and response, creative imagery, and biblical content signal educational devices such as dialogue, imagination, and narrative that are themselves inherent within the spirituals. Such devices can assist educators in determining subject matter and creative approaches to the educational process.

In this chapter, I will introduce four teaching strategies that emerge from the characteristics of a triple-heritage model of Christian education that is grounded in the African American spirituals. I will then discuss various aspects of the course "Christian Education in the African American Experience" and illustrate how these strategies have shaped and informed my teaching of the course. The primary purpose of this essay is to examine the teaching/learning process that emerges throughout the course.

Teaching Strategies

I am often asked whether I have used the ideas that I have proposed in the triple-heritage model of Christian education in my classes. While I had incorporated some of the ideas in classes as well as in workshops and seminars conducted for various churches and conferences prior to my involvement in the "Mining the Motherlode" workshop, I had not yet developed a course that drew insights from the model throughout the content and methodology. My participation in the workshop gave me an opportunity to create a course that would explore these and other ideas by drawing upon sources that naturally arise from the African American experience, not only as sources for content but also as sources for exploring creative approaches throughout the educational process. The triple-heritage model has provided the foundation for this reflection, particularly since the aim of the model is to assist educators in gleaning insights for what we teach (content) and strategies for how we teach (practice) in the African American experience.

While there are a number of sources that could inform a triple-heritage model of Christian education (e.g., music, dance, ritual, folklore, etc.), I have focused on the spirituals because they embody all three components of the triple heritage—African, African American, and Christian. Maud Cuney Hare, an African American writer, lecturer, and concert pianist during the early twentieth century, recognized this integration of traditions within the spirituals throughout her writings. While she emphasized the African origins as the foundation of these songs, she also noted that the spirituals, which were born out of the American experience of slavery, were significantly shaped by Christian doctrine.[1] The spirituals can thus be a vehicle for exploring the triple heritage in a manner that allows all three aspects of the heritage to be reflected fully in relation to one another. This full representation is essential so that one aspect of the heritage does not dominate the curriculum while other aspects are lost. The aim is to see the triple heritage as a whole, with interrelated components, rather than as three separate and distinct elements.

The spirituals also lend themselves easily to critical analysis of the culture and reflection upon personal and collective responsibility within the community. Indeed, according to Wyatt Tee Walker and Jon Michael Spencer, the spirituals, since their inception, have been used as a form of social critique. This critique can be seen in numerous songs that embody a spirit of protest and a challenge to bring about transformation and social change.[2] Social analysis and critique is an important part of Christian education in the African American experience because they can empower contemporary African Americans to identify, challenge, and change oppressive systems and structures.

In addition, the spirituals can facilitate the church's reflection on the move-

ment of the Holy Spirit in the life of the African American church. The movement of the Holy Spirit through music and song united the slave community,
provided comfort in the midst of hardship, and deepened the church's sense
of spirituality.[3] Reflection on the theology embodied in the spirituals can shed
light on how the church has been empowered and inspired by the Spirit with
a sense of hope for the future: a hope that has allowed African Americans to
envision liberation and freedom from oppression. Furthermore, the spirituals
have already been accepted and integrated into the life of the African American
church. While we must continue to examine and critique the theology of the
spirituals to reinterpret them for contemporary African Americans, they can
be a familiar way to engage some of the critical issues and concerns facing the
African American church and community. And, finally, on a more personal
note, I am drawn to the spirituals because they have inspired a deeper sense
of the presence of God in my life; they have given me a sense of connection
with, as well as a profound respect for, my ancestors; they have allowed me to
experience a deeper sense of community within the African American church;
and they have helped me to gain a sense of pride in my African American
heritage. The spirituals, then, are a natural place to begin reflecting on a model
of Christian education that embodies a more authentically African American
mode of Christian education because they naturally arise out of the African
American experience. Furthermore, they affirm and celebrate the rich heritage
of African people on the continent and in the Diaspora.

In my research, I have identified at least four characteristics that describe
a triple-heritage model of Christian education that is informed by the spirituals.
The model is communal, creative, critical, and cooperative. The teaching strategies that emerge from these characteristics include communal dialogue, creative engagement, critical reflection, and cooperative action.[4]

Communal Dialogue

Since the spirituals were created and sung in community, they inspire a
sense of community through the educational process. This sense of community draws students and teachers together in a mutual dialogue, or call
and response. The call and response, commonly seen in the spirituals and
grounded in African music, usually begins with a chant, sung by a leader or
soloist that is answered by the group or congregation. This rhythm, seen in
the spiritual "Swing Low, Sweet Chariot," reveals the communal nature of
the spirituals.

LEADER   Swing low, sweet chariot,

RESPONSE   Coming for to carry me home,

LEADER   Swing low, sweet chariot,

RESPONSE   Coming for to carry me home.[5]

The call and response promotes a communal dialogue that encourages both students and teachers to fully participate in the educational process. Since each person brings something valuable to the dialogue, anyone may begin the call and response at any time, engaging the entire community in a dynamic exchange of ideas and experiences. In the course "Christian Education in the African American Experience," communal dialogue has taken many forms, including a choral reading, responsive reading, litany, small and large group discussion, individual sharing, and role play.

Creative Engagement

Zora Neale Hurston noted that the spirituals are always in the process of creation.[6] Since a common characteristic of the spirituals is improvisation, they can be shaped and reshaped to accommodate a particular situation or event. For example, the words in the spiritual "Don't You Let Nobody Turn You Round" were adapted to "don't let segregation turn you around" and used during the Civil Rights movement in the 1960s. Freedom fighters such as Fannie Lou Hamer and Bernice Johnson Reagon were intimately involved in transforming these songs into freedom songs that ultimately undergirded the movement. These women embodied the spirit of the movement through their commitment to the survival and liberation of their people. They expressed their commitment not only through music but also through their creative participation in the marches, rallies, and sit-ins. In a similar fashion, I view the teaching/learning process as a creative one. The content, practice, and participants are shaped and reshaped throughout the educational process. Drawing upon resources that naturally emerge from the African, African American, and Christian traditions, I have been inspired by this improvisational strategy to incorporate creative ideas, creative methodology, and creative programming that often includes music, dance, ritual, proverbs, parables, communal learning, experience, and learning by example. Consequently, I frequently use these and other creative expressions throughout the course to meet the educational demands of the moment.

Critical Reflection

Some spirituals possess a dual or hidden meaning, which allowed the enslaved community to communicate secret messages with one another without being detected by their masters. This feature, grounded in African traditions, allowed the slave community to relate words of insult, history, wisdom, humor, and critique. For instance, the words "ev-'ry-bod-y talk-in' 'bout heav-'n ain't go-in' there"[7] were often used to mock slaveholders and to critique their religious hypocrisy. Just as the slave community critiqued their world through the spirituals, this strategy seeks to engage students in a serious critique of the barriers, obstacles, systems, and structures that lead to oppression. The aim of this strategy is to empower students to become actively involved in transforming their communities.

Cooperative Action

The desire for freedom, "Oh freedom! Oh freedom all over me!"[8] motivated many who were enslaved to resist the bonds of slavery. Consequently, the slave community joined together in a cooperative effort to assist in the escape of hundreds of slaves. One of the most successful efforts was the Underground Railroad led by Harriet Tubman, who participated in the liberation of over three hundred slaves.[9] In her efforts to guide others to freedom, Tubman reportedly incorporated numerous spirituals. Through cooperative action, the community united in the struggle for liberation and social change. In a similar fashion, this historical strategy can be used to challenge students to reflect critically on ways to engage in cooperative action today that will bring about transformation and change in their communities. One way that this has been done in the course, particularly through student presentations, is by exploring the gifts and contributions of African and African American people past and present who have participated in transforming their communities (e.g., Nelson Mandela, Desmond Tutu, Thurgood Marshall, Martin Luther King, Jr., Malcolm X, Hatshepsut of Kemet (Egypt), Amina of Hausaland (now Nigeria), Sojourner Truth, Ida B. Wells Barnett, Mary McLeod Bethune, Mary Church Terrell, Fannie Lou Hamer, etc.). Sharing these and other stories can help to instill not only a sense of pride and appreciation for African and African American people but also a sense of responsibility for the well-being of one's community. This strategy challenges us to move beyond the classroom to explore active involvement in both local and global settings.

Establishing the Context

I have taught the course "Christian Education in the African American Experience" at Iliff School of Theology in Denver, Colorado, and most recently (spring semester 2002) at Yale University Divinity School (YDS) in New Haven, Connecticut, where I am currently on the faculty. The context of these two institutions is very different. For example, Iliff is a freestanding United Methodist seminary, located on the campus of (and working in partnership with) Denver University. Although Iliff is a United Methodist school, many other denominations and faith traditions are also represented among the student body, faculty, and staff. At the time that I taught at Iliff (1998–2000), over half of the students were women. Eighty-one percent were European American, 6 percent were African American, and the remaining 13 percent represented racial/ethnic groups that included Asian American, Latino/a, Native American, and international students. Moreover, Iliff demonstrated a strong commitment to diversity around sexual orientation. Of the twenty-three persons on the faculty, eight were persons of color (two African Americans), eight were women, and seven were European American.

Yale Divinity School, on the other hand, is an interdenominational and nonsectarian graduate professional school of Yale University with access to the entire university. The YDS community reflects the primary Christian traditions, as the faculty and students embody forty denominations and assemblies. In the 2001 entering class, 10 percent represented racial/ethnic minority groups (e.g., African American, Latino/a, Native American, Asian American, etc.), 12 percent represented international students, and the remaining 78 percent represented European American students. There are approximately thirty-three persons on the faculty. About nine are white women, six are persons of color (three African Americans—with one being adjunct), and eighteen are white men. The school also has a strong commitment to diversity around sexual orientation. While both schools struggle with many of the issues that emerge within diverse communities, both seem to be committed to promoting an educational environment that is supportive, challenging, and transformative. In addition, they see their mission as training leaders for lay and ordained ministry by providing degree programs on both the master's and doctoral levels.

I have taught "Christian Education in the African American Experience" as an elective at both Iliff and Yale, and the course has attracted students from a variety of racial/ethnic backgrounds, including African American, European American, Korean, and African. While I have made revisions in the course since I taught it at Iliff, I will reflect primarily on my experience of teaching the course at Yale and refer only periodically to various experiences at Iliff.

"Christian Education in the African American Experience"

This course is an introduction to the educational ministry of the African American church. The primary purpose of the course is to examine major components of African American Christian education by providing a general overview of historical developments, contemporary models, and common teaching practices in the African American church. While a number of topics could have been included in this course, I developed the course around several educational themes that provide a lens for examining key aspects of African American Christian education. These themes include: a historical overview, education through the Sunday school, educational practices in the African American Church, educating African American children and youth, contemporary approaches to Christian education, teaching scripture, teaching through the oral tradition, teaching and theological reflection, and the practice of teaching. Throughout the course, students are encouraged not only to engage the content but also to think pedagogically by exploring possibilities for how the content might be used, presented, or taught creatively in their particular settings.

When I've taught the course in the past, the required readings included all or portions of a number of books, including: Karen Baker-Fletcher, *A Singing Something,* to explore the oral tradition and the use of metaphor in the African American experience; Keith Chism, *Christian Education for the African American Community,* to examine a pastoral perspective on the educational practices in the African American church; Joseph Crockett, *Teaching Scripture from an African American Perspective,* to explore the role of scripture in the teaching/learning process; Charles Foster and Grant Shockley, *Working with Black Youth: Opportunities for Christian Ministry,* to identify issues, concerns, and approaches for educating African American children and youth; Janice Hale-Benson, *Black Children: Their Roots, Culture, and Learning Styles,* to consider the unique challenges that confront African American children and how educators can provide a more holistic educational experience for black children by honoring their particular learning styles; bell hooks, *Teaching to Transgress: Education as the Practice of Freedom,* to introduce the notion of engaged pedagogy and the importance of critical reflection throughout the educational process; Lynne Westfield, *Dear Sisters: A Womanist Practice of Hospitality,* to explore the relationship between black theology, womanist theology, and Christian education; and Anne Wimberly, *Soul Stories: African American Christian Education,* to discuss diverse models of African American Christian education. Additional articles related to the various themes throughout the course were also included in a course packet.

I incorporated a number of requirements for the class. Students were expected to participate fully in the class discussions and activities. These activities included an opening and closing ritual, as well as preparation exercises designed to connect us with the material in a practical way. To prepare for class discussions, each person was required to write and bring to class a one-page reflection paper on the major reading assignments. In these papers I asked students to write a brief summary of the book or articles, to identify the major issues and concerns raised by the author, to list questions for clarification, and to develop at least two questions to bring to the class for discussion. In addition, I asked them to think about their general response to the readings by reflecting on the following questions: Do you agree/disagree? Why? Why not? What are major points of interest? What new revelations does the author raise for contemporary Christian education in the African American context? What do you see as the strengths and/or challenges of the reading? What additions, changes, recommendations (if any) would you make to the readings? How has the reading informed and/or transformed you? And, in light of this, reflect on what these revelations/insights mean to your ministry in your particular context. The reading assignments and reflection papers counted toward the overall participation grade.

Each person was also asked to visit the Sunday school department of an African American church and present that experience to the class. The purpose of this assignment was to examine the role of the Sunday school in local African American churches throughout the community. I asked students to pay particular attention to the nature and purpose of the Sunday school as articulated by the churches they visited, the structure of the program, key educational issues that emerged within these programs, and the strengths and challenges confronting these Sunday schools. I also encouraged them to interview the Sunday school superintendent or primary person responsible for the program, to sit in on a class, to secure and examine a sample of the curriculum resources, and to tour the facilities. In addition, each person was required to write a reflection paper that included a description and analysis of the experience, as well as possible recommendations for strengthening these programs.

To explore a wide range of resources for African American Christian education, I required students to develop an annotated bibliography of at least four sources emerging from or reflecting upon the African American experience. Along with the written annotations, students were asked to creatively introduce one of their resources for the benefit of the class. I emphasized that this presentation was *not* a book report. In other words, I did not want them to simply articulate the title, author, content, and their reactions to the book. Instead, I wanted them to think creatively and pedagogically in order to lead the class in a teaching/learning experience that embodied the essence of the book and then discuss its usefulness for Christian education in the African American church. For example, one student presenting bell hooks's book *All about Love* led the class in an exploration of various images of love. The class compared several concepts presented in hooks's book with the teachings of love presented in the Bible, with particular attention to 1 John 4:17–21. She incorporated a variety of teaching aids, including a poster with various images of love, Bible verses, and music. She also led the class in a discussion of the usefulness of this book for adult and adolescent Bible study groups on love.

Another student presenting June Lee and Matthew Parker's edited volume *Evangelism and Discipleship in African American Churches* examined the book's ideas on Christian education and youth ministry and the use of music in reaching today's youth. In this presentation, the class, taking on the role of teenagers, listened to different types of music (both secular and gospel) to examine the message embodied in the music in light of one's faith. This presentation led the class in a broader discussion of the book, its usefulness for Christian education in the African American church, and creative approaches for teaching today's youth. Although some students were nervous about this assignment initially, they were ultimately amazed by their own creativity when asked to think both creatively and pedagogically about the material.

All of my classes incorporate a teaching component so that students have an opportunity to practice teaching in the class. In the final project of this class, students were asked to develop a forty-five-minute lesson (to be presented in class) that embodied one aspect of African American Christian education. This presentation included a reflection paper that incorporated the purpose and goals of the lesson, the educational assumptions that informed the structure of the lesson, a reflection on how the lesson embodied African American experience, and an analysis of how the lesson might inform contemporary Christian education theory and practice. After each presentation, I encouraged students to reflect on the experience as both teachers and learners. As a major requirement of the class, the final project provides an opportunity for students to integrate insights from the class lectures, readings, presentations, and outside resources to develop a creative teaching/learning experience that they might be able to use in their future ministries. In addition, this project gives students an opportunity not only to explore creative ideas but also to develop their skills as Christian educators. The final project is worth 40 percent of the grade.

Revisiting the Teaching Strategies: Insights for Teaching the Course

As I mentioned previously, the teaching strategies of communal dialogue, creative engagement, critical reflection, and cooperative action have shaped and informed my teaching of this course. In this section, I will illustrate how I have incorporated insights from the teaching strategies.

Communal Dialogue

In recent years, some scholars have begun to focus their attention on the ways adults learn. In his work on adult learners, for example, Malcolm Knowles introduces four characteristics of adult learners. These characteristics suggest that adults are self-directed, they have a desire to share their experience, they have a readiness to learn based on need, and they desire more immediate learning.[10] Building upon Knowles, Christine Blair in her discussion on teaching the Bible to adults discusses several elements that should be taken into consideration to help adults learn best. First, the learning environment must feel safe and adults must feel a sense of community, respect, collaboration, and guidance. Second, adults must have their interest engaged through critical thinking and intellectual analysis coupled with reflection and an openness to the unexpected. Third, adults need to have their learning grounded in experience. This means that educators must provide space for adults to relate their learning to their everyday life situations while respecting them as "knowers" in the teaching/learning process. Fourth, adults are self-directed and should have a voice in helping to shape the educational process. And fifth, education for adults should speak to the mind, heart, and soul through symbol and story, imagination, ritual, and action.[11] If adults are to be successful in theological education, religious educators must attend to the needs of adult learners and create an environment that will facilitate their learning. Communal dialogue is one way to honor the gifts that adult students bring to the classroom because it respects their learning styles and their needs as adult learners and it engages their interest on a personal level. In short, communal dialogue emphasizes a mutual partnership between students and teachers.

One of my primary concerns is to build a sense of community that encourages communal dialogue throughout the course. I begin this task on the first day by inviting students to participate in an opening ritual that includes listening to music from the African American tradition, reading an inspirational scripture, praying for guidance, and participating in a ritual designed to welcome each person to the teaching/learning experience. Students are given an opportunity to share their reflections on the scripture and song, as well as to name one gift that they have received from the African American church and one gift that they would like to give back. The purpose of this opening ritual is to help students focus on the theme for the day and to set the tone not only for the remainder of the class session but also for the entire semester. In a similar fashion, I end the class with a closing ritual that often includes prayer, reflection questions, music, poetry, silence, or other activities. The closing ritual is designed to reinforce the lesson and to move the class to a natural conclusion. After the first class session, each student in the class is responsible for leading an opening and closing ritual for subsequent classes. In general, the opening and closing rituals usually incorporate the theme for the day and draw upon the gifts, traditions, and passions of the person presenting.

Another vehicle that I use for building a sense of community and nurturing communal dialogue early in the semester is the introduction of class participants.[12] During the first (and sometimes the second) class session, each person, including the instructor, is asked to respond to a number of questions, such as:

1. What is your name and where are you from?
2. What is your faith tradition?
3. Name a memorable teaching and/or learning experience in an African American setting (if applicable; if not, share an experience in a diverse cultural setting). How did this experience affect you? What was the significant learning that you gained from this experience?

4. What degree are you pursuing? What influenced you to pursue this degree? What is your greatest hope for yourself, your ministry/work, and the African American church?

5. Why are you taking this course? What would you like to gain from this teaching/learning experience?

During the first class, we typically spend the first half reflecting on these questions, and I generally do not introduce the syllabus until after the break. At the end of the class, time permitting, I lead the class in a brainstorming exercise that encourages students to begin reflecting on some of the themes that will emerge throughout the class, such as the role of Christian education in the African American experience, the context out of which we do Christian education in the twenty-first century, the dominant issues surrounding Christian education in the Black Church, and the emerging models of Christian education in the African American experience. This exercise has been helpful in preparing students for the class discussions that will follow.

Throughout the course, I also draw upon a number of elements, including preparation exercises, discussion questions, teaching/learning activities, and interactive lectures to encourage communal dialogue.

Creative Engagement

Religious educators generally agree that people learn in a variety of different ways; and to be effective in our teaching, we must take into consideration the unique learning styles that each person brings to the teaching/learning process. Although learning styles are formed and informed by a number of elements, including heritage, cultural context, personality, life experiences, and various learning situations, each person embraces certain preferences in his or her approach to learning.[13] While the major learning styles are usually identified as visual, auditory, and kinesthetic, a number of scholars have expanded this list to include several categories that encompass our five senses (Waynne James and Michael Galbraith)[14] and our multiple intelligences (Howard Gardner and Thomas Armstrong).[15]

In his article "Reaching African-American Students in the Classroom," Jonathan Collett notes that African American students, as well as other students of color, are performing poorly in higher education because most college professors do not take into consideration "culturally based learning styles." He challenges faculty members to consider a number of teaching strategies for the culturally diverse classroom. These strategies include: awareness of our own culture-bound learning style, tolerance of "disorder" and emotion, high expectations, friendly intervention, class sessions on cultural diversity, frequent class evaluations, and a pedagogical mix.[16] Janice Hale-Benson addresses similar concerns in *Black Children: Their Roots, Culture, and Learning Styles*. She examines the impact of African and African American heritage (including slavery, discrimination, and racism) on the way African American children learn. She argues that black children do in fact learn differently and that these differences must be taken into consideration. She goes on to suggest several characteristics of a model of education that is sensitive to the concerns of African American children. Although Hale-Benson's model is designed for public schools, the basic concepts of the model can also be applied to Christian education. The characteristics of this model include: high effective support, self-concept development, creative expression, arts and crafts, activities, study of African culture and African American culture, extracurricular experiences, and the politics surrounding various holidays. She also recommends teaching strategies that are culturally specific, such as body language as incorporated by black children, Standard English, equal talking time, group learning, a variety of learning activities, and music in the classroom.[17]

Addressing learning styles in the classroom, with particular attention to African American students, challenges us as educators to integrate creative engagement throughout the teaching/learning process. Although creative engagement includes creative ideas, creative methodology, and creative programming, it is not limited to these components. For example, creative engagement may move us to a new location, which may entail a field trip or outing. Last semester, the class visited the Nannie Helen Burroughs School, a private elementary school sponsored by the Community Baptist Church of New Haven, in order to explore issues, concerns, and approaches for educating African American children and youth. The school is distinctive in that it integrates aspects of African American and Christian traditions throughout its curriculum. After the field trip, we went to a soul food restaurant to reflect on our general impressions of the school and to continue our discussion of the readings.

Creative engagement may also inspire us to include other voices in the form of experts and resource persons. For instance, while teaching at Iliff, I invited Dr. Rachel Harding, author of the book *A Refuge in Thunder: Candomblé and Alternative Spaces of Blackness,* to speak to the class about African religious traditions and how these traditions have informed our ways of knowing and learning in the African American experience. I also invited Dr. Paul Martin, pastor of the Macedonia Baptist Church in Denver, to speak to the class about his experiences in the civil rights/Black Power movement, the emergence of black theology, and how those experiences have informed his preaching and teaching. Since I have been teaching at Yale, I have invited Dr. Lynne Westfield, assistant professor of religious education at Drew University and author of *Dear Sister: A Womanist Practice of Hospitality,* to share with the class, as well as the YDS community, on engaged pedagogy, womanist thought, and Christian education. Dr. Westfield's presentation included a poetry reading, a book signing, and a reception. Dr. David Bartlett, the dean of academic affairs and the Lanz professor of preaching and communication at YDS, has also served as a guest speaker in the class. In his presentation, he reflected on preaching/teaching in the oral tradition. Other voices may also be included through case studies, video presentations, music, art, poetry, and other artistic expressions.

Finally, creative engagement challenges us to use our space creatively and to experiment with creative activities within the space. I tell students on a regular basis that we are not bound to the space. We can reshape it by moving tables and chairs, we can incorporate visual aids and music, or we can go outside of our regular space to another space. One of the major topics that we covered in the class was "Teaching through the Oral Tradition." This particular class focused on reclaiming the oral tradition through music, storytelling, metaphor, and ritual as a viable mode of education in the African American church. After a brief interactive lecture and discussion of the reading assignment, I invited students to participate in a reflective exercise that allowed them to experience different aspects of the oral tradition. This exercise consisted of six learning stations that were set up in several locations. Some were set up in the classroom, others were set up in the hallway, and still others were set up in various rooms throughout the building. The learning stations contained a variety of materials, including books, art supplies, videos, CDs, cassette tapes, hymnals, poetry, pictures, and other symbols from the African American tradition.

First, I asked students to walk around to all of the locations and to briefly explore each of the learning stations. Then I asked them to settle on one of the stations that they would like to explore in more detail. Each station included a worksheet that guided them through a creative learning experience. For example, one of the learning stations was entitled "Remembering Our Story." This learning station engaged students in an exploration of the slave narrative through the following activity.

> Read through (or listen to a cassette recording of) several slave narratives. Hear the voices that are represented in the narratives. Allow yourself to be present with the voices.
>
> 1. What images emerge for you as you listen to the narratives?
> 2. What issues or problems emerge as you listen to the voices?
> 3. What lessons did you glean from the narratives?
> 4. How might the slave narratives be used as an effective teaching tool in contemporary Christian education?
> 5. Create a symbol of remembrance in honor of an ancestor who has special meaning for you.
> 6. Using your symbol, create a ritual of remembrance and lead the class in this ritual. You may use music, dance, prayer, communal sharing, or any other mode of expression to create your ritual.

The other five learning stations were entitled: "Metaphors in Our Tradition," "Musical Expressions," "Ritual and Dance," "Literature Corner," and "Sharing Our Story."

Critical Reflection

In his book *Pedagogy of the Oppressed*, Paulo Freire strongly critiques the banking model of education (teachers pour knowledge into students, who are empty vessels, and they repeat the information back without critical analysis or creativity), which dominates American approaches to education. Freire argues that the banking model is oppressive and dehumanizing, as students are objects of their education in this approach. He proposes a problem-posing model of education that allows students to be subjects rather than objects and teaches them to develop skills in critical thinking, problem solving, and strategizing for social change. Freire's model emphasizes praxis (action and reflection) as a critical component of education that is transformative and life giving.

One way that I incorporate critical reflection is through the use of case studies. In the class session that focuses on contemporary approaches to Christian education, we examined several models of African American Christian education, including Grant Shockley's intentional engagement approach, Olivia Pearl Stokes's Saturday ethnic school approach, James Harris's community-based Afrocentric approach, Anne Wimberly's story-linking approach, and my triple-heritage approach to Christian education. After exploring the major components of each model, students were divided into five groups and assigned one of the educators. Each group was given the following case study and asked to examine it through the lens of their assigned educator.[18]

CASE STUDY

Baby J is an African American teenager who lives in the projects of South Central Los Angeles. Her father is a drug dealer and a gang member serving time in prison. Her mother is a crack addict and is rarely at home to tend to Baby J and her little brother Tommy, who is 5 years old. At age 10 Baby J took to the streets to sell drugs to keep the family together. At age 11 she joined a gang for fellowship, protection, and a sense of community. At age 12 Baby J was arrested and sent to live in a group home for 2 years. At the group home Baby J met other young women like herself who needed a sense of direction and purpose in their lives. As she began to share her story with the other women in the group home, she found that she wanted to make a change in her life. Although she had not spent much time in church or pondering spiritual things, she began to have a hunger for a sense of spirituality and peace in her life. Baby J was pleased with this new desire to change her life; however, she struggled with poor self-esteem. How might the views of Wimberly/Shockley/Harris/ Stokes/Smith help Baby J find a sense of liberation and vocation in order to take action toward changing her lifestyle and becoming a productive member of society?

REFLECTION EXERCISE

1. Read through the case study together.
2. Identify and discuss the major issues that emerge for Baby J.
3. Discuss ways that Wimberly's/Shockley's/Harris's/Stokes's/ Smith's model of education might help to address Baby J's struggle with poor self-esteem.
4. Develop a lesson/activity that addresses this issue (self-esteem) by implementing the various aspects of your educator's model.
5. Share with the large group.

I also encouraged critical reflection around all of the reading assignments and oral presentations. In these discussions, I stressed both an individual and social orientation to the class reflections.

Cooperative Action

Examples of cooperative action in the class can best be seen through some of the final projects that students have been inspired to develop. Many students use this assignment as an opportunity to develop programs that they would like to implement in their churches or communities. For example, one student developed a proposal for a nonprofit organization that she is developing for African American adolescents. The name of the organization is GIRLS MIN-ISTRY; GIRLS is an acronym for "God is real love sisters." This organization is based on a mentoring approach to working with African American women whereby the elder women support and encourage younger women ages four-teen to twenty-one to succeed in today's world. Through the educational com-ponent of this ministry, young women will be exposed to a number of topics, including: self-awareness through cultural heritage and biblical development, relationship building (God, self, others), managing emotions, communica-tions, conflict resolution, health/fitness and etiquette, college preparation, ca-reer development, financial management, leadership development, time man-agement, and theater/arts/sports.[19] GIRLS MINISTRY will work in cooperation with churches, schools, community organizations, and other agencies in Hart-ford, Connecticut, to provide education, scholarships, materials, and other serv-ices for mentoring young African American women.

Another student developed a similar outreach ministry for African Amer-ican men entitled *Menistry*. This program was designed as an actual program for a congregation in Colorado Springs. The primary goal of this ministry is to provide opportunities for black men to explore the African American experience in light of their Christian faith. Lessons are based on scriptures, video presentations, music, art, individual experiences, and critical issues and concerns surrounding black men in the African American community. This program, however, goes beyond the classroom to active involvement in prison ministry, food and clothing drives, mentoring black boys, community involvement, and other areas of outreach.[20]

Still another student developed an educational outreach program for African American youth in New Haven. This program is being implemented through the New Haven library. The program is designed to teach African American youth about their heritage through various persons in history and in their contemporary lives (e.g., Thurgood Marshall, Malcolm X, Martin Luther King, Jr., M. C. Hammer, Puffy Combs, etc.). During his first presentation with the youth (which was also given in class), this student introduced young people to various personalities through music, speeches, biographical sketches, and critical analysis of each person's life, legacy, and contributions. These activities were also designed to develop critical thinking, analytical skills, and strategies for creative engagement in transformative action and reflection within the community. Additional topics, teaching strategies, and hands-on activities will also be incorporated throughout the program. This student plans to work not only with the library but also with schools, churches, and other community organizations.[21] Through cooperative action, these students are striving to transform their communities through education, active involvement, and empowerment of African American women, men, and children.

Implications for Contemporary Christian Education Theory and Practice

Teaching "Christian Education in the African American Experience" has been rich and rewarding. From this experience, I have gained new insights into African American religious traditions and explored creative approaches to studying these traditions. Through this course, I have also observed several implications for contemporary Christian education theory and practice. First, teaching Christian education from an African American perspective challenges Christian educators to provide numerous opportunities for African American students to learn about their heritage and the unique contributions made by their African foreparents, religious educators, and scholars in the field. It also challenges us to introduce students to a wide range of books, journal articles, video documentaries, curriculum resources, music, art, and other sources by and about African American people. These sources should portray positive and realistic images of African Americans, highlighting not only their strengths and challenges but also their unique contributions to society.

Second, a course on Christian education in the African American experience should not be limited to African American students. Indeed, the class should be inclusive of all students who are interested in learning about diverse African American religious traditions through the lens of Christian education. In teaching "Christian Education in the African American Experience," I discovered that one of the benefits of exploring African American Christian heritage through the spirituals is that they can serve as inspiration for persons of other cultures to explore their own religious and cultural heritage. For instance, our reflection through the spirituals inspired some students to identify specific elements within their own culture that have special meaning, just as the spirituals have significant meaning within the African American community. Sometimes storytelling or a unique form of dance or art in someone's tradition would take the place of the spirituals and form the central point of reflection on both the content and practice of education. Moreover, these sources invited persons into a dynamic dialogue that involved sharing stories, music, art, dance, and various forms of cultural and faith expressions. This dialogue promoted a greater sense of understanding and appreciation for other traditions while dispelling misleading myths and stereotypes. This experience affirmed for me that Christian education from an African American perspective can play a key role in equipping students to engage in a serious critique of the systems and structures that lead to oppression. To this end, the aim of the course should not only be to help students gain a deeper understanding of African people in the Diaspora but also to empower them to struggle against oppression and to bring about liberation and social change. "Christian Education in the African American Experience" can therefore provide a model of Christian education that may be adapted by diverse groups of people desiring to explore and celebrate their own heritage.

Third, embracing the spirituals as a viable source of Christian education can enhance creativity in the classroom. For the spirituals not only inspire us to draw upon sources that naturally arise from African American religious traditions, such as music, dance, story, proverbs, and ritual, but they also sensitize us to the importance of considering communal dialogue, creative engagement, critical reflection, and cooperative action when making decisions about content and the best approaches for communicating that content. To ensure a well-rounded teaching/learning experience, grounded in African American heritage, Christian educators must draw upon a variety of teaching methods and techniques. This approach to Christian education can also assist teachers in honoring the various gifts and learning styles that students bring to the teaching/learning experience.

Fourth, the dynamic character of the spirituals motivates us as teachers and students to go beyond the classroom to participate more fully in the broader society. The spirit of protest and social critique embodied in these songs awakens us to the realities of injustice and oppression that continue to affect people all over the world. Transcending various beliefs and backgrounds, the spirituals have the ability to unite and empower individuals in the struggle toward social change. For instance, when the freedom songs were sung during the civil rights movement, the community immediately came together to challenge racism, discrimination, and oppressive social systems and structures. These songs, as they were shaped and reshaped to address various situations, spontaneously created a sense of community among diverse groups of people who were ready to act on behalf of freedom and justice. Thus, the spirituals served not only as a form of social critique but also as a source of inspiration and motivation in the struggle toward liberation. Education that moves us beyond the classroom can provide dynamic learning experiences that are often creative, spontaneous, and grounded in real-life, hands-on learning. This approach to education not only has the potential to benefit the community and larger society but also encourages educators and learners to participate more fully in the educational process by embracing each moment as an opportunity for learning.

Fifth, contextualized approaches to Christian education can promote holistic teaching/learning experiences. For example, a major component of my course "Christian Education in the African American Experience" was to provide an element of inspiration that would allow students to deepen their sense of spirituality and their relationship with God. This component was often reflected through the opening and closing meditations, music, prayer, and moments of reflection. I also wanted the element of inspiration to encourage a deeper sense of appreciation not only for African American heritage but for other cultures and traditions as well. "Christian Education in the African American Experience" also incorporated an element of information that was intended to inform students about African American Christian heritage. This element was designed to stimulate intellectual inquiry and discourse regarding education for blacks in America. Moreover, "Christian Education in the African American Experience" embodied an element of transformation. This element challenged us throughout the course to seek transformation not only on a personal level but also with regard to the church and the academy, the African American community, and the broader society. Incorporating an element of transformation required serious reflection on how to encourage and equip students for the process of transformation. A holistic approach to Christian education that embodies inspiration, information, and transformation can offer new possibilities for the theory and practice of Christian education.

Finally, the spiritual "I Want to Be Ready!" used in the title of this essay suggests that one must be ready to embrace new opportunities as they emerge. The creators of this song wanted to be ready "to walk in Jerusalem just like John,"[22] for they believed that they would one day live in a new world free from the bonds of oppression and injustice. In order to be ready to inhabit this new world, they had to think in new ways, incorporate new behaviors, and move in new directions. In a similar fashion, if contemporary Christian education theory and practice is to be relevant for the twenty-first century, it must also be ready to move in new directions and to embrace new insights that emerge from African American Christian education. These insights may help to address the problem of diversity in Christian education and the need for appropriate models and curriculum resources that are relevant for diverse populations. Insights from the African American experience may also inform educational programs that embody a multicultural orientation and are grounded in a liberative praxis. And finally, Christian education in the African American experience may spark new ideas for guiding individuals in their faith journeys and equipping them to be agents of change in the wider society. Contemporary Christian educators must, therefore, be ready to engage in this important dialogue if they are to prepare individuals to participate more fully in life and social transformation.

NOTES

A small portion of this article is excerpted and adapted from Yolanda Y. Smith, *Teaching through the Spirituals: New Possibilities for African American Christian Education* (Cleveland: The Pilgrim Press, 2004), pp. 4–5, 17–20, 97, 153. Adapted by permission.

1. Maud Cuney Hare, "The Source," in *The Negro in Music and Art*, Lindsay Patterson, ed., International Library of Negro Life and History (New York: Publishers, 1967; originally published 1935), 21–22.

2. See Wyatt Tee Walker, *"Somebody's Calling My Name": Black Sacred Music and Social Change* (Valley Forge, PA: Judson Press, 1979); Jon Michael Spencer, "Freedom Songs of the Civil Rights Movement," *Journal of Black Sacred Music* 1,2 (1987): 1–16; Jon Michael Spencer, *Protest and Praise: Sacred Music of Black Religion* (Minneapolis: Fortress Press, 1990).

3. Melva Wilson Costen, *African American Christian Worship* (Nashville: Abingdon Press, 1993), 44–47.

4. See Yolanda Y. Smith, *Teaching through the Spirituals: New Possibilities for African American Christian Education* (Cleveland: The Pilgrim Press, 2004).

5. "Swing Low, Sweet Chariot," in *Songs of Zion* (Nashville: Abingdon Press, 1981), 104.

6. Zora Neale Hurston, "Spirituals and Neo-Spirituals," in Patterson, *Negro in Music and Art*, 15.

7. "I've Got a Robe," in *Songs of Zion*, 82.

8. "Oh Freedom," in *Songs of Zion*, 102.

9. Sarah Bradford, *Harriet Tubman: The Moses of Her People* (Secaucus, NJ: Citadel Press, 1961); M. W. Taylor, *Harriet Tubman* (New York: Chelsea House, 1991).

10. See Malcolm Knowles, *The Adult Learner: A Neglected Species* (Houston: Gulf, 1973), and Malcolm S. Knowles and Associates, *Androgogy in Action: Applying Modern Principles of Adult Learning* (San Francisco: Jossey-Bass, 1984).

11. Christine Blair, *The Art of Teaching the Bible: A Practical Guide for Adults* (Louisville, KY: Geneva Press, 2001), 24–49.

12. This exercise is most effective in smaller classes. Ten to twelve students is ideal. This exercise can also be done in larger classes by dividing the class into smaller groups and then having the groups report briefly to the larger group. Another way of incorporating this exercise in large classes is to limit the number of questions (it is best to focus on 1 or 2 key questions) and the time for responses from each student (each person should speak for no more than 2 or 3 minutes).

13. Karen Tye, *Basics of Christian Education* (St. Louis, MO: Chalice Press, 2000), 82.

14. Waynne James and Michael Galbraith, "Perceptual Learning Styles: Implications and Techniques for the Practitioner," *Lifelong Learning* (January 1985), 20–23, cited in Tye, *Basics,* 82–84.

15. See Howard Gardner, *Multiple Intelligences: The Theory in Practice* (New York: Basic Books, 1993), and Thomas Armstrong, *Multiple Intelligences in the Classroom* (Alexandria, VA: Association for Supervision and Curriculum Development, 1994).

16. Jonathan Collett, "Reaching African-American Students in the Classroom," *To Improve the Academy* 9 (1990): 179–186.

17. Janice Hale-Benson, *Black Children: Their Roots, Culture, and Learning Styles* (Baltimore: Johns Hopkins University Press, 1986), 163–165.

18. I was inspired to develop this case study after reading an article on African American girls and gang membership. The article, which appeared in *Essence* magazine, highlighted a myriad of challenges that these girls face and the often difficult task of leaving the gangs. As I began to reflect on the various models of African American Christian education, I was struck by the fact that each of the models incorporates some form of liberation and that they might offer some insights for supporting African American youth who are struggling with difficult circumstances in their lives. See Allison Abner, "Gangsta Girls," *Essence* 25 (1994): 64–66, 116–118.

19. *GIRLS MINISTRY* handout developed by Joan Burnett.

20. *Ministry* lesson plan and handout developed by Benjamin Reynolds.

21. Class presentation by David Watts.

22. "I Want to Be Ready!" in *Songs of Zion,* 151.

REFERENCES

Armstrong, Thomas. *Multiple Intelligences in the Classroom.* Alexandria, VA: Association for Supervision and Curriculum Development, 1994.
Bradford, Sarah. *Harriet Tubman: The Moses of Her People.* Secaucus, NJ: Citadel Press, 1961.
Collett, Jonathan. "Reaching African-American Students in the Classroom." *To Improve the Academy* 9 (1990): 177–188.
Costen, Melva Wilson. *African American Christian Worship.* Nashville: Abingdon Press, 1993.
Gardner, Howard. *Multiple Intelligences: The Theory in Practice.* New York: Basic Books, 1993.
Hale-Benson, Janice. *Black Children: Their Roots, Culture, and Learning Styles.* Baltimore: John Hopkins University Press, 1986.
Hare, Maud Cuney. "The Source." In *The Negro in Music and Art,* Lindsay Patterson,

ed., 19. *International Library of Negro Life and History*. New York: Publishers, 1967; originally published 1935.

Hurston, Zora Neale. "Spirituals and Neo-Spirituals." In *The Negro in Music and Art*, Lindsay Patterson, ed., 15–17. *International Library of Negro Life and History*. New York: Publishers, 1967; originally published 1933. James Waynne, and Michael Galbraith, "Perceptual Learning Styles: Implications and Techniques for the Practitioner," *Lifelong Learning* (January 1985). Cited in Karen Tye, *Basics of Christian Education*. St. Louis: Chalis Press, 2000.

Knowles, Malcolm S. *The Adult Learner: A Neglected Species*. Houston: Gulf, 1973.

Knowles, Malcolm S., and Associates. *Androgogy in Action: Applying Modern Principles of Adult Learning*. San Francisco: Jossey-Bass, 1984.

Spencer, Jon Michael. "Freedom Songs of the Civil Rights Movement." *Journal of Black Sacred Music* 1, 2 (1987): 1–16.

————. *Protest and Praise: Sacred Music of Black Religion*. Minneapolis: Fortress Press, 1990.

Songs of Zion. Nashville: Abingdon Press, 1981.

Taylor, M. W. *Harriet Tubman*. New York: Chelsea House, 1991.

Tye, Karen. *Basics of Christian Education*. St. Louis, MO: Chalis Press, 2000.

Walker, Wyatt Tee. *"Somebody's Calling My Name": Black Sacred Music and Social Change*. Valley Forge, PA: Judson Press, 1979.

PART II

Challenges to the Textual Canon and the Regnant History

6

"Testifying" and "Testimony": Autobiographical Narratives and African American Religions

Moses N. Moore Jr.

Autobiographical narratives and related materials such as journals and diaries have proved to be valuable—but often problematic—resources for studying and teaching African American religious experiences. This chapter identifies a number of these resources and attempts to illuminate some of the historiographical and pedagogical issues related to their use. For the purposes of this essay, "testifying" alludes to the confessional tradition within the black religious experience and is used in reference to the "subjective" self-representations, interpretations, and experiences recounted in autobiographical narratives and related materials. "Testimony," meanwhile, has more "factual" connotations and refers to resources and interpretations that are ostensibly more "objective" and hence readily subject to the traditional canons of critical historical assessment. Both types of materials are presented as valid, valuable, complementary, and often mutually corrective resources for exploration of the African American religious experience. This essay also incorporates pedagogical reflections on my varied classroom experiences as I have attempted to incorporate both types of resources in courses situated in two university departments of religious studies. Of particular concern for this essay is the development of a course entitled "Black Religion: An Autobiographical Approach." This course has been in constant evolution and dates back to my earliest attempts to develop undergraduate courses focused on the black religious experience.

Although I was trained in American and African American church history during graduate studies at Yale Divinity School and Union Theological Seminary during the late 1970s and early 1980s, subsequent appointments in the religious studies departments at two large public universities required that I quickly expand my disciplinary range to include non-Christian traditions and, thereby, to re-create myself as both a student and instructor of American and African American religious history. In keeping with this metamorphosis, I was challenged to develop courses in African American religious history that: (1) would be consistent with the methodological standards of the discipline of religious studies as embraced within my departments; (2) would expand these often narrowly focused standards to include treatment of religion as more than simply social or cultural "epiphenomena" (a crucially important challenge in relation to the study and teaching of African American religions, inasmuch as their study in the public university context has often tended to encourage sociocultural and institutional perspectives and methodologies that, according to Charles H. Long, fail to "come to terms with the specifically religious elements in the religion of black Americans"); (3) would be broadly focused and include a variety of religious experiences and traditions; and (4) would creatively and critically engage students as they were introduced to the varieties of African American religious experience.[1]

Addressing these multiple goals required me to employ resources and materials that would illuminate the complexity and multiple dimensions of the African American religious experience—materials and resources that would illuminate not only the intensely personal nature of "the encounter with the divine" but also the broader communal, institutional, cultural, and social impact of this encounter. The course "Black Religion: An Autobiographical Approach" was the result of this pedagogical and methodological imperative; through it I attempted to employ as primary texts and resources the autobiographical "testifying(s)" of "major figures" of the African American experience.

A rich corpus of autobiographical narratives and related materials were readily available for this pedagogical experiment. Consequently, the earliest versions of the course included, in various combinations, such familiar narratives as *The Interesting Narrative of the Life of Olaudah Equiano or Gustavus Vassa the African, Written by Himself; The Life Experiences and Gospel Labours of Rt. Rev. Richard Allen; The Fugitive Blacksmith, or Events in the History of James W. C. Pennington, Pastor of a Presbyterian Church, New York, Formerly a Slave in the State of Maryland, United States*; Samuel R. Ward, *Autobiography of a Fugitive Negro; Narrative of the Life of Frederick Douglass, An American Slave; The Life and Religious Experience of Jarena Lee, A Coloured Lady, Giving an Account of Her Call to Preach the Gospel As Revised and Corrected from the Original Manuscript, Written by Herself; Recollections of Seventy Years; With Head and Heart: The Autobiography of Howard Thurman; The Autobiography of Malcolm X; Stride Toward Freedom: The Montgomery Story*; and *My Soul Looks Back*.[2] These "testifying(s)," supplemented by slave narratives contained in works such as *The American Slave: A Composite Autobiography* and miscellaneous addresses such as David Walker's "Appeal" and Henry Highland Garnet's "Address To The Slaves," provided the initial foundation for "Black Religion: An Autobiographical Approach."[3] This demanding upper-level undergraduate seminar with its daunting list of required readings would become the flagship of my curriculum offerings on the African American religious experience.

Issues and concerns such as "subjectivity" and "agenda" often rendered much of this material methodologically and pedagogically challenging. However, I quickly discovered that its pedagogical and historiographical contributions usually minimized and transcended most of the difficulties and liabilities associated with its use. Crucially, this material gave voice and agency to black men and women who "testified" in their own words to the profound impact and influence that religious experiences, beliefs, ideas, values, traditions, rituals, and institutions had upon both their personal and corporate existence. Use of this material also enabled the course to subvert some of the usual limitations imposed on religious studies offerings in public universities as it encouraged and allowed students (and the instructor) to encounter the black religious experience at its most basic and profound level—as "lived faith." In addition, use of autobiographical material as the primary text of the course served as an effective pedagogical antidote to the attempt by many students to evade encounter with the less pleasant realities of the black experience—especially as related to the ordeal of slavery. The often poignant and powerful "testifying" of these authors forced students to both intellectually and emotionally engage, many for the first time, the historical and theological essence of the African American religious experience. Moreover, the use of autobiographical material as the primary texts of the course provided students with a richly textured introduction to the history and complexity of the African American religious experience while introducing them at the same time to important historiographical and methodological issues related to its study. For example, the autobiographical and comparative reflections of Equiano introduced students not only to the African religious and cultural prologue but also to the "origins" and "survivals" debate that explored the extent to which African American religion has been influenced by African religious and cultural retentions; the conversion narrative of the slave Morte provided crucial insight into the spiritual, psychological, and even social impact of the conversion phenomenon as experienced by both slave and master; and the narrative of Richard Allen not only recounted the faith journey of a former slave who became a bishop but also focused attention upon the Northern urban religious experience and the emergence of the "black independent church movement."[4] Similarly, Jarena Lee's poignant witness to the personal and public struggles for the validation of her faith and spiritual gifts introduced the problematic of gender. The narrative of Howard Thurman exploded preconceived and stereotyped notions of the black minister, as it introduced students to traditions of black religious intellectualism, mysticism, and ecumenism. The autobiographical reflections of Malcolm X and Martin Luther King illuminated not only their personal religious, intellectual, and ethical odysseys but also provided critical insight into historiographical treatments of the black Islamic tradition and the contemporary civil rights movement. Finally, the autobiographical musings of James Cone illuminated the racial, religious, intellectual, and academic issues that shaped the history and agenda of the black theology movement.

It was clear from the inception of the course that these selective and subjective "testifying(s)" (though "self-validating" at the deepest level of religious meaning and significance) would have to be complemented by more critical and "objective" (though not necessarily more accurate) "testimony." The latter was provided by the burgeoning library of critical studies that issued forth by the mid-1980s, heralding a "golden era" in the study of black religion.[5] In an ever-changing variety of combinations and formulas, both types of resources ("testifying(s)" and "testimony") would be employed in an effort to introduce students to the complexity and scope of the African American religious experience.

Despite a reading list that was especially demanding, students responded positively to the course. Moreover, since the course required that students critically engage not only the readings but also each other's interpretation of the readings, its seminar format proved ideal. Success of the course also required a concerted effort to help students become aware of the various methodological and historiographical advantages and disadvantages associated with the use of autobiographical materials. Consequently, students were immediately engaged in critical reflection related to the use of this material as they encountered, for example, John Blassingame's insightful essay "Black Autobiographies as History and Literature."[6] This work not only affirmed the legitimacy of black autobiographical materials but also confronted students at a deeper level with its suggestions as to why the autobiographical testifying(s) of blacks had been routinely neglected and dismissed while those of their white contemporaries were readily validated and incorporated into the historical and literary canon. Efforts to further involve students in this important debate that established the critical norms of the course were aided by the additional "testimony" of scholars such as William Andrews and Stephen Butterfield.[7] Also of special importance were critical reflections specifically regarding religious and spiritual autobiographies contained in Angelo Costanzo's *Surprizing Narrative: Olaudah Equiano and the Beginnings of Black Autobiography* (1987) and William Andrews's collection *Sisters of the Spirit: Three Black Women's Autobiographies of the Nineteenth Century* (1986).[8]

By the early 1990s the course description read as follows:

Through the critical study of autobiographical and related materials this 300/400 level undergraduate seminar will examine the experiences, motivations, and contributions of a number of major figures associated with African American religious experience. The varied influence of religious beliefs, traditions, and institutions upon the personal and social lives of these figures and the broader culture (both black and white) will be emphasized. This course will also provide an overview of the history and development of African American religion and an introduction to historiographical and methodological issues related to its study and impact within the broader discipline of religious studies.

The syllabus indicated that the "general course objectives" were as follows.

1. To provide students with a critical introduction to the African American religious experience
2. To provide a general knowledge of the various roles played by religious beliefs and institutions in African American and American life and culture
3. To provide basic awareness of theoretical and methodological issues involved in the study of African American religious history
4. To encourage development of critical interpretive, evaluative, and communication skills (oral and written) related to the study of African American religious history
5. To prepare students to be informed participants in contemporary discourse related to the role and function of religion in contemporary American life and culture

As the course evolved over the next decade, under the prodding of students, colleagues, and my own pedagogical maturation, it became clear that constant adaptation was required. The evolving course would draw upon the increasing availability and diversity of additional testifying(s) and related primary source materials, as well as a plethora of critical interpretive scholarship ("testimony") that included a new generation of biographical studies.[9] The emergence of new historiographical and methodological issues and topics such as pluralism and regionalism, coupled with my own increasing sensitivity to pedagogical and historiographical issues and topics that were ignored or minimized in original versions of the course, also demanded efforts to make the course much more inclusive.[10] For example, conspicuously absent in earlier versions of the course were autobiographical materials pertaining to the Holiness and Pentecostal tradition. Moreover, the predominately Protestant and Christian orientation of the course resulted in exclusion of the experiences of black Catholics and black Jews—not to mention the reconfigured African religious traditions such as

Santeria and Voudun.[11] Similarly, it was apparent that the course had not paid adequate attention to the varied religious experiences of black women and the broader historiographical problematic and treatment of gender. The pedagogical prescription for this deficiency required not only the inclusion of additional testifying(s) by figures such as Julia A. J. Foote and Zilpha Elaw but also the incorporation of the insights of a new generation of critical scholars who examined the many facets of black women's religious and spiritual autobiographies from a variety of methodological perspectives.[12]

Unexpectedly, the course underwent additional transformation as it became apparent that the gender issue (originally isolated in a section of the course titled "To Be Black, Female, and Called") also provided an entrée into numerous additional issues. For example, my belated inclusion of *The Story of the Lord's Dealing with Mrs. Amanda Smith the Colored Evangelist* provided critical insight into the early history of the Holiness and Pentecostal movement as well as black missiological efforts and attitudes.[13]

Also critical to the continued evolution of the course was my gradual awareness of the need to move beyond an implicit "great person" bias and the related reliance on the presumed primacy of written and literary resources. In response to the demand for resources that more accurately reflected and illuminated the religious lives and experiences of a broader segment of the black religious community, traditional autobiographical materials were supplemented and often displaced by prayers, songs, sermons, stories, and narratives rooted in the black oral and folk tradition.[14] In addition, the powerful visual testimonies of religion-based folk art, such as paintings, sculptures, quilts, graveyard decorations, and even photographs, increasingly became important primary resources for the course. This material proved invaluable in helping to reveal the varied religious experiences, voices, and agency of "regular" black folk in contrast to those traditionally designated as the "movers and shakers" of the African American religious experience. Consequently, the autobiographical writings of figures such as Richard Allen, Daniel Payne, and even Martin Luther King found themselves competing with more diverse and inclusive materials pertaining to less well-known—indeed, often anonymous—figures.

The insistent expansion of the course and the need to provide students with an affordable and readable number of texts was aided immensely by the collection of autobiographical excerpts compiled and made available by Milton C. Sernett in *African American Religious History: A Documentary Witness*.[15] Sernett's text, now in its second edition, supplemented by an extensive "course reader" that contains an ever-changing variety of additional "testifying(s)" and "testimony," has helped to keep the course economically feasible as well as pedagogically flexible.[16]

Finally, changing course demographics related to wider university developments have also played an important role in the continued evolution of "Black Religion: An Autobiographical Approach." The welcomed, though belated, development of an African American studies program at Arizona State University provided competing course options for the relatively small number of African American students on campus. An unexpected result was a shift in the demographic (ethnic, religious, and racial) profile of students enrolled in "Black Religion: An Autobiographical Approach." Anglo, Latino/Latina, Asian, and even Native American students now made up the majority of the course's enrollment. In response, the course was redesigned so that it would remain true to its original goals but also address the needs and concerns of a broader cross-section of the student population. Consequently, "Black Religion: An Autobiographical Approach" would be increasingly presented and taught as a "case study" approach to the broader dynamic and dialectic of religion, race, ethnicity, and culture. While the black religious response to this dialectic remained central and at the forefront of the course, this more expansive methodological and pedagogical paradigm provided students from different racial, ethnic, and religious orientations with an opportunity to more closely relate, compare, and contrast "testifying(s)" and "testimony" emanating from their particular ethnic and religious backgrounds. Thus for example, the autobiographical narrative and addresses of Martin Luther King also became an opportunity to explore in addition the religious and ethical orientations of figures as diverse as Cesar Chavez, Abraham Heschel, and even Jimmy Carter. Similarly, the autobiographical narrative of James Cone often occasioned discussions and research papers focused on liberation theologians of various ethnic, gender, and cultural orientations. Autobiographical narratives pertaining to the religious and spiritual experiences of black women have also provided exceptionally rich entrée into a broader ethnic and gender perspective.

As "Black Religion: An Autobiographical Approach" nears the end of its second decade, it has evolved into an important undergraduate (and occasional graduate) seminar. Still very much "in process," this seminar continues to draw upon the multifaceted African American religious experiences present in both "testifying(s)" and "testimony" as a rich and expansive pedagogical template. As such, it provides students from a variety of religious, racial, ethnic, and cultural backgrounds with an opportunity to critically and comparatively reflect on the personal and communal nature of religion and the religious experience, as well as on the multifaceted dialectic of race, ethnicity, religion, and culture.

NOTES

1. See Charles H. Long, "Perspectives for a Study of African American Religion in the United States," in Timothy E. Fulop and Albert J. Raboteau, eds., *African-American Religion: Interpretive Essays in History and Culture* (New York: Routledge, 1997), 23–35.

2. Olaudah Equiano, *The Interesting Narrative of the Life of Olaudah Equiano or Gustavus Vassa the African, Written by Himself* (New York: W. Durell, 1791); Richard Allen, *The Life Experiences and Gospel Labours of Rt. Rev. Richard Allen* (Philadelphia:

Martin and Boston, 1833); James W. C. Pennington, *The Fugitive Blacksmith, or Events in the History of James W. C. Pennington, Pastor of a Presbyterian Church, New York, Formerly a Slave in the State of Maryland, United States*, 2nd ed. (London: Charles Gilpin, 1849); Samuel R. Ward, *Autobiography of a Fugitive Negro*, 1855 (New York: Arno Press, reprint, 1968); Frederick Douglass, *Narrative of the Life of Frederick Douglass, An American Slave* (Boston: Anti-Slavery Office, 1845); Jarena Lee, *The Life and Religious Experience of Jarena Lee, A Coloured Lady, Giving an Account of Her Call to Preach the Gospel As Revised and Corrected from the Original Manuscript, Written by Herself* (Philadelphia, 1836); Daniel A. Payne, *Recollections of Seventy Years* (New York: Arno Press; reprint, 1969); Howard Thurman, *With Head and Heart: The Autobiography of Howard Thurman* (New York: Harcourt Brace Jovanovich, 1979); Malcolm X, *The Autobiography of Malcolm X*, with Alex Haley (New York: Ballantine Books; reprint, 1973); Martin Luther King, Jr., *Stride Toward Freedom: The Montgomery Story* (New York: Harper, 1958); and James Cone, *My Soul Looks Back* (Nashville: Abingdon Press, 1982).

3. George P. Rawick, ed., *The American Slave: A Composite Autobiography* (Westport, CT: Greenwood; reprint, 1971); David Walker, *Walker's Appeal, in Four Articles; Together with Preamble, to the Coloured Citizens of the World, But in Particular, and Very Expressly, to Those of the United States of America. Written in Boston, State of Massachusetts, September 28, 1829*, 3rd ed. (Boston: D. Walker, 1830); and Henry Highland Garnet, "An Address to the Slaves of the United States of America (1843)," reprinted in Henry H. Garnet, *A Memorial Discourse by Rev. Henry Highland Garnet, Delivered In The Hall Of The House Of Representatives* (Philadelphia: Joseph M. Wilson, 1865).

4. On Morte see "I Am Blessed but You Are Dead," in George P. Rawick, *God Struck Me Dead* (Westport, CT: Greenwood, 1941), 3–6. For additional insight into the value of comparative methodology in autobiographical materials see James Olney, "The Value of Autobiography for Comparative Studies: African vs. Western Autobiography," in *African American Autobiography: A Collection of Critical Essays*, William Andrews, ed. (Englewood Cliffs, NJ: Prentice Hall, 1993).

5. See Fulop and Raboteau, *African-American Religion*, 1.

6. John Blassingame, "Black Autobiographies as History and Literature," *Black Scholar* (December 1973–January 1974), 2–9.

7. See William Andrews, "The First Century of Afro-American Autobiography: Theory and Explication, *Studies in Black Literature* 1 (1983): 4–42, and William L. Andrews, *To Tell a Free Story: The First Century of Afro-American Autobiography, 1760–1865* (Urbana: University of Illinois Press, 1986). See also Stephen Butterfield, *Black Autobiography in America* (Amherst: University of Massachusetts Press, 1974), and Russell C. Brignano, *Black Americans in Autobiography: An Annotated Bibliography of Autobiographies and Autobiographical Books Written Since the Civil War* (Durham, N.C.: Duke University Press, 1974). A broader critical dialogue regarding the use of autobiographical material continues to be advanced in more recent texts such as William Andrews, ed., *African American Autobiography: A Collection of Critical Essays* (Englewood Cliffs, NJ: Prentice Hall, 1993); Herb Boyd, *Autobiography of a People: Three Centuries of African American History Told by Those Who Lived It* (New York: Doubleday, 2000).

8. See Angelo Costanzo, *Surprising Narrative: Olaudah Equiano and the Begin-

nings of Black Autobiography (Westport, CT: Greenwood Press, 1987) and William Andrews, ed., *Sisters of the Spirit: Three Black Women's Autobiographies of the Nineteenth Century* (Bloomington: Indiana University Press, 1986).

9. Although this material presents its own historiographical, pedagogical, and methodological challenges, it nevertheless inspired creation of a related course entitled "Black Religion: A Biographical Approach." This course employs critical biographies as its primary texts and now competes with "Black Religion: An Autobiographical Approach" in my curriculum offerings and rotation.

10. See *African-American Religion: Research Problems and Resources for the 1990s* (New York: Schomburg Center for Research in Black Culture, New York Public Library, 1992).

11. Valuable resources pertaining to the Holiness and Pentecostal Tradition include: Elsie W. Mason, *The Man, Charles Harrison Mason, 1866–1961* (Memphis: Church of God in Christ, 1979); Ithiel C. Clemmons, *Bishop C. H. Mason and the Roots of Church of God in Christ* (Bakersfield, CA: Pneuma Life, 1997); J. O. Patterson, German R. Ross, and Julia Atkinson, eds., *History and Formative Years of the Church of God in Christ with Excerpts from the Life and Works of Its Founder-Bishop C. H. Mason* (Memphis: Church of God in Christ, 1969); and Cheryl Jeanne Sanders, *Saints in Exile: The Holiness-Pentecostal Experience in African American Religion and Culture* (New York: Oxford University Press, 1996). See also Sherry S. DuPree, ed., *Biographical Dictionary of African-American Holiness-Pentecostals, 1880–1990* (Washington, DC: Middle Atlantic Regional Press, 1989). Insight into the traditions and peculiar experiences of black Catholics and black Jews was provided by works such as Howard Brotz, *The Black Jews of Harlem* (New York: Free Press of Glencoe, 1964); James E. Landing, *Black Judaism: Spread of a Movement* (Durham, NC: Carolina Academic Press, 1998); and Elly M. Wynia, *The Church of God and Saints of Christ: The Rise of Black Jews* (New York: Garland, 1994). On the Catholic experience see Cyprian Davis, *The History of Black Catholics in the United States* (New York: Crossroad, 1990) and Stephen J. Ochs, *Desegregating the Altar: The Josephites and the Struggle for Black Priests, 1871–1960* (Baton Rouge: Louisiana State University Press, 1990). Resources pertaining to Santeria and Voudun include Karen McCarthy Brown, *Mama Lola: A Vodon Priestess in Brooklyn* (Berkeley: University of California Press, 1991); Suzanne Preston Blier, *African Vodun: Art, Psychology, and Power* (Chicago: University of Chicago Press, 1995); and Irving I. Zaretsky, *Spirit Possession and Spirit Mediumship in Africa and Afro-America* (New York: Garland, 1978).

12. Julia A. J. Foote, *A Brand Plucked from the Fire: An Autobiographical Sketch by Mrs. Julia A. J. Foote*, and Zilpha Elaw, *The Memoirs of the Life, Religious Experience, Ministerial Travels and Labours of Mrs. Zilpha Elaw, an American Female of Colour* (London: 1846) both reprinted in Andrews, *Sisters of The Spirit*, 49–234. See also Joanne Braxton, *Black Women Writing Autobiography: A Tradition within a Tradition* (Philadelphia: Temple University Press, 1989); Phebe Davidson, *Religious Impulses in Selected Autobiographies of African Women (c. 1630–1893): Uses of the Spirit* (Lewiston, NY: Edwin Mellen Press, 1993); Gloria WadeGales, *My Soul Is Witness: African-American Women's Spirituality* (Boston: Beacon Press, 1996); Judith Weisenfeld and Richard Newman, *This Far by Faith: Readings in African-American Women's Religious Biography* (New York: Routledge, 1996); and Richard J. Douglass-Chin, *Preacher Woman Sing the*

Blues: The Autobiographies of Nineteenth-Century African American Evangelists (Columbia: University of Missouri Press, 2001).

13. Amanda Smith, *An Autobiography: The Story of the Lord's Dealing with Mrs. Amanda Smith the Colored Evangelist* (Chicago: Meyer, 1893). Note the similar contributions to these topics by the narratives of Zilpha Elaw and Julie Foote. See Andrews, *Sisters of the Spirit,* 1–10; 49–234.

14. Among available resources were Ira Berlin, Marc Faureau, and Steven F. Miller, eds., *Remembering Slavery: African American Talk about Their Personal Experiences of Slavery and Emancipation* (Washington, D.C.: New Press, 1998); James Washington, *Conversations with God: Two Centuries of Prayers by African Americans* (New York: HarperCollins, 1994); and Bettye Collier-Thomas, *Daughters of Thunder: Black Women Preachers and Their Sermons, 1850–1979* (San Francisco: Jossey-Bass, 1997). See also Marie Jeanne Adams, "The Harriet Powers Pictorial Quilts," in Weisenfeld and Newman, *This Far by Faith,* 21–31, and Glayds-Marie Fry, "Harriet Powers: Portrait of a Black Quilter," in *Missing Piecies: Georgia Folk Art* (Atlanta: Georgia Council for Arts and Humanities, 19). See also Yvonne Chireau, "Hidden Traditions: Black Religion, Magic and Alternative Spiritual Beliefs in Womanist Perspectives," in *Perspectives on Womanist Theology,* Jacquelyn Grant, ed. (Atlanta: ITC Press, 1995), and Richard J. Powell, "Conjuring Canes and Bible Quilts: Through the Prism of Nineteenth Century African American Spirituality," in *African Americans and the Bible: Sacred Texts and Social Textures,* Vincent Wimbush, ed. (New York: Continuum, 2000), 342–354. See also Maude Wahlman, "Religious Symbolism in African American Quilts," *Clarion* 14 (summer 1989): 36–43.

15. Milton C. Sernett, ed., *African American Religious History: A Documentary Witness* (Durham, NC: Duke University Press, 1985).

16. Milton C. Sernett, ed., *African American Religious History: A Documentary Witness,* 2nd ed. (Durham, NC: Duke University Press, 1999).

REFERENCES

Allen, Richard. *The Life Experiences and Gospel Labours of Rt. Rev. Richard Allen.* Philadelphia: Martin and Boston, 1833.
Andrews, William, ed. *African American Autobiography: A Collection of Critical Essays.* Englewood Cliffs, NJ: Prentice Hall, 1993.
———, ed. *Sisters of the Spirit: Three Black Women's Autobiographies of the Nineteenth Century.* Bloomington: Indiana University Press, 1986.
———. *To Tell a Free Story: The First Century of Afro-American Autobiography, 1760– 1865.* Urbana: University of Illinois Press, 1986.
Austin, Allan D. *African Muslims in Antebellum America: Translantic Stories and Spiritual Struggles.* New York: Routledge, 1997.
Blassingame, John. "Black Autobiographies as History and Literature." *Black Scholar* (December 1973–January, 1974): 2–9.
———, ed. *Slave Testimony: Two Centuries of Letters, Speeches, Interviews, and Autobiographies.* New Orleans: Louisiana State University Press, 1977.
Blier, Suzanne Preston. *African Vodun: Art, Psychology, and Power.* Chicago: University of Chicago Press, 1995.

Boyd, Herb. *Autobiography of a People: Three Centuries of African American History Told by Those Who Lived It.* New York: Doubleday, 2000.

Braxton, Joanne. *Black Women Writing Autobiography: A Tradition within a Tradition.* Philadelphia: Temple University Press, 1989.

Brotz, Howard. *The Black Jews of Harlem.* New York: Free Press of Glencoe, 1964.

Brignano, Russell C. *Black Americans in Autobiography: An Annotated Bibliography of Autobiographies and Autobiographical Books Written since the Civil War.* Durham, NC: Duke University Press, 1974.

Brown, Karen McCarthy. *Mama Lola: A Vodon Priestess in Brooklyn.* Berkeley: University of California Press, 1991.

Butterfield, Stephen. *Black Autobiography in America.* Amherst: University of Massachusetts Press, 1974.

Chireau, Yvonne. "Hidden Traditions: Black Religion, Magic and Alternative Spiritual Beliefs in Womanist Perspectives." In *Perspectives on Womanist Theology,* Jacquelyn Grant, ed. Atlanta: ITC Press, 1995.

Clemmons, Ithiel C. *Bishop C. H. Mason and the Roots of Church of God in Christ.* Bakersfield, CA: Pneuma Life, 1997.

Collier-Thomas, Bettye. *Daughters of Thunder: Black Women Preachers and Their Sermons 1850–1979.* San Francisco: Jossey-Bass, 1997.

Cone, James. *My Soul Looks Back.* Nashville: Abingdon Press, 1982.

Costanzo, Angelo, *Surprizing Narrative: Olaudah Equiano and the Beginnings of Black Autobiography.* Westport, CT: Greenwood Press, 1987.

Davidson, Phebe, *Religious Impulses in Selected Autobiographies of African Women (c.1630–1893): Uses of the Spirit.* Lewiston, NY: Edwin Mellen Press, 1993.

Davis, Cyprian. *The History of Black Catholics in the United States.* New York: Crossroad, 1990.

Douglass, Frederick. *Narrative of the Life of Frederick Douglass, An American Slave.* Boston: Anti-Slavery Office, 1845.

Douglass-Chin, Richard J. *Preacher Woman Sing the Blues: The Autobiographies of Nineteenth-Century African American Evangelists.* Columbia, MO: University of Missouri Press, 2001.

DuPree, Sherry S., ed. *Biographical Dictionary of African-American Holiness Pentecostals, 1880–1990.* Washington, DC: Middle Atlantic Regional Press, 1989.

Elaw, Zilpha. "Memoirs of the Life, Religious Experience, Ministerial Travels and Labours of Mrs. Zilpha Elaw, an American Female of Colour." *In Sisters of the Spirit,* William Andrews, ed. Bloomington: Indiana University Press, 1986.

Equiano, Olaudah. *The Interesting Narrative of the Life of Olaudah Equiano of Gustavus Vassa the African, Written by Himself.* New York: W. Durell, 1791.

Foote, Julia A. J. *A Brand Plucked from the Fire: An Autobiographical Sketch by Mrs. Julia A. J. Foote.* In *Sisters of the Spirit,* William Andrews, ed. Bloomington: Indiana University Press, 1986.

Fulop, Timothy E., and Albert J. Raboteau, eds. *African American-Religion: Interpretive Essays in History and Culture.* New York: Routledge, 1997.

Garnet, Henry Highland. "An Address to the Slaves of the United States of America." In Henry H. Garnet, *A Memorial Discourse by Rev. Henry Highland Garnet, Delivered in the Hall of the House of Representatives.* Philadelphia: Joseph M. Wilson, 1865.

King, Jr., Martin Luther. *Stride Toward Freedom: The Montgomery Story.* New York: Harper, 1958.

Landing, James E. *Black Judaism: Spread of a Movement.* (Durham, NC: Carolina Academic Press, 1998.

Lee, Jarena. *The Life and Religious Experience of Jarena Lee, A Coloured Lady, Giving an Account of Her Call to Preach the Gospel. As Revised and Corrected from the Original Manuscript, Written by Herself.* Philadelphia, 1836.

Lester, Julius. *To Be a Slave.* New York: Dell, 1968.

Long, Charles H. "Perspectives for a Study of African American Religion in the United States." In *African American-Religion: Interpretive Essays in History and Culture,* Timothy E. Fulop and Albert J. Raboteau, eds., 233–235. New York: Routledge, 1997.

———. *Significations: Symbols and Images in the Interpretation of Religion.* Philadelphia: Fortress Press, 1986.

Malcolm X. *The Autobiography of Malcolm X* (as told to Alex Haley). New York: Ballantine, 1988; originally published 1965.

Mason, Elsie W. *The Man, Charles Harrison Mason (1866–1961).* Memphis: Church of God in Christ, 1979.

Murphy, Joseph M. *Working the Spirit: Ceremonies of the African Diaspora.* Boston: Beacon Press, 1994.

Ochs, Stephen J. *Desegregating the Altar: The Josephites and the Struggle for Black Priests, 1871–1960.* Baton Rouge: Louisiana State University Press, 1990.

Olney, James. "The Value of Autobiography for Comparative Studies: African vs. Western Autobiography." In *African American Autobiography: A Collection of Critical Essays,* William Andrews, ed. Englewood Cliffs, NJ: Prentice Hall, 1993.

Payne, Daniel A. *Recollections of Seventy Years.* New York: Arno Press, 1969.

Pennington, James W. C. *The Fugitive Blacksmith, or Events in the History of James W. C. Pennington, Pastor of a Presbyterian Church, New York, Formerly a Slave in the State of Maryland, United States.* London: Charles Gilpin, 1849.

Rawick, George P. ed. *The American Slave: A Composite Autobiography.* Westport, CT: Greenwood, 1971.

———. *God Struck Me Dead.* Westport, CT: Greenwood, 1941.

Sanders, Cheryl J. *Saints in Exile: The Holiness-Pentecostal Experience in African American Religion and Culture.* New York: Oxford University Press, 1996.

Sernett, Milton C. ed. *African American Religious History: A Documentary Witness.* 2nd ed. Durham, NC: Duke University Press, 1999.

Smith, Amanda. *The Story of the Lord's Dealing with Mrs. Amanda Smith the Colored Evangelist.* Chicago: Meyer, 1893.

Thurman, Howard. *With Head and Heart: The Autobiography of Howard Thurman.* New York: Harcourt Brace Jovanovich, 1979.

Wade-Gales, Gloria. *My Soul Is Witness: African-American Women's Spirituality.* Boston: Beacon Press, 1996.

Walker, David. *Walker's Appeal, in Four Articles; Together with Preamble, to the Coloured Citizens of the World, But in Particular, and Very Expressly, to Those of the United States of America. Written in Boston, State of Massachusetts, September 28, 1829.* 3rd ed. Boston: D. Walker, 1830.

Ward, Samuel R. *Autobiography of a Fugitive Negro*. New York: Arno Press, 1968; originally published 1855.

Washington, James M. *Conversations with God: Two Centuries of Prayers by African Americans*. New York: HarperCollins, 1994.

Weisenfeld, Judith, and Richard Newman. *This Far by Faith: Readings in African-American Women's Religious Biography*. London: Routledge, 1996.

Wimbush, Vincent, ed. *African Americans and The Bible: Sacred Texts And Social Textures*. New York: Continuum, 2000.

Wynia, Elly M. *The Church of God and Saints of Christ: The Rise of Black Jews*. New York: Garland, 1994.

7

Rethinking the Core: African and African American Religious Perspectives in the Seminary Curriculum

Edwin David Aponte

The classroom remains the most radical space of possibility in the academy.

—bell hooks, *Teaching to Transgress*

Conventional and Alternative Perspectives

This chapter explores some pedagogical challenges and responses to, and strategies for, the inclusion of African and African American cultural perspectives into the required core curriculum courses at a graduate theological seminary. This essay represents my longstanding personal interest in African and African American religions and cultures—an interest that was deepened through participation in the workshop "Mining the Motherlode of African American Religious Life." I wanted to take this personal commitment and see how I could construct graduate seminary courses that draw on African American religious life to strengthen pedagogical integrity and effectiveness, as well as increase contextual relevance.[1] Simultaneously, I wanted to broaden the core curriculum through the inclusion of courses with such perspectives. In my teaching context, part of the challenge of rethinking the core curriculum is the particular nature of theological education.

In theological seminaries, like many postsecondary schools, there are sets of standard required courses that students must take as part of a common core curriculum. In the educational setting in which I am an instructor, I teach three core courses regularly: a two-semester survey of the history of Christianity and a basic course in social analysis for ministry. After a few years of teaching "Christian Heritage 1 and 2" (the history of Christianity core course survey), I have come to expect student skepticism and wonder at several points in the discussion. One key point is when we review the early church leaders, thinkers, martyrs, and dissenters such as Tertullian, the biblical scholar Origen of Alexandria, the martyrs Felicitas and Perpetua, Cyprian, bishop of Carthage, Anthony of Egypt, Clement of Alexandria, Athanasius, bishop of Alexandria and champion of Nicaean orthodoxy, the famous Augustine, bishop of Hippo, who was to have ongoing influence on Christianity in the West, and Valentinians and Donatists, relegated to the category of heretics.[2] As I introduce these figures from early church history, I ask students to take note that these people were from Africa and that many of the events of their lives took place in Africa. While this may seem like an obvious observation, it consistently evokes surprise and occasionally objection.

Something similar happens in the second semester of this required core survey of Christian history that experience has taught me to anticipate. Given the pressure to review two thousand years of complicated and wide-ranging history, by the final weeks of the course there is some rushing and cramming, but I try to get as far as the early twentieth century. One reason for this is that I want to review the roots of the largest religious movement in history, Pentecostalism. I mention in my lectures the different factors that prepared the way and eventually led to the great Azusa Street revival of 1906 in Los Angeles. I then say that Pentecostalism in many contemporary settings can trace a connection to Azusa Street, where the key initial leader was William Seymour, an African American Holiness preacher. At this point some students express surprise, including some students who are Pentecostal, who knew of Azusa Street, and perhaps even heard of William Seymour, but never knew that he was African American.

I regularly teach a third required core course at my institution, "The Church in Its Social Context." This course was developed and added by the faculty to the curriculum with input from a curriculum review committee, students, and external constituencies of the school. Generally it was assumed that there was a need to better prepare students to assess, understand, and respond to the social situations of their ministries, as well as to the cultural and social contexts of their congregations and communities. It was determined that students needed to consider the church as a social situation in a wider society and that there was a need for preparation in analyzing groups, communities, and social processes. The expectation was that this addition to the core curriculum would serve as a gateway for students to begin their basic ministry courses and advanced studies. One of the things I do in this social analysis course is have students read works by African American authors and some works that describe social and cultural contexts of African American communities. Occasionally a very few students muse out loud as to why they have these assignments since (1) they are not African American and (2) they do not plan to do ministry in an African American community. This is a required core course, one very different from the history of Christianity survey, with an ambitious set of goals and representing a different set of pedagogical challenges. In it, as in all three core courses, I am committed to introducing perspectives that draw upon African or African American religious heritage and that elicit curiosity, surprise, or even complaint.

My pedagogical approach includes both the specific study of African and African American religious traditions, as well as consideration of broader topics originating from alternative perspectives of African American life and culture. The former is a more direct approach to broadening the core curriculum while the latter is more implicit. My focus in this essay is to describe my efforts with the latter, that is, to value African and African American religious traditions as resources to understand a variety of subjects. Therefore, the ultimate goal is to help influence the whole seminary curriculum to take seriously African, African American, and African Diaspora religious perspectives and history.

My sense is that the goals I set for myself are not usually considered in the formulation and functioning of core curricula. What is called for is a fundamental rethinking of the nature and function of core courses. In the introduction to his documentary reader on African American religious history, Milton C. Sernett called for rethinking American religious history. He writes:

> It is not satisfactory simply to doctor up the standard texts by adding a paragraph or two about slave religion, Richard Allen, or Father Divine. The problem is more than inclusion as opposed to exclusion. If the African American religious experience is allowed to stand on its own merit, not as a footnote to someone else's story, then we will discover a great deal about American culture that is opaque unless seen from the vantage point of those who, according to a nineteenth-century spiritual, have "been in the storm so long."[3]

This presents a crucial reminder and a needed challenge in my rethinking three required core courses. The rethinking and reshaping needed to be more than "politically correct" window-dressing or a sprinkling of a few names across one or two lectures that then trumpeted a false inclusivity. Rethinking these core courses certainly meant reshaping course content, but it also meant addressing the context of teaching.

The Teaching Context

This exercise in rethinking the core emerges from several years of teaching the three courses I have just discussed, which are part of the required core curriculum for master of divinity students at Perkins School of Theology at Southern Methodist University. The courses can be used as test cases at this historic "mainline" Protestant theological seminary.[4] The historical survey ("The Christian Heritage 1 and 2") and the basic course in social analysis for ministry ("The Church in Its Social Context") are prerequisites for other courses in the curriculum. The seminarians who attend these courses reflect the broadest range of students in the school in terms of different backgrounds. The majority of the enrolled students are white/Anglos from the United States. There are also African Americans, Latinos and Latinas, Asian Americans, and some international students. In addition, the majority of the students regardless of cultural background enrolled in these core courses are either engaged in, or preparing for, some type of pastoral ministry.

A longstanding diversity commitment of the Perkins faculty is expressed in a formal "statement," "Minority Concerns and the Perkins Curriculum," which is to be included in every Perkins syllabus. According to this statement,

> Instructors are urged to make every effort to provide—in the syllabi, assignments and formats of their courses—opportunities (1) for women students and students from ethnic minority groups to pursue their study with special reference to their own status or tradition and (2) for all students to become acquainted with the special problems and conditions that affect women and ethnic minority groups in human society.

Rethinking these core courses from African, African American, and African Diaspora religious perspectives and histories became a way to carry forward that faculty commitment and responsibility.

Student body diversity leads to one of the pedagogical challenges for the inclusion of African American and African religious traditions. From one viewpoint, the students are in these courses because they are required in order to complete their degrees. Students came into the courses with varying levels of interest and expectations. For these reasons, some have started the semester with a certain amount of disinterest, resistance, or even animosity toward the subject matter, not an uncommon response to core requirements. These factors present a twofold challenge to the professor: first, to help the students see value in the subject matter in general, and second, to embrace the possibility of viewing course materials through African and African American perspectives, thereby expanding their theological education. This approach is influenced by the observation of Katie G. Cannon that

> African American women scholars created new modes of inquiry for dealing critically with the tradition, structure, and praxis for our fields. These modes invite women and men of contemporary faith communities to a more serious encounter with the contribution African American women have made—and continue to make—to theological studies. The imperative suggested by this pedagogy is an engaged scholarship that leads us to resist domination through mindful activism and helps all of us to live more faithfully the radicality of the gospel.[5]

Building on Cannon's goal for a serious encounter with the contributions of African American women, I have attempted an engaged scholarship and pedagogy, dealing with the tradition, structure, and praxis in the fields of Christian history and the cultural analysis for ministry—a scholarship and pedagogy that seriously considers the contributions of African Americans and Africans.

In committing myself to incorporate African American and African religious perspectives and themes into these core requirements I have three hopes. The first hope is to affirm the legitimacy of multiple perspectives on the subjects studied, while demonstrating that social and cultural location does make a difference for the study of the past as well as for the study of the present. This addresses the previously unquestioned hegemony of certain dominant disciplinary perspectives. Second, it is my hope to lift up African American perspectives and contributions in these courses in a positive way. Third, I hope to nurture the desire to pursue further study in African American religious traditions in students' minds. Finally, the different methodological approaches employed will be reviewed with attention to how such a pedagogical orientation impacts the rest of the curriculum and the approaches of teaching colleagues.

Furthermore, rethinking the core curriculum in this way has wider implications for the vocation of a theological educator as teacher, scholar, and mentor.[6] It means being cognizant of the sense of vocation of the institution as a whole, as well as those diverse callings of individual students. This intentional focus on vocation also supports an approach that seriously engages the various social and cultural contexts of ministry for which the students are being prepared through their theological education.

The Nature of the Core at Theological Seminaries

Considering African and African American religious perspectives in the teaching of the history of Christianity certainly means adjusting the content of the course. It also means giving attention to the processes of teaching, learning, research, and student formation. By mentioning formation, there is then the reminder that a particular core course or core sequence plays a role in the formation of the student for the major field of study, for general education, and for future work upon completion of the program. Faculties decide upon a core curriculum because they want their future graduates to receive a shared basic understanding that they can draw upon in the future.

Part of the pedagogical context is that Perkins School of Theology is both a graduate school and a school for the professional and theological preparation for Christian ministries, set within the larger context of a research university. The mission statement of Perkins School of Theology says that "as a community devoted to theological study and teaching in the service of the church of Jesus Christ, [the mission of Perkins] is to prepare women and men for faithful leadership in Christian ministry." It is common for the alumni/ae of graduate schools of theology to proceed to parish ministry as pastors or to further graduate work in theology or religious studies, as chaplains, in para-church ministry, in international ministry, or in a wide variety of church-related vocations. In preparing future graduates for these diverse callings, many graduate seminaries commonly employ a fourfold division of the curriculum: biblical studies, history, theology, and practical theology. Each of these has subcategories, as well as studies with a curious divisional home. Commenting on the traditional division of seminary curricula, Charles Wood says that

> the fourfold pattern of theological studies—biblical, dogmatic/systematic historical, and practical—which has dominated curricular organization into our own day . . . had its origins in the Reformation, and more specifically in the effort to equip Protestant pastors and teachers with certain requisite knowledge, abilities, and understandings. The persistence of this pattern ever since, despite the many ways in which both theological studies and church leadership have changed over the years, is attributable in part to the power of a common perception that its divisions still represent what the church's leaders need.[8]

Like Wood, I also wonder about the persistent power of this fourfold pattern. It is not clear to me that it is the most effective way to organize theological education and preparation for ministry for the twenty-first century, or that it adequately reflects the needs of contemporary faith communities. Nevertheless, it seems unlikely that there will be a pedagogical revolution any time soon on this point, so this exercise in rethinking the core needed to be done within the parameters of the fourfold pattern of theological education.

Building upon the common fourfold division, master of divinity students at Perkins School of Theology are required to take courses in basic theological studies, the history of Christianity, theology, basic ministerial studies, contextual studies, and a supervised internship. However, master of divinity candidates are not the only students in my classrooms. A number of students in other master's degree programs, as well as individuals seeking personal or professional enrichment, are present. Persons in these alternative categories may or may not have Christian ministry as a goal, and this complicates the pedagogical task further.

Generally, survey courses at theological seminaries must take a broad approach while presenting a great deal of material to a student body at different levels of interest and with different senses of vocations and expectations in a perennially inadequate amount of time. The nature of theological seminaries dictates that core courses will have a dimension of student formation. This student formation is certainly intellectual, as one would expect in graduate school. On the other hand, the course must address the personal and spiritual dimensions of student formation. Accordingly, study in any course at a theological seminary has both educational and formation dimensions.

A further pedagogical challenge in teaching the core survey is that the professor may be asked to cover material that is not in his or her primary area of specialization. Some core courses are the result of group decisions and require that professors extend their teaching beyond their chosen specialties. At Perkins School of Theology both "The Church in Its Social Context" and the "Christian Heritage 1 and 2" sequence developed as a result of group faculty consultations and negotiations as part of a revised curriculum at the seminary. This sequence in the history of Christianity is a core requirement and therefore a gateway into the rest of the seminary curriculum.

Two categories of required courses might be explored by students. The first type is composed of the specific core requirements designed to provide a foundational survey and introduction into a particular discipline and methodology. These courses must be taken before students can progress in their degree programs. Second, there is the core elective that meets a core distribution requirement. All three courses chosen for this project were core requirements.

Seminaries, in some sense, operate as "communities of faith and learning."[8] Perkins School of Theology is a self-confessed Christian community of faith and learning while simultaneously a graduate school within a research university. Accordingly, while there is some variety of commitment and connection, there is nonetheless an investment in the telling of the story of Christianity and the goal of social and cultural analysis that may not be present in other educational settings. This complex teaching context impacts not only the pedagogical methodologies employed generally but also specifically how to have a more serious encounter with African American religious perspective throughout the curriculum.

Reflections on Teaching Strategies

As a professor, drawing upon African and African American religious traditions and perspectives was for me a concrete, measurable first step in rethinking and restructuring the core curriculum. Furthermore, it was a step in shaping core courses in a way that addresses present and future multicultural realities in theological education in the United States. Another concern of this effort was to see what differences it made—for both professor and students—as other cultural perspectives were brought to bear on the traditional ways of teaching the core.

This short listing draws on teaching strategies I used before I started on this path. Furthermore, suggestions and reflections from colleagues and other resources were incorporated while I was fleshing out this teaching emphasis. Finally, these strategies reflect some of my continuing reflections on the praxis of teaching in this way. Central to this teaching approach is building community in the classroom in which both instructors and students are teachers and learners. Regarding this point, bell hooks writes:

> When education is the practice of freedom, students are not the only ones who are asked to share, to confess. Engaged pedagogy does not seek simply to empower students. Any classroom that employs a holistic model of learning will also be a place where teachers grow, and are empowered by the process.[9]

By implementing an engaged pedagogy, one opens the possibility for growth by all within the community that is the classroom.

Nurturing a classroom of possibility, I try to cultivate a collaborative way of learning and a collegial atmosphere in my classes. In this I draw on my own cultural location as a Puerto Rican Latino scholar of religion and on a vital feature of Hispanic/Latino theology, its collaborative methodology, known as *teología en conjunto*. As a shared endeavor, Latino/a collaborative theology arises both from the historical contexts of Hispanics/Latinas and Latinos in the United States, as well as a set of commitments, one of the foremost of which is a commitment to community.[10]

Part of the reality of the Latino/a communities in the United States is that we are exceedingly diverse, more so than is usually acknowledged in the dominant public spheres. What does a second-generation, English-dominant Puerto Rican from Connecticut have in common with a recently arrived Miskito immigrant in Houston, Texas, from Nicaragua—for whom Spanish is a second language (to say nothing of English)—or a Chicana in California whose family has been in the United States for generations? What does it mean that some of the largest communities of Salvadorans are in the United States or that there are growing populations of Mexicans in North Carolina and Arkansas? And yet all these and more are clustered as one under the rubric Hispanics or Latinos. One dimension of the existential reality of being grouped together is discovering what it means to be part of a community that is simultaneously imagined and real, imposed and embraced. *Teología en conjunto* seeks to explore and articulate the theological dimensions of this diverse and constantly developing life together in the United States.

Another part of Latino/a communities in the United Stated is that many of the issues facing them still are not adequately addressed by the larger society and church. Contributions of Hispanics, particularly in theology, history, liturgy, and pastoral ministry, continue to be haphazardly and systematically ignored. *Teología en conjunto* seeks to correct this oversight and to make positive contributions to the life, thought, and ministry of the wider Christian church. Recognizing that all theologies arise out of some particular cultural context, *teología en conjunto*, with its intentional emphasis on the value of cooperative work and commitment to community, seeks to add its voice to wider discussions, all the while trying to be faithful to the perspectives and experiences of the diverse Hispanic/Latino/a communities in the United States. Such a scholarly approach is more than the parochial concerns of a marginalized community. Doing history or cultural analysis in a collaborative way, *en conjunto*, is another way of doing engaged pedagogy, one in which both students and instructors are learners together, fostering an educational community within the classroom.

Building upon a commitment to work *en conjunto*, several connections were made with African American and African religious life in the presentation of the material in each of these courses. This included required readings and lectures that addressed these topics. After a few sessions, some students recognized this emphasis and ensured its place in our discussions.

For all three classes I made two major pedagogical commitments for classroom presentation: I developed Power Point slides to give a visual dimension for all the lectures, and I intentionally drew upon African American rhetorical traditions. Most of my interaction with students is through oral discourse via lectures and discussions. The lectures in "The Church in Its Social Context" and the "Christian Heritage 1 and 2" classes, rather than an inflexible unidirectional delivery of information, took on more of the appearance of both an extemporaneous performance and a multivoice conversation as we became teachers, learners, story tellers, and interpreters together.[11] Both the historical survey courses and the course in cultural analysis had large enough enrollments that a lecture approach was more suitable than a seminar one. The lectures were prepared ahead of time and therefore not improvised, but rather in the delivery there was an intentional attempt to be more engaging. This reflected an effort to emphasize the importance of the spoken word in African American religious tradition. Related to this performance style of lecturing was my sharing my own personal stories as was appropriate to the subject. I intentionally allowed for more discussions during class and a way to affirm our being learners together and to cultivate a community of learning rather than of competition. My persistence in encouraging student interaction led to community-building. Small groups were created and assigned common starter questions to foster discussion in "Christian Heritage 1 and 2" classes.

Student semester projects were of two types. For "The Church in Its Social Context," I assigned semester-long project papers that required field research. While most students have chosen to do this individually, in one offering of the course two students chose to do their project together, taking collaborative learning a step further. I assigned a research paper in "Christian Heritage 1 and 2." This reflected both my assessment of the nature of the course and the departmental negotiations on course methodology. I had students make in-class presentations based on semester projects in earlier offerings of "The Church in Its Social Context"; however, enrollment in the course increased to the degree that this became unmanageable. Short papers that focused on engagement with the textbooks were required in all three courses.

Both the history of Christianity survey and "The Church in Its Social Context" made use of internet course websites. The course sites provided lists of required readings, announcements, chat rooms, primary resources, illustrations, supplemental materials, and links to other sites. Although it was required, not all students used the site. Those who used this resource said that they found it valuable for their study.

I attempted to recognize and honor the importance of different learning styles, for example, that some people do well with oral discourse, while others are more visual learners. It is not that one is better than another; they are just different. As mentioned, all the core courses had visual lectures through Power Point slides that I developed. These slides provided not only bullet points but also charts, artwork, and maps that were part of the classroom conversations. I made greater use of the syllabus as a learning tool and document rather than as a simple list of readings, so that in the first class session I would "exegete" the syllabus and my plan for the course and thereby share with the students aspects of my pedagogical plan for our work together. I embraced the fact that there are certain rituals in the classroom, including the first and last sessions of the course, so that there were opportunities for us to become acquainted with each other and to be introduced into this temporary community, as well as an opportunity for us to say goodbye at the end of the semester. I incorporated more film, video, music, and art. For example, in discussing church art I would show Coptic icons as well as western European medieval painting. All this is an ongoing process, in which I need the help and encouragement that I receive through continuing dialogue with like-minded instructors who are also interested in an engaged pedagogy.

Of course, the challenge of rethinking the core curriculum is not restricted to the areas of history of Christianity, or cultural analysis for ministry, or even to theological education. It is part of a broader pedagogical challenge whenever individual instructors and faculties as a group develop a single course or a curriculum that asserts a desire to engage difference and diversity as well as the received tradition in the formation of students.

Teaching these core courses in light of African American religious tradition means recognizing that this is a counter-hegemonic effort. There is a type of hegemony behind the mainline/mainstream Protestant theological curriculum that places Eurocentric traditions in the position of privilege to the exclusion of all other traditions. Courses that do not seem to be within the dominant central tradition are assigned marginal space while the "real work" is done elsewhere. The challenge and the excitement appears when an Afrocentric perspective is brought into the discussion and thereby opens up the legitimacy of multiple perspectives in the classroom. Molefi Kete Asante defines Afrocentricity as "placing African ideals at the center of any analysis that involves African culture and behavior."[12] Bringing the light of African American religious tradition to these core courses means recognizing that these courses are in many ways a crossroads for everyone. And because of the emphasis of community, teaching these core courses in light of African American religious tradition means that this is not an individual effort.[13]

In the history of Christianity survey, my Afrocentric approach sought to bring into new light the history of African Christianity in contrast with the way Christian church history is commonly taught. While this concern started with a concern for drawing on African American religious heritage, it was suggested to me that it was an opportunity for highlighting African perspectives. Although for many observers it may seem to be common knowledge that Christianity in Africa commenced with European contact and later colonization beginning in the fourteenth and fifteenth centuries, in actuality Christianity in the continent has a much longer history. Frequently the history of Christianity in Africa is taught in a way that stresses the missionaries of the nineteenth and twentieth centuries, overlooking the history of Christianity in Africa prior to modern colonization, or seeing Christianity in North Africa as part of greater European Mediterranean world. Indeed there has been a continuous Christian presence in Africa since the early years of Christianity in antiquity right up to the present. One of the challenges in embracing this fact is defining what one means by Africa. Often northern Africa (Egypt, Libya, Tunisia, Algeria, Morocco) gets treated historically and theologically as an extension of Europe and/or the Islamic world, whereas Sudan and Ethiopia may not be discussed at all until they enter stories of European colonization in that part of the world. What some historians call a discontinuity paradigm is quite common—that is, a view that sees a gap between early Christianity in Africa and contemporary African Christianity. The discontinuity paradigm assumes a disappearance of Christianity from Africa with the advent of Islam, followed by a reintroduction of Christianity in Africa (especially sub-Saharan) by modern Western missionaries. J. Joseph Hoffman notes that

> European church historiography has not only encouraged the discontinuity paradigm with its failure to emphasize the distinction between missionary history and African church history but has largely been responsible for propagating the view that the "real" history of Christianity in Africa belongs roughly to the last century and a half. Thus while defending an ignorance of indigenous culture by the early missionaries which was "partly blameworthy, partly inevitable," Adrian Hastings asserts that in 1875 "African Christianity barely existed," on the premise that the state church of Ethiopia and the Coptic church of Egypt—two of the most ancient Christian foundations in the world were in no way in contact with the rest of the continent.[14]

There is no one story of Christianity, but in fact there are many stories, sometimes overlapping, at other times pursuing concurrent alternative story lines, not always aware of the existence of others. Approaching the history of Christianity with greater appreciation for the antiquity of Christianity in Africa is not only important for a fuller historical understanding of Christianity; the expansion of Christianity in Africa in the twentieth and early twenty-first century has global significance. Crafting these core courses with the African religious perspectives in view provides students with more tools to engage a global community in both a historical and contemporary sense.

This approach embraces a different perspective from the one found in the common telling of early Christian history, theology, and cultures. It asks us to consider whether telling the Christian story from the geographical perspective of Africa may bring new insights and appreciation not only for African Christianity but also for broader understanding of the history of Christianity. By not divorcing ancient northern Africa from its connections to Mediterranean and Asian civilizations and taking seriously that North Africa was simultaneously African, learners gain access to a different angle on the importance of social and cultural context of the church in its early period.[15] From this point of view, questions of culture, ethnicity, class, and gender are considered in addition to questions of regional orientation.

African American religions and the social context for ministry were addressed in the third core course I taught, "The Church in Its Social Context," a required course at Perkins School of Theology. This course is intended to be an examination of social structures, trends and dynamics affecting contemporary life, local communities, and the mission of the church, with the goal of preparing students to understand and respond to specific sources of social structure and power, including economic, racial, ethnic, and gender differences. In my approach to this course, my objectives for the students are as follows:

1. To become acquainted with critical tools and methods to assess, understand, and thereby respond to the social contexts of congregations and their communities
2. To examine contemporary society with regard to trends in the population, economic aspects, culture and social life, including examination of larger societal structures as they shape the social context within which the church is in ministry
3. To analyze the church as a social institution in a wider diverse society.
4. To become familiar with ways to analyze groups, communities, systems, and social processes
5. To consider the "problem of the color-line," that is, racism, and how the church responds to this challenge in its ministry in society
6. To consider the issues of sexism present in contemporary society and identify ways to address it in ministry contexts
7. To be introduced to congregational studies as a tool for ministry

I use different texts each time I teach this course, but I have settled on a few that engage a dominant explanation of Christianity and culture. These texts provide an extremely helpful gateway to the methodologies of congregational studies, and a challenging engagement with issues of race and racial reconciliation.[16]

Distinctively, a major component of student work in this course is the congregational and contextual analysis project. Students are to submit a semester project paper analyzing the characteristics, context, and nature of mission of a particular congregation or other ministry context. This is an opportunity to apply congregational studies perspectives and to interact with some of the themes discussed in class. This congregational and contextual analysis project will focus a particular ministry setting, for example, a local congregation, church agency, or faith-based service provider, chosen in consultation with the instructor. The final project should directly address at least one of the aforementioned course objectives. In addition, it should be in conversation with H. Richard Niebuhr's five "types" of interactions between Christian communities and their specific social contexts, as enumerated in *Christ and Culture*, and should make use of additional rubrics for analysis found in other course textbooks.[17] We draw upon African American religious traditions through lectures, assigned readings, and a semester-long focus on the theme of race and racial reconciliation in the United States.

Reflections on the Praxis of Teaching African American Religious Life

Throughout these three core courses I seek to draw upon African American religious life. The Latino theologian Samuel Solivan writes of orthodoxy (teaching, body of knowledge), orthopraxis (doing, practice), and orthopathos (feeling).[18] Solivan holds that each is needed for a more balanced and fuller articulation of theology as a whole, not just Latino theology. Without pressing the parallel too far, my intentionally Afrocentric teaching experience has impressed upon me that teaching and learning about African American religious life is more than acquiring and disbursing a body of knowledge (*doxy*) or an appreciation of how it is done (*praxis*). A fuller appreciation of African American religious life also involves helping the student tap into the *pathos*—the "feeling"—of African American religious life. The role of community ascends as a key aspect of bringing the student into the experience of African American religious life. Throughout my courses I have tried to cultivate a sense of community in the classroom, so that this small, temporary community would become another portal in appreciating African American religious life.

A serendipitous result was the response of the majority of my African American students in my first class, who said in their class evaluations that the "classroom community" was a safe, welcoming, relevant place that connected with their own experiences of African American religious life. This student response from both African Americans and others has been repeated consistently.

On a personal level, being able to focus on African American religions and culture has reminded me how important this area of knowledge is to me and has made an impact my own major field of research. It has reminded me how important the study of Latino/a religion and culture and North American religion and culture are to me as a scholar of North American religious history and culture with specializations in Latino/a religions and African American religions. My initial basic knowledge for "The Church in Its Social Context" came from the methodology employed in my major area of research; but teaching the course expanded my own interest and proficiency, especially in the interdisciplinary approaches of congregational studies.

In taking such an approach to classroom learning there is the need to guard against the temptation to slide into essentialism and "presentism." Essentialism often is understood as a view that defines, and even restricts something to a certain set of essential properties or characteristics. In this regard, when seeking to be in dialogue with African and African American religious traditions in the teaching of the core curriculum, there is a need to be vigilant against succumbing to stereotypes that do not allow for the rich diversity of the traditions. The historian Lynn Hunt articulates the challenge facing historians in the form of presentism. Hunt writes, "presentism besets us in two different ways: (1) the tendency to interpret the past in presentist terms; and (2) the shift of general historical interest toward the contemporary period and away from the more distant past."[19] Again, without care, an Afrocentric emphasis in the core curriculum may fall victim to this type of presentism.

Nevertheless, rethinking the core curriculum through an emphasis on African American religious tradition and perspectives has had a radical impact on the academic discourse and pedagogical strategies for teaching in my setting. And as a result, together with my students, I have enjoyed a classroom of radical possibilities, not only for the subjects at hand but also for the whole curriculum.

NOTES

1. See Robert Banks, *Reenvisioning Theological Education* (Grand Rapids, MI: Eerdmans, 1999), 11.

2. A convert to Christianity, Tertullian (c. 160–220 C.E.) was from Carthage and exerted great influence as a Christian theologian and biblical exegete. Origen (c. 184–254) was known both for his teaching of the subordination of the Son to the Father and of being accused of universalism. Felicitas and Perpetua were early Christian martyrs (d. 203); the account of their deaths had wide influence on the development of Christianity. Cyprian of Carthage (200–258) was a bishop during periods of persecution; he emphasized the authority of the Church. The hermit Anthony (c. 250–356) was influential in the development of ascetic Christianity in the movement of the Desert people (traditionally "Desert Fathers"). Athanasius, bishop of Alexandria (293–373), campaigned for the Christological views of the Council of Nicaea (325); he was an opponent of Arianism. Augustine, bishop of Hippo (354–430), addressed a number of topics, including the Fall and human depravity, salvation, and predestination. The Valentinians were the followers of the theologian Valentinus of Alexandria (d. 165); they were accused of being Gnostics. The Donatists were members of a large movement that actually preceded the leadership of Donatus. Donatus and other church leaders in North Africa opposed the readmittance to the Church of those who had "lapsed" during the persecution of Christians in North Africa. Although condemned by Augustine, Donatist Christianity survived for an additional three hundred years until the appearance of Islam. See Elizabeth Isichei, *A History of Christianity in Africa: From Antiquity to the Present* (Grand Rapids, MI: Eerdmans, 1995).

3. Milton C. Sernett, ed., *African American Religious History: A Documentary Witness* (Durham, NC: Duke University Press, 1999), 9.

4. Terms such as "mainline" and "mainstream" are themselves problematic and can obscure as much as they define. See Douglas Jacobsen and William Vance Trollinger, Jr., ed., *ReForming the Center: American Protestantism 1900 to the Present* (Grand Rapids, MI: Eerdmans, 1998), and Edwin David Aponte, *Mainstreams, Mainlines, and Margins: Latino Protestantism in Philadelphia* (Waco, TX: Baylor University Press, forthcoming).

5. Katie G. Cannon, *Katie's Canon: Womanism and the Soul of the Black Community* (New York: Continuum, 1995), 137–138.

6. For more on theological education as vocation see L. Gregory Jones and Stephanie Paulsell, eds., *The Scope of Our Art: The Vocation of the Theological Teacher* (Grand Rapids, MI: Eerdmans, 2002); Robert Banks, *Reenvisioning Theological Education: Exploring a Missional Alternative to Current Models* (Grand Rapids, MI: Eerdmans, 1999).

7. Charles M. Wood, *Vision and Discernment: An Orientation in Theological Study* (Eugene, OR: Wipf and Stock, 1985), 3.

8. See Michael Gilligan, "Diversity and Accreditation: A Measure of Quality," *Theological Education* 38, 2 (2002): 2.

9. hooks, *Teaching to Transgress*, 21.

10. For more on *teología en conjunto* see José David Rodríguez and Loida I. Martell-Otero, eds., *Teología en Conjunto: A Collaborative Hispanic Protestant Theology* (Louisville, KY: Westminster John Knox Press, 1997); see also the preface to Miguel A. De La Torre and Edwin David Aponte, eds., *Introducing Latino/a Theologies*, (Maryknoll, NY: Orbis Books, 2001), xi–xiii.

11. In this approach Will Coleman's hermeneutics are particularly influential. See Will Coleman, *Tribal Talk: Black Theology, Hermeneutics, and African/American Ways of "Telling the Story"* (University Park: Pennsylvania State University Press, 2000). In describing his project Coleman says: "This book explores the relationship between black theology, hermeneutics, and the idiom of African American discourse. In doing so, it strives to demonstrate a 'mulitvoiced' praxis of storytelling and interpretation" (vii).

12. Molefi Kete Asante, *The Afrocentric Idea*, rev. and expanded ed. (Philadelphia: Temple University Press, 1998), 2.

13. See Coleman, *Tribal Talk*, 193.

14. R. Joseph Hoffmann, "Beyond the Discontinuity Paradigm: Toward a Pan-African Church," *Journal of Religious History* 21, 2 (June 1997): 142–143.

15. This in no way denies Hellenistic and Roman influence in North Africa. Not only were there expatriate communities but also many indigenous peoples of North Africa were Romanized and Hellenized. At the same time many indigenous languages and cultural patterns coexisted with the Romanized communities, and this cultural diversity may have been a factor in the theological disputes in Christian North Africa. For more on the African dimensions on North African Christianity, see Isichei, *History of Christianity in Africa*, and Maureen A. Tilley, *The Bible in Christian North Africa: The Donatist World* (Minneapolis: Fortress Press, 1997).

16. Textbooks used regularly include H. Richard Niebuhr, *Christ and Culture* (San Francisco: HarperSanFrancisco, 2001; originally published 1951); Spencer Perkins and Chris Rice, *More Than Equals: Racial Healing for the Sake of the Gospel*, rev. and expanded ed. (Downers Grove, IL: InterVarsity Press, 2000); Evelyn L. Parker, *Trouble Don't Last Always: Emancipatory Hope among African American Adolescents* (Cleveland: Pilgrim Press, 2003); Cheryl J. Sanders, *Saints in Exile: The Holiness-Pentecostal Experience in African American Religion and Culture* (New York: Oxford University Press. 1996); Emilie M. Townes, ed., *Embracing the Spirit: Womanist Perspectives on Hope, Salvation, and Transformation* (Maryknoll, NY: Orbis Books, 1997); and Nancy Tatom Ammerman, Carl S. Dudley, and Jackson W. Carroll, eds., *Studying Congregations: A New Handbook* (Nashville: Abingdon Press, 1998).

17. Niebuhr, *Christ and Culture*; Nancy Tatom Ammerman and Arthur Emery Farnsley, *Congregation and Community* (New Brunswick: Rutgers University Press, 1997); Harold J. Recinos, *Jesus Weeps: Global Encounters on Our Doorstep* (Nashville: Abingdon Press, 1992).

18. Samuel Solivan, *The Spirit, Pathos, and Liberation* (Sheffield, UK: Sheffield Academic Press, 1998).

19. Lynn Hunt, "Against Presentism," *Perspectives: Newsmagazine of the American Historical Association* 40 (May 2002): 7.

REFERENCES

Ammerman, Nancy Tatom, Carl S. Dudley, and Jackson W. Carroll, eds. *Studying Congregations: A New Handbook*. Nashville: Abingdon Press, 1998.

Ammerman, Nancy Tatom, and Arthur Emery Farnsley. *Congregation and Community*. New Brunswick, NJ: Rutgers University Press, 1997.

Aponte, Edwin David. *Mainstreams, Mainlines, and Margins: Latino Protestantism in Philadelphia*. Waco, TX: Baylor University Press, forthcoming.

Asante, Molefi Kete. *The Afrocentric Idea*, rev. and expanded ed. Philadelphia: Temple University Press, 1998.

Bakke, Ray. *A Theology as Big as the City*. Downers Grove, IL: InterVarsity Press, 1997.

Banks, Robert. *Reenvisioning Theological Education*. Grand Rapids, MI: Eerdmans, 1999.

Cannon, Katie G. *Katie's Canon: Womanism and the Soul of the Black Community*. New York: Continuum, 1995.

Coleman, Will. *Tribal Talk: Black Theology, Hermeneutics, and African/American Ways of "Telling the Story."* University Park: Pennsylvania State University Press, 2000.

De La Torre, Miguel A., and Edwin David Aponte, *Introducing Latino/a Theologies*. Maryknoll, NY: Orbis Books, 2001.

Gilligan, Michael. "Diversity and Accreditation: A Measure of Quality." *Theological Education* 38, 2 (2002), 1–13.

Hoffmann, R. Joseph. "Beyond the Discontinuity Paradigm: Toward a Pan-African Church." *Journal of Religious History* 21, 2 (June 1997), 138–158.

hooks, bell. *Teaching to Transgress: Education as the Practice of Freedom*. New York: Routledge, 1994.

Hunt, Lynn. "Against Presentism." *Perspectives: Newsmagazine of the American Historical Association* 40 (May 2002), 7–9.

Isichei, Elizabeth. *A History of Christianity in Africa: From Antiquity to the Present*. Grand Rapids, MI: Eerdmans, 1995.

Jacobsen, Douglas and William Vance Trollinger, Jr., eds. *Re-Forming the Center: American Protestantism 1900 to the Present*. Grand Rapids, MI: Eerdmans, 1998.

Jones, L. Gregory and Stephanie Paulsell, eds. *The Scope of Our Art: The Vocation of the Theological Teacher*. Grand Rapids: Eerdmans, 2002.

Lischer, Richard. *Open Secrets: A Spiritual Journey through a Country Church*. New York: Doubleday, 2001.

Niebuhr, H. Richard. *Christ and Culture*. San Francisco: HarperCollins, 2001.

Parker, Evelyn L. *Trouble Don't Last Always: Emancipatory Hope among African American Adolescents.* Cleveland: Pilgrim Press, 2003.

Perkins, Spencer and Chris Rice. *More Than Equals: Racial Healing for the Sake of the Gospel.* Rev. and expanded ed. Downers Grove, IL: InterVarsity Press, 2000.

Recinos, Harold J. *Jesus Weeps: Global Encounters on Our Doorstep.* Nashville: Abingdon Press, 1992.

Rodríguez, José David and Loida I. Martell-Otero, eds. *Teología en Conjunto: A Collaborative Hispanic Protestant Theology.* Louisville, KY: Westminster John Knox Press, 1997.

Sanders, Cheryl J. *Saints in Exile: The Holiness-Pentecostal Experience in African American Religion and Culture.* New York: Oxford University Press. 1996.

Sernett, Milton C., ed. *African American Religious History: A Documentary Witness.* Durham, NC: Duke University Press, 1999.

Solivan, Samuel. *The Spirit, Pathos, and Liberation.* Sheffield, UK: Sheffield Academic Press, 1998.

Tilley, Maureen A. *The Bible in Christian North Africa: The Donatist World.* Minneapolis: Fortress Press, 1997.

Townes, Emilie M., *In a Blaze of Glory: Womanist Spirituality as Social Witness.* Nashville: Abingdon Press, 1995.

———, ed. *Embracing the Spirit: Womanist Perspectives on Hope, Salvation, and Transformation.* Maryknoll, NY: Orbis Books, 1997.

Wood, Charles M. *Vision and Discernment: An Orientation in Theological Study.* Eugene, OR: Wipf and Stock, 1985.

8

Acknowledging Diversity in the American Catholic Experience

Bernadette McNary-Zak

"But the Emperor is naked!" cried an innocent child. "He hasn't got anything on!"

—Hans Christian Andersen,
The Emperor's New Clothes

Like those who heard and understood this child's cry, I have come to learn through participation in the "Mining the Motherlode" teaching workshop that challenges to our operative assumptions—"those taken-for-granted ideas, commonsense beliefs, and self-evident rules of thumb that inform our thoughts and actions"—may come in unexpected forms.[1] I applied for this workshop when I was teaching as an adjunct instructor at a small Catholic university in the Northeast and wanted help with a course called "History of American Catholicism." My proposed project had clear goals for course revision that included locating neglected resources on the African American Catholic experience for two of the course units and building this material in to the existing course structure. However, within the first few days of the workshop, I realized the extent to which my operative assumptions about the existing course and my own pedagogy were seriously flawed. Nevertheless, in my misguided and ill-conceived attempt to think about diversity in terms of additional books and other sources, another more promising guiding question had emerged: how might an upper-level, undergraduate, religious studies course in the history of American Catholicism be framed in order to foster academic engagement with the diversity in this faith tradition in a way that minimizes marginality and invites interaction?[2]

When my institutional affiliation changed during the course of the workshop, I needed to expand this question to include how the course might be framed for a non-Catholic, Protestant, and Southern context. I have located an initial response to my methodological questions through developing an entirely new course, "Histories of American Catholicism," which will strive to address diversity by problematizing American Catholic identity. This chapter discusses several of these methodological issues with a particular focus on how they have shaped my own thinking about how to teach this course. Since the course has not yet been taught in either a Catholic or a non-Catholic context, this essay is a working proposal that offers a preliminary road map. Like all maps, it will require adjustment when borders are ill defined, when directions are faulty, and when paths go astray.

The Study of History

In *Lumen Gentium*, one of the sixteen principal documents produced by the Second Vatican Council, the Roman curia advanced a model of the Roman Catholic Church as the people of God. This theoretical model intentionally shifted the focus from a church identified principally with the hierarchy to one identified principally with the laity. Almost twenty years after the council the historian Jay P. Dolan observed: "The spirit of Vatican II and the new vision it inspired has had a profound effect on the study of the Bible, theology, ethics, and church law. Less publicized but no less real is its effect on the study of history. A new understanding of the church demands a new history of American Catholicism."[3]

The construction of this "new history" requires, at least in my mind, a more explicit expression of how I understand the tasks of historical investigation. The classical historian E. H. Carr offered a definition of history that grounds my thinking in and orientation to this course. Carr notes that history is "both the inquiry conducted by the historian and the facts of the past into which he inquires"; Moreover, it

> is a social process, in which individuals are engaged as social beings. . . . The reciprocal process of interaction between the historian and his facts . . . the dialogue between past and present . . . is a dialogue not between abstract and isolated individuals, but between the society of today and the society of yesterday.[4]

An emphasis on history as dialectical process entails participation on the part of the instructor and student; their work is both a particular understanding of the past and the present as well as a contribution to the ongoing assessment and evaluation of past and present in the future. Such emphasis grounds in a necessary way the notion that ideas, beliefs, and values originate in a given context, are shaped by that context, and contribute to that context. In this, such emphasis upholds specificity while concretizing a fundamental sameness between the student and the subject; in the process of studying the past the student is challenged to understand the self as historical being.

By extension, historical investigation construed in this way also implies that in this course, and in my teaching in general, I offer a way of approaching and perceiving the world and our places in it. As Lynn Weber Cannon observes, "the process of critical thinking begins by recognizing that as the teacher in the classroom I am a key actor in the classroom dynamics that evolve. I must recognize who I am, where I teach, and whom I teach."[5] Who I am establishes a certain positioning with respect to religion, culture, gender, society, education, and politics. It entails naming clearly those experiences and values that are essential to my own personhood and then remaining aware of why I think how I think when I am in the classroom. Where I teach establishes a specific positioning with regard to context and space. It involves attentiveness to the mission of my department and of my institution. Here, again, I need to consider if, and how, the course might contribute to the specific goals of a liberal arts education as advanced by my college or university. Whom I teach determines my position with respect to the students. How do their values and ideas inform their understanding of the course material and how do these shape the teaching-learning relationship?

Cannon's charge further requires that I must also recognize my role "in transmitting a dominant cultural system."[6] The unveiling of my own operative assumptions during initial syllabus reconstruction of this course challenged me to confront my understanding of diversity in the context of a faith tradition. As Nancy Van Note Chism and Anne S. Pruitt admonish:

> College teachers should examine their own thoughts and actions. The more reflective they are about biases, the more they are able to deal with them. The more they convince themselves of the importance of valuing other perspectives and socially different people, the more willing they will be to take extra measures to foster inclusion.[7]

I realized early in the process of drafting the course that the term "American Catholicism" was a misnomer. Any effort to unpack the standard scholarly identification of the American Catholic as an individual affiliated with the Roman Catholic Church who resides in the United States confronts the inaccurate prioritization of experience at the expense of marginalizing and, in many instances, silencing the experiences of others residing in the Americas. The problem, however, is not only that the term is found widely in discourse about Catholicism in the United States but that it can be reinforced and normalized easily in undergraduate courses in the history of American Catholicism where the dominant chronological scheme for understanding the European American Catholic paradigm is upheld. Such courses depict an inaccuracy and may even foster further alienation from the Catholic faith tradition. To avoid this, I needed to consider carefully course content and its relation to diversity as a central interpretive paradigm of a course.

The Study of American Catholic History

Cannon's claims about positioning reveal how the effectiveness of Carr's framework for historical investigation depends on whether I am explicit about the operative assumptions that frame my own perceptions and those contained in the course. The way I appropriate myself as a historical being engaged in the social process of history, and the way the course construes historical investigation, significantly impacts the teaching-learning relationship and the way the students approach the course material. To take this task seriously is to equip the student with the tools necessary for constructively evaluating the faith tradition. To this end, the proposed course situates at its center the misnomer that is American Catholicism; it is framed by the questions "What is American Catholicism?" and "Who is the American Catholic?" The complexities that lie at the core of these questions will be mirrored by course structure— a conceptually based course model that organizes "units around major ideas or concepts of the field so that understanding of these concepts evolves in a manner that represents important relationships."[8] In this, the four primary areas of American Catholic history recognized by scholars (i.e., the colonial period, the republican period, the immigrant period, and the modern period) will be assessed by utilizing texts reflective of the five principal groups of American Catholics by population size: African American Catholics, Asian American Catholics, European American Catholics, Hispanic American Catholics, and Native American Catholics.[9]

Because the course seeks to explore factors of diversity and factors of unity within American Catholicism in coverage of each of these periods, the intention is to preserve each of these groups as an independent manifestation of American Catholicism. So, rather than attempting to plug some representative voice or text from each group into a strict chronological survey, the course follows several chronological currents within each broad period. This structure diffuses the notion of any of these groups as marginal to the history of the tradition; their active presence since the inception and throughout the sustenance of the faith tradition in the United States is evidence of their value and role in shaping what is American Catholicism.[10]

Such a paradigm shift responds to the false depiction of American Catholicism as European American Catholicism and the minority status of all other manifestations of the faith tradition. Furthermore, it avoids repeating consideration of these manifestations in the context of a European American Catholic paradigm. Several noteworthy ramifications follow. Although aspects of African American Catholic experience such as unfair treatment by a largely conservative European American Catholic episcopate and populace certainly are not dismissed, they no longer can stand as the only assessment. In a similar way, the relegation and isolation of Hispanic American Catholicism and of Native American Catholicism to the context of colonization is no longer the only perspective.

One potential result of this conceptually based course model becomes, then, an emphasis on what is commonly shared among these groups of American Catholics, that is, a set of dimensions, in the words of Ninian Smart, that define a worldview (in this application, a specifically Catholic one).[11] Let me offer two illustrations from the proposed course syllabus that bear particular importance to the teaching and learning of African American religious experience in order to suggest how this may occur.

To challenge the assumption that the early European missionary movements to Native Americans are the sole foundation for American Catholicism, I intend to follow an introductory lecture with four class sessions devoted to "Roots of American Catholicism." The first of these sessions is titled "African Roots," after the first chapter in Cyprian Davis's book *The History of Black Catholics in the United States*, one of the reading assignments for this class period. Here students encounter explicit connection with the origins of Christianity. Davis claims that the

> black Catholic community in America . . . sought its roots in the religious experience of Africa and its self-definition in the African saints of the early church. American blacks, both Protestant and Catholic, found their roots in the black Africans who appeared in the pages of the Scriptures, both in the Old Testament and the New, and most particularly in the many references to Ethiopia in the Psalms and Prophets.[12]

Similar claims are voiced in readings for the second session, "Hispanic Roots," which include the first two chapters of Moises Sandoval, *On the Move: A History of the Hispanic Church in the United States*, and the first chapter of Jeanette Rodriguez, *Our Lady of Guadalupe: Faith and Empowerment among Mexican American Women*. This is followed by treatment of "European Roots" and of "Native American Roots."

Likewise, in an effort to witness engagement between several of these primary groups of American Catholics and to reconsider the tensions between black and white Catholics prior to the civil rights movement, students will read accounts of racial segregation in the churches, racial exclusion at Catholic educational institutions, and the violent antagonism toward black Catholics in the late nineteenth century.[13] Textual treatment can be coupled with case studies from the local region about parochial school integration and the role of religious orders like the Josephites. So, for example, for students at an institution in the mid-South, text material might be supplemented with evidence for the creation of separate churches and schools for blacks, such as St. Anthony of Padua in Memphis (1909), run by the Josephites, and with evidence for the racial riots in Memphis (1866).[14]

Histories of American Catholicism

Theoretical expansion of the notion of canon and of text has the effect of diffusing the notion of any type of evidence, including personal experiences, as marginal to the faith tradition. Such multitextuality reflects how diversity is expressed, interpreted, and understood, as it ensures that "one group's experience is not held up as the norm or the standard against which everyone else is defined."[15] When multitextuality is accompanied by appropriate assignments, the course can invite students, as learners, to address the same questions that I faced about operative assumptions. Here the student is offered a process for preparing the self to think critically. This process is concretized in the presentation of many opportunities for concrete experience, reflective observation, abstract conceptualization, and active experimentation.[16]

Concrete experience can incorporate the rich material culture of the faith tradition. The use of material culture can empower the students to critically engage diversity constructively. In my opening remarks in previous versions of the course, I presented several objects sacred to Catholics and explained that such objects are " 'symbols of' unity" that, along with the sacraments, provide common ways of framing experience of the divine, doctrinal beliefs, myths, ethics, social constructions, and ritual practices. Such objects can include, among others, a holy card, a catechism, a medal, a rosary, a chaplet. I encourage students to read such objects as texts and to notice how they are used, who uses them, and why they are used. Students not familiar with such objects are often most interested in moving beyond sight to the feel of the object; they often ask if it is worn, and they try to make correlations with other more familiar objects. Discussion of what makes an object sacred tends to follow and supplies an easy segue into the role of public validation and the need for communal identity in faith traditions. This opens the class to the idea that the story of Catholics in the United States is, to a large extent, the story of how groups of Catholics have defined their identity as ethnic, American, and Catholic (thereby introducing the question of what constitutes an American Catholic). The symbolic dimensions (i.e., the doctrine and ritual practices represented by such objects, as in prayer, sacraments, etc.) of the worldview to which these objects point might be the site where bridges between groups of American Catholics can be built. A discussion of symbolism, toward the end of the course, might also address the supposed crisis of American Catholicism. While such objects are commonly deemed sacred among Catholics, the role and weight given them in popular practice differs among manifestations of the faith tradition.

Likewise, concrete experience might include sound recordings, videos, and art. A class that addresses the period of mass immigration of European Catholics to the United States can be illustrated in a way that invites conversation, for instance, by reading letters of immigrant women alongside visual components of photography and video. Small group work, in which students work through specific questions that force them to make connections and to explore consequences, enables them to engage problems and issues raised by the material.

Finally, visitation to an off-campus Catholic parish might also be included to address this learning stage. Student visits are coordinated ahead of time and are processed in writing and in group discussion. The larger educational goals of this form of fieldwork are

> to broaden, extend, and deepen the intellectual content of undergraduate instruction by integrating theory and practice in a particular subject area; to increase students' motivation to engage in academic work through the experience of applying knowledge; and to encourage students to develop their skills as independent scholars and researchers.[17]

By visiting a local congregation, students can witness how American Catholicism is defined in a specific geographic locale. Many times, such visits combat relativism and oversimplification.

The processing of these concrete experiences in writing and in discussion affords opportunity for reflective observation. However, an additional occasion for this might emerge by inviting contemporary voices who reflect the lived experience of the faith tradition. Here, selected members of the local Catholic community might share their perspectives in the classroom. Reading assignments and written responses from works like John Deedy, *American Catholics: What Went Wrong*, or William J. Bausch, *Catholics in Crisis: The Church Confronts Contemporary Challenges*, works that address the apparently growing divide between "orthodox" and "heterodox" American Catholics, can become the basis of a discussion that names and explores generational issues, for instance, in a fruitful way.

Research papers are a common vehicle of abstract conceptualization. Another written form that might be incorporated here is a book review. As a faith tradition that originates in, and continues to be shaped by, a Protestant context, American Catholicism retains a minority status. Novels, in particular, are a highly effective form of evidence for encountering, problematizing, discussing, and understanding this status. I assign a book review as one of the course requirements, and at the beginning of the course I provide a list of representative works from each of the groups of American Catholics to be studied.

Works I have suggested include: Pietro Di Donato, *Christ in Concrete*; Virgil Elizondo, *The Future Is Mestizo: Life Where Cultures Meet*; Mary Gordon, *The Company of Women*; *Taking Down Our Harps*, edited by Diana L. Hayes and Cyprian Davis; Ada Maria Isasi-Diaz and Yolanda Tarango, *Hispanic Women: Prophetic Voice in the Church*. Book reviews offer an important type of engagement, as students are required to supply an analysis, and not a summary, of the content of the work that entails some awareness of their own operative assumptions about the material. Students often discover through this assignment an accessible way of grounding the discourse about the lived tension between religion and culture and, in some cases, about negotiating an American and a Catholic identity, an affiliation to Rome and to the United States.

Because it is my intention to supply the students with both an understanding of a specific history and a model for doing history, I also emphasize the use of case studies, in particular, as a means of active experimentation. Case studies encourage multilevel thinking, and as a result they tend to engage students in the details of an issue without sacrificing the broader context in a highly effective way. For example, students might begin to appreciate the tensions that surfaced in immigrant efforts to forge identity in the United States as they are embedded in parish histories from the late nineteenth century.

Active experimentation is also possible through course projects. Such projects, like many of the examples already supplied, really employ several learning stages. Students should explore a feature of American Catholicism by crafting and implementing a project of interest to them. This might entail conducting interviews or campus surveys, for example. Brief presentations of completed projects can be incorporated into the syllabus. Discussions about ethical and social issues are grounded when the reading assignment is supplemented with the results of a student project that culled information about such issues on campus. Likewise, the topic of devotional Catholicism might take on new meaning when the memories of one student's grandparents flood the classroom via a videotaped interview created for the project.

Conclusion

By problematizing what constitutes an American Catholic and by expanding notions of canon and of text, "Histories of American Catholicism" seeks to acknowledge what remains hidden, namely, that diversity within the faith tradition, has been there from its inception in the United States (only needing to be brought to the fore). The depiction of a multivariant, multitextual, multidimensional, multiethnic, and multiracial faith tradition in which there is both distinctiveness and fluidity among and within various groups of American Catholics reflects accurately and well the current state of the post–Second Vatican Council Catholic Church. Furthermore, I hope, through this course, to challenge students to think about their operative assumptions and those in the texts they read. In this, the course strives to empower students to participate in and to assess the nature of historical investigation. Equipped with the insight of the innocent child in Hans Christian Andersen's fable, the course strives to embrace the future with an understanding of the past.

NOTES

1. Stephen Brookfield, "Using Critical Incidents to Explore Assumptions," in *Excellence in University Teaching*, Thomas H. Buxton and Keith W. Pritchard, eds. (Columbia: University of South Carolina Press, 1975), 177.

2. This question, I realized much later, might also be contextualized by discussions about cultural pluralism and higher education. As Dwight Boyd writes, when "increasing public recognition of the cultural diversity that now characterizes many societies . . . intersects with an appreciation that educational claims are necessarily prescriptive . . . the question of whose culture/whose values should guide educational prescriptions cannot be escaped." He continues: "This is, of course, not to say that in practice this question does not get circumvented or ignored. Rather, it is to say that doing so seriously undermines the legitimacy of the institution of education for many segments of society (though not in the minds of those in the dominant culture)." See Dwight Boyd, "Dominance Concealed Through Diversity: Implications of Inadequate Perspectives on Cultural Pluralism," *Harvard Educational Review* 66, 3 (1996): 609–630; quotations from p. 610.

3. Jay P. Dolan, *The American Catholic Experience: A History from the Colonial Times to the Present* (Garden City, NY: Doubleday, 1984), 10.

4. Edward Hazlett Carr, *What Is History?* (London: Macmillian, 1961), 5.

5. Lynn Weber Cannon, "Fostering Positive Race, Class, and Gender Dynamics in the Classroom," *Women's Studies Quarterly* 1 and 2 (1990): 128. See also: Carol A. Jenkins and Deborah L. Bainer, "Common Instructional Problems in the Multicultural Classroom," *Journal on Excellence in College Teaching*, vol. 2 (1991): 77–88. I have addressed the methodological dimension of this course in particular in "Wading through the Quagmire of Religious History," *Teaching Theology and Religion* 5, 2 (2002): 101–104.

6. Maurianne Adams, "Academic Culture: The Hidden Curriculum," *Teaching Excellence* 3, 6 (1991): 6.

7. Nancy Van Note Chism and Anne S. Pruitt, "Promoting Inclusiveness in College Teaching," in *Teaching Improvement Practices: Successful Strategies for Higher Education*, E. Alan Wright, ed. (Bolton: Anker, 1999), 332. They write: "Decisions about what shall be taught reflect the decision makers' values about what knowledge is most worthy. These values are rooted in the societal traditions, mainstream scholarship, and personal preferences of those who make curriculum choices" (328). See also Adams, "Academic Culture."

8. Malcolm A. Lowther, Joan S. Stark, and Gretchen G. Martens, *Preparing Course Syllabi for Improved Communication* (Ann Arbor: University of Michigan, Na-

tional Center for Research to Improve Postsecondary Teaching and Learning), 19. See also Howard B. Altman and William E. Cashin, "Writing a Syllabus," Center for Faculty Evaluation and Development, Kansas State University, IDEA Paper no. 27 (1992).

9. The identification of these types is intended to help make categories for the purpose of discussion; in the course, attention is given to the reality of diversity among Catholics within each type and to the inaccuracy of these types for categorizing many modern American Catholics.

10. In "Walking on Eggs: Mastering the Dreaded Diversity Discussion," *College Teaching* 43, 3 (1995): 84–85, Peter Frederick writes, "Without minimizing the realities of oppression, privilege, and power, as teachers, we must affirm both the particularities of distinctive cultural and human differences and the universalities of the human person and condition . . . we need to help students appreciate cultural issues at three levels: individual uniqueness; complex group identity, including ultra-group differences, and those common human characteristics and behaviors we share across cultural and individual differences."

11. Ninian Smart, *Worldviews: Crosscultural Explorations of Human Beliefs* (New York: Scribner's, 1983). These dimensions include the experiential, the mythic, the doctrinal, the ritual, the ethical, and the social.

12. Cyprian Davis, *The History of Black Catholics in the United States* (New York: Crossroad, 1988), 1.

13. See Maria Caravaglios, *The American Catholic Church and the Negro Problem in the Eighteenth to Nineteenth Centuries* (Charleston, SC: Caravaglios, 1974) and Joseph Anciaux, *De Miserabili Conditione Catholicorum Nigrum in America* (Namur, Belgium: Typis Jac. Godene, n.d.). A brief presentation of Anciaux's work is found in Davis, *History of Black Catholics in the United States,* 196–198.

14. Thomas Stritch, *The Catholic Church in Tennessee* (Nashville: Catholic Center, 1987), 99.

15. Barbara Gross Davis, *Tools for Teaching* (San Francisco: Jossey-Bass, 1993), 44. I would suggest that such multitextuality can also contribute to what Jonathan Collett calls an "awareness of our own culturebound learning style." See "Reaching African-American Students in the Classroom," *To Improve the Academy* 9 (1990): 182.

16. On the learning cycle, see D. A. Kolb, *Experiential Learning: Experience as the Source of Learning and Development* (Englewood Cliffs, NJ: Prentice-Hall, 1984). On practices pertaining to each phase of the learning cycle, see M. D. Svinicki and N. M. Dixon, "The Kolb Model Modified for Classroom Activities," *College Teaching* 35 (1997): 141–146.

17. Svinicki and Dixon, "The Kolb Model," 146.

REFERENCES

Adams, Maurianne, ed. *Promoting Diversity in College Classrooms: Innovative Responses for the Curriculum, Faculty, and Institutions.* San Francisco: Jossey-Bass, 1992.
Altman, Howard B., and William E. Cashin, "Writing a Syllabus," Center for Faculty Evaluation and Development, Kansas State University, IDEA Paper no. 27 (1992).

Boyd, Dwight. "Dominance Concealed through Diversity: Implications of Inadequate Perspectives on Cultural Pluralism." *Harvard Educational Review* 66, 3 (1996): 609–630.

Buxton, Thomas H., and Keith W. Pritchard, eds. *Excellence in University Teaching*. Columbia: University of South Carolina Press, 1975.

Cannon, Lynn Weber. "Fostering Positive Race, Class, and Gender Dynamics in the Classroom." *Women's Studies Quarterly* 1 and 2 (1990): 126–134.

Carr, Edward Hazlett. *What Is History?* London: Macmillian, 1961.

Collett, Jonathan. "Reaching African-American Students in the Classroom." *To Improve the Academy* 9 (1990): 177–188.

Davis, Barbara Gross. *Tools for Teaching*. San Francisco: Jossey-Bass, 1993.

Davis, Cyprian. *The History of Black Catholics in the United States*. New York: Crossroad, 1988.

Dolan, Jay P. *The American Catholic Experience: A History from the Colonial Times to the Present*. Garden City, NY: Doubleday, 1984.

Frederick, Peter. "Walking on Eggs: Mastering the Dreaded Diversity Discussion." *College Teaching* 43, 3 (1995): 83–92.

Jenkins, Carol A., and Deborah L. Bainer. "Common Instructional Problems in the Multicultural Classroom." *Journal on Excellence in College Teaching* 2 (1991): 77–88.

Kolb, D. A. *Experiential Learning: Experience as the Source of Learning and Development*. Englewood Cliffs, NJ: Prentice-Hall, 1984.

Lowther, Malcolm A., Joan S. Stark, and Gretchen G. Martens. *Preparing Course Syllabi for Improved Communication*. Ann Arbor: University of Michigan, National Center for Research to Improve Post-Secondary Teaching and Learning, 1988.

Smart, Ninian. *Worldviews: Crosscultural Explorations of Human Beliefs*. New York: Scribner, 1983.

Stritch, Thomas. *The Catholic Church in Tennessee*. Nashville: Catholic Center, 1987.

Svinicki, M. D., and N. M. Dixon. "The Kolb Model Modified for Classroom Activities." *College Teaching* 35 (1997): 141–146.

Wright, E. Alan, ed. *Teaching Improvement Practices: Successful Strategies for Higher Education*, Bolton, MA: Anker, 1999.

9

"Making a Way Out of No Way": Interpreting the Praxis of the Black Church for Theological Education

Daphne C. Wiggins

One of the challenges of theological education in the twenty-first century is preparing a generation of ministerial leaders who are spiritually formed and anchored in the Christian faith and who are equipped with theological and practical resources to lead the people of God into faithful service. This is a unique contemporary challenge at a time when trust in churches and their leaders has eroded and new church models and organizational structures are emerging. Denominations do not have the hold upon the clergy in their ranks they once had. Frustrated clergy move among denominations looking for a context in which to minister effectively. Members shop for a congregation where they can encounter the spirit, be a part of a meaningful fellowship, give support without giving up all their discretionary time, and experience a minimum of conflict.

In the Black Church these changes and more are taking place. By "Black Church" I mean that cluster of denominations that have shared the commitments to a socially relevant gospel that meets the material and spiritual needs of its members. The majority of these congregations stem from the seminal movement of the Free African Society of 1787. Thus, the seven major denominations that comprise the Black Church are the African Methodist Episcopal Church, African Methodist Episcopal Zion Church, Christian Methodist Episcopal Church, National Baptist Convention, USA, Inc., National Baptist Convention of American Unincorporated, Progressive National Baptist Convention and the Church of God in Christ. No definition, whether coined by a historian, sociologist, or theologian, is going to be inclusive of all black congregations. For instance, my usage excludes the smaller Pentecostal and Holiness sects, as well as black congregations in predominantly white denominations. Yet, to describe the church sociologically, we must have some parameters. This definition suggests a common heritage, culture, and ongoing commitments. The Black Church defined as such, encompasses over 30,000 congregations and claims an estimated 80 percent of African American Christians.[1] It has been the cornerstone of African American communities for nearly 150 years. It has counted among its ranks persons officially on the rolls and the infrequent visitors. Its mission has encompassed the well-being of African Americans in particular and others in general. Situated as the cultural womb and spiritual progenitor of so many other organizations and entrepreneurial efforts, African American religion via the Black Church is a rich repository for preparing theological students for ministry in the church and the academy.

African American Christianity is a distinctive context to engage the questions of social practice and theology. From a variety of sources, the Black Church has constructed practices that counter and subdue oppressive forces felt by African Americans while simultaneously establishing a context for a more abundant life. This chapter presents a model for teaching that examines those contexts. I present the rationale and several of the strategies I used in my course "The Social Contexts of the Black Church." The model requires students to ground their ministerial vision in a dialectical understanding of the Black Church. Moving between the contemporary interdisciplinary interpretation of the sociocultural contexts of African Americans and the history and established theological teachings of the Black Church, I present an approach that equips theological students to construct a ministerial direction and praxis.

Black Church As "Text"

In the fall 2000 semester, I taught a class entitled "African American Women in Christianity." On the first day I went around the room and asked persons to tell us a little about themselves and why they signed up for the class. I knew my class fulfilled a prerequisite and expected some of the students to be forthright about this. One student, a white male, told us a little about himself, and then said: "Well I had to take my Black Church course requirement; 'Black Preaching' was being offered, but since I'm not going to preach to black people, I decided to not take that course. Yours was the other option I could take." I recall being jarred by his words because they implied that black preaching is about how to preach to black people. Did that mean that my colleague who taught "Introduction to Preaching," a white male, was teaching content applicable to everyone, or was he teaching "white preaching"? This student implied there was nothing he could learn about African American homiletics that might hold him in good stead in his white congregation. If he really believed this, what was he going to do with a course about black women's religious journeys and contributions? Certainly, he did not expect many black women would be present in his congregations either.

I share this vignette not to embarrass the student—who has since graduated and who actually slowly let down some of his resistance to the content of that class—but because it highlights an often-unstated reality of the academy in general and theological education in particular. If the subject matter overtly concerns a racial, ethnic, or gender constituency—feminist theology or Black Church studies, for example—the course is marginalized not only in the minds of the students but often in the curriculum as well. This was not a new revelation to me, but it did take me aback. I might have expected such a comment from the undergraduates I had taught at a Christian college in the Southwest. Now these few words confronted me afresh with the challenges I was facing. How does one teach about the church from the particularity of the black experience in a predominantly white divinity school to students with limited exposure to the African American experience? It raised questions for me about the role of Black Church studies as a requirement in a theological school curriculum, the validation process of knowledge, and the legitimization given to some disciplines and not others. It reminded me of a theme I reflected upon during the year-long seminar "Mining the Motherlode": the authenticity of African American religious experience and its often pejorative interpretation by scholarly investigators. It reminded me again of the racial and intellectual superiority accrued to "whiteness" that makes "double consciousness" a necessary analytical stance for black students in the academy.[2] It fundamentally challenged me to consider the effectiveness of my teaching about the Christian church through investigation of the Black Church.

I did not shrink from teaching my course, nor did I embark on a personal crusade to convince that student (and perhaps others present who were not courageous enough to voice the same "convictions") he could indeed learn something from the contexts of African American religion. I did not want to freeze-frame that student in my mind or be tempted to grade him differently. I did not want to engage him any differently from others in the class. I decided that the best method for countering such perceptions was to present the history and work of the Black Church with skill so that it would be persuasive and produce transformative learning. Thus, I began the course with several of my foundational remarks about the Black Church as a viable context for understanding ministry and for the students' theological formation.

The Black Church is a vital context for ministerial education for several reasons. One, it is a religious institution with its own raison d'être. The Black Church exists because African Americans desire it to. Its genesis was an act of self-determination, influenced by the negative forces of racism and the positive force of a theological mandate to respond holistically to the needs of the community. The Black Church is the manifestation of a quest for a viable faith community by Africans and African Americans. C. Eric Lincoln described the quest in this manner:

> First, a viable religion will be one that has a working reciprocity with the culture that produces it or with which it interacts. This is not to say that it needs to be a culture religion in the sense that the values of the society and those of the religion are indistinguishable. It is to suggest, however, that religion must be firmly rooted in the needs and the expectations of the society that it both molds and reflects. Further, if a religion is to flourish, the needs and conditions, the fears, the anxieties, the hopes and aspirations to which it is addressed must be real in the experience of the believers. If it is not, the faith will never be more than an aberration, unless by some miracle the culture itself modified to fit the faith.[3]

Born in the crucible of racism and national disenfranchisement, the Black Church sought to embody the ethical mandate of "the parenthood of God and the kinship of all peoples."[4] As a consequence of African Americans' search for a vehicle to hold together and transport their conceptions of God, the Black Church is more than just a cultural institution; it is a spiritual one that gives expression to the tensions of believing in the Eternal in the midst of a confining social world. The Black Church is not simply a clone of white religious institutions. Neither does one find replication of African rituals, sacred practices, or direct descendants of African sensibilities in the modern day Black Church. Wilmore argues the lack of such retentions can be explained by the hostility toward African traditions.

> It was from within an African religious framework that the slaves made adjustments to Christianity after hearing the gospel. The influences of the African religious past extended into their new life, first in the Caribbean and later in the United States. . . . But instead of decaying there [after exposure to Christianity], the African elements were enhanced and strengthened in the subterranean vaults of the unconscious from whence they arose—time and time again during moments of greatest adversity and repression—to subvert the attempt to make the slave an emasculated, depersonalized version of a white person.[5]

Wilmore reminds us that in the study of black religion we have to make sure to neither romanticize the past in order to validate its African heritage nor deny the impact of the processes of acculturation whereby one culture intentionally dominated another. Rather, we can accept that the Black Church is a "new," albeit reconstructed, and appropriate response of Black Americans to their new environment.

> The slaves had two choices: they could resign themselves to their fate without struggles, or they could make a conscious effort at the redetermination of their destiny and their identity within the context of their developing body of Western experience. They did both, and in the process they became a distinctive subculture, rooted in the African heritage, and developed in the black experience in America. They became Black Americans, and as the first expression of their new identity, they created a Black Church: spiritually, theologically, and idealistically independent of any previous cultural commitment, and transcending the circumstances which called it into existence.[6]

Second, the Black Church is a rich context for theological reflection because its history and ministry manifests the dialectical tensions between society and religion. The Black Church has taken prophetic stances, and it has been silent at times it should not have been. Sometimes it has acquiesced to the survivalist impulse. At other times it has been in the vanguard of declaring God's liberating work in the world. The church has been constituted by a membership that knows experientially the impact of multiple oppressive forces: sex, class, and race oppression. Yet, it has sometimes marginalized its own members because of one or more of these classifications. The church has had to interact with alternative religious traditions within the bounds of African American communities and to communicate a realistic view of God and the world in the context of the increasing individualistic spirituality gaining sway in America.

One thing that pertains to all peoples regardless of their race or ethnicity is that their religious beliefs and rituals are intertwined with the material and psychological realities of their daily lives. That is to say, what people believe about God, how they worship God, and what they desire their religious communities to be are informed by their position, privilege, resources, and sense of security in the world. For example, questions that middle-class persons ask about God are going to be somewhat different from the queries or needs a homeless person brings to God. A person who is tenth-generation native born has a different concept of God from the recent immigrant coming from a country where Christianity is not the dominant faith or where religious persecution prevails.

People whose religious lives have been shaped decisively by their common history of oppression and experience in America populate the Black Church. I am not suggesting that white Americans have never had to ask where their next meal was coming from, or how to raise their children safe from the assaults of bigotry. The black religious experience, however, has been fraught with these questions and many others. How do you make sense out of life when you know the larger society devalues your very being? How do you attempt to be economically successful when there are institutionalized practices to keep you from getting ahead? What kind of God would allow your racial community to be the underdog? Is it possible for Black Christians to relate to white Christians on a group level without paternalism being present? All these queries have been part of the theological and ideological contemplation of Black Americans. The social, cultural, and economic practices of this nation (legal and de facto) have made these questions pertinent to what it means to be an African American person of faith.

Third, African American lives and the Black Church are invaluable for theological preparation because they have always been engaged in a practical theology. Olin Moyd describes the work of the Black Church as grounded in the intersection of reflection and praxis. Practical theology is interpreting the Christian faith established in the past for the contemporary human condition in the present. It is the movement between the poles of eternal truth and temporary situations. Molin sums up the Black Church's work in these words:

> Practical theology reflects upon the divine mandate for ministries through the church. It examines both the biblical mandate and the present human condition and attempts to correlate the two, giving divine sanction to the mission and ministries of the church in every current world situation. . . . Practical theology in the African American perspective does not study the history of the meaning of God as understood by the church down through the years. . . . [It] affirms the God of history. Practical theology also affirms the attributes of God. In history, God is the One who, according to his own plan of redemption, redeemed the Israelites from Egyptian bondage. God is the One who redeemed the Hebrew children from the fiery furnace. Thus, God is the One who has ordained a plan of redemption and is in the process of redeeming the dispossessed from human-caused suffering now.[7]

In *The Sacred Art*, Moyd asserts that we can uncover the tenets of an African American practical theology through the lens of printed sermons and the preached word. In other words, if you want to know what the Black Church stands for, you have to know what has been preached in the church. Although I concur with his identification of practical theology as a basic quality of the Black Church, his approach for articulating that theology raises some concerns. When one equates the preached word with the theological worldview of the Black Church, it seems that one inherently is suggesting that the theology is articulated exclusively by the clergy. Focus on the preached word also serves to minimize the way that black women have done theology and shaped a praxis-based theology, since women have not had responsibility for articulating the theology from the pulpit. Furthermore, it assumes that thought circumscribes action, rather than action and theological thought maintaining more of a dialectical relationship. I believe students serving the Christian church today have to be anchored in practical theology. However, I don't think this is found only in the documented preaching of the church or its sermons. Such a focus confines theology to a body of verbal pronouncements rather than an embodied praxis. There is sufficient evidence available to challenge this common equation. Thus when we look at the practical theology of the Black Church we must point students to what is being done, not solely what is being said.

The Instructor in Course Preparation

I initially started to develop this course because I was changing the context of my teaching. I moved from teaching in an undergraduate religion department to a divinity school faculty. I entered the "Mining the Motherlode" workshop knowing this change was on the horizon. My project for the workshop was to transform what was primarily a historical course called "The Black Church in America" into a learning experience for ministers in training. In the process of the Lilly workshop, two core insights kept resurfacing for me.

The first pertained to how one teaches African American religions as authentic and legitimate in their own right. My own training has been in predominantly white institutions, and my religious upbringing had instilled in me values of integration and Christian racial reconciliation. In the course of the workshop, I had to confront my own realization that I considered the Black Church a hybrid of sorts, an institution that I was obscuring by my constant evaluation of it in light of theoretical frames largely developed from mainline religious congregations. The absolute day and lecture in which this learning took place escapes me. It was a synthetic and cumulative realization rather than immediate insight. I recall sitting around that large table in the conference room on the third floor of Union Theological Seminary and realizing many of my colleagues were starting from a different place from mine as we talked about African American religions, Christianity, and related topics. I realized that reconstructing this course was difficult for these reasons. In addition, my training in an interdisciplinary liberal arts program did not seem to neatly conform to the disciplinary divisions of the divinity school. Moreover, I realized I was intellectually and personally a Christian triumphalist. Our sessions on African traditional religions in the Diaspora were challenging these loyalties.

The workshop also assisted me in clarifying my role as professor. My commitment became to form students, not merely disseminate information. This seems obvious to me now (and perhaps to persons reading this), but at the time it felt like a weight being lifted. My self-understanding as a teacher was tainted by my reservations and internalized anxiety about being the only African American female on the faculty, proving myself as a junior faculty member, and being an interdisciplinarian with a bent toward the sociology of religion (not an area wholeheartedly embraced in theological education). As I interrogated my overprescribed notions of objectivity and neutrality and my feelings of marginality, and as I took seriously bell hooks's concept of *teaching to transgress*, I embraced the teaching task with renewed vigor. I was able to develop my own *voice* and professional posture. I felt better prepared for male students, like the one mentioned earlier, because I believed his education—as well as the education of African American students—could be refracted through the Black experience.

As a teacher, I no longer regard myself as a funnel for a measured amount of knowledge or a barometer for truth claims. I am a presenter/investigator/facilitator of ideas, "facts," and paradigms. I help students understand social and historical facts, relevant constructs and theories, theological frameworks—and their own experiences. I push them to interrogate this data rather than digest it whole. I do not presuppose there is one right way to do ministry, and I want my students to embrace that idea. I also want them to have an experience that does not require a dichotomy between secular and sacred, or faith and reason.

Teaching the Black Church

The new version of that earlier course became "The Social Contexts of the Black Church." This course combines scholarship on African American Protestant religious experience with the contemporary contexts of the lives of African Americans. This course was developed in several stages and with consultation from others. One context I've already mentioned was the "Mining the Motherlode" workshop. The other was the Duke University Divinity School, in Durham, North Carolina, where I taught for four years.

This course has been offered three times; it continues to undergo refinement. I will focus primarily upon the second version since I decided this was the more nuanced adaptation of the course and it met my teaching goals. The constituencies for each class were different. It was offered as an intermediate-level course in my second semester at the school. Our school requires all master of divinity students to take an elective in the area of Black Church studies. This course was one of the options they had in the spring of 2000, fall of 2001, and fall of 2002.

The enrollment of the course was a workable-size seminar. In spring 2000, I had sixteen students, eight white, seven black, and one Native American. The next term I had twelve students, ten white, and two black. The third time I had nine students, four black and five white. The dynamics were different in each course. The first time the students had a greater exposure to African American churches or communities than in the subsequent sections. The African American members of the class also were more evenly engaged in the class discussion and contributed insights about the dynamics of Black Church life. This minimized the occurrence of a particular student assuming the burden of having to speak for the black community or to defend the Black Church's posture on some issue. Through these students, the class reaped the benefits of the diversity of insights, analysis, and perspectives among black students. This diversity was also evident among the white students, but since white students are the majority of the student body, it is not often regarded as distinctive for this difference to be present.

In my teaching I start with the presupposition that students do not just want to be told what to remember or do. They are more apt to retain new learning if they exercise some control over the content and where to continue searching in the days to come. I also begin from the premise that faith does not have to impede analytical inquiry. To help them master this, I intentionally disagreed with authoritative positions or a student's presentation at times. My goal was to encourage the students to more adequately defend positions they held or identify their inherent presuppositions, that is, foster a healthy suspicion of their authoritative claims or sources. On the other hand, I believe that knowledge has to be "tested" not only by other reasoned arguments but also by experiential knowledge and insights. To that end, I have always included some aspect of this course called "field research" and invited student input rooted in students' own religious experiences (or lack thereof).

This course has always had a mixed enrollment of black and white students. I inform students that intricate knowledge of African Americans or experience in the Black Church is not a prerequisite for engaging its heritage and completing the course work. I have said in class: "Many of us have had to enter into the world of seventeenth-century England to appreciate the lines of Shakespeare's *Macbeth* or *Hamlet*. Thus I assume we can build a sufficient bridge for you to enter the more contemporary world of black America and the Black Church; after all, it is not so distant as the world of Shakespeare." These words are not meant to be snide or rude. They are meant to help us unmask the role we give to experience as a prerequisite for learning. Often when subject matter pertains to marginalized groups, dominant-group students (and professors) want to utilize the category of experience as the reason why some information cannot be engaged. I recognize that feminists and some people of color have exploited this premise to their advantage. As a black female professor, I could have done so as well. I choose rather to lift up that "whiteness" is no better a marker for what is universal than "blackness" is. The Christian church is currently experiencing challenges to its modernist assumptions about universal principles and truth claims. Some bemoan this challenge. I embrace it in the expectation that the generations of parishioners my students will engage well into the twenty-first century will be shaped by postmodern assumptions.

Creating the Syllabus

When I created the syllabus, I was guided by several questions. How can I expose students to the scholarship on African American churches? How do I structure this class so that each student experiences some dimension of African American community and church? What skills can I provide students with for social analysis and theological reflection? How do I encourage students to engage in theological reflection when they are part of the group identified as "the other"? I also considered which students might best take advantage of this type of learning experience. Three factors informed my design: their academic preparation, their time flexibility, and their inclinations toward social justice ministry. Let me offer a word about each.

I made our introductory course on American religious history a prerequisite for this course. In lieu of that course, a competency (interpreted loosely) in American or Black Church history substituted. This prerequisite is desirable because of the necessary understanding of cultural dynamics, the history of racism and its legacy for African Americans and the church. A student needs to be somewhat fluent in twentieth-century sociocultural history. If a student is limited in her or his knowledge or needs a refresher, I suggest several key texts to enhance the student's competency: John Hope Franklin, *From Slavery to Freedom,* and C. Eric Lincoln, *Race, Religion and the Continuing American Dilemma,* are two of them. In addition, Anthony Pinn, *Fortress Introduction to Black Church History,* is a good starter text on the Black Church.[8]

Time flexibility was another consideration in developing this course. In our school culture, what is considered out-of-the-classroom work usually means reading a text or doing library research. I was asking students to do more than that. They had to look up very specific data on a geographic community, or identify and meet with community resource persons, and possibly visit churches or events held in the community—all this in addition to the typical research one can access through databases. Thus I tried to present parameters for the course without boxing students in. To make it accessible to them, I allowed them to pick a topic in a specific area of North Carolina (one student did his in Virginia). They were researching social issues the Black Church presumably would have an interest in responding to within a particular county or smaller area. I guided them through a process of contacting local agencies, pastors, and community resources. They also used African American periodicals and internet sources to ascertain how the black community (religious and otherwise) regarded this issue. I provided a list of possible topics, including feminization of poverty, environmental racism, incarceration, homelessness, AIDS, secularization and the Black Church, violent crime, domestic violence, educational inequities, political apathy, medical access, racial profiling, hiphop culture, and homosexuality. To encourage peer learning and the art of theological reflection, I required students to make class presentations on their topics. I introduced the project this way in the syllabus:

> This project is entitled "Ministry in Contemporary Times." The first step is to choose a current issue or social phenomenon that is presently impacting African Americans lives and the Black Church. Select an issue specific enough that you can complete significant research on it. This issue should also be local to an area you can get to geographically. Some possibilities are listed below but you may choose another one. This is your opportunity to do some field work and independent research. You will write this paper in 5 stages and turn it in incrementally. The sections are outlined further on the additional handout. A grade will be assigned to the final paper. I will give you feedback on your assignments along the way. All of the stages must be turned in to be eligible for full credit. After completing the incremental phases, you will write a comprehensive paper of 20–25 pages with a bibliography to turn in at the end of the term.

The third variable—their orientation toward social justice ministry—I could neither plan around nor predict. I never knew until I got the class roster and met the students whether they had any inclination toward socially engaged ministry. As it turns out there has been a variety of personal convictions. Some students were clearly headed toward the pastorate; others were contemplating doctoral work. Another segment planned on working in social service agencies or for their denominations.

There is nothing particularly novel about the teaching strategies I used in this course. They included critical reflection papers, class discussion, and a research project with in-class presentation. I have used critical reflection papers in two different ways. One semester the papers were assignments to help students reflect on the readings and integrate their own experiences in the Christian faith. I gave them questions each week to write on. Another semester I used critical reflection papers to have students engage the weekly readings. They had to write an essay that pursued a substantial theme in one or more of the readings for the week. In both instances, the students had to do several papers, and they were able to decide when they turned them in.

Students had assigned readings that introduce them to the origins of the Black Church and its historic commitments. All have *required* readings, and there are additional *recommended* readings for the more intellectually aggressive students. The course readings are from historical, theological, and sociological sources. I intentionally do not give them too much in the way of "how to fix things." I have looked for articles and texts that promote critical examination of the African American community/church. Some of the readings have been case studies of black churches.

Central to this course are the class lectures and discussions. Each week I introduce the topic for the week. I have found myself lecturing more in the beginning third of the semester and less often as the term progressed. The course starts with a brief introduction to the historical origins of the Black Church, followed by sociological frameworks for interpreting the church. I structure the rest of the class after the dialectical framework developed by C. Eric Lincoln and Lawrence Mamiya in *The Black Church in the African American Experience*. I present the contours of a social concern relative to the black community one week and the church's response to that concern the following week.

There is no assumption on my part that students will develop a better response, or a "solution." My goal is that they take seriously the complexity of developing an appropriate Christian ministerial response. This approach often elicits lively discussion. Here is where the professor can decide how best to address the topic or which topics to include. The goal is to open the issue, engage students about what has been done, and what theological concepts have directed this response, or would inform what they would posit as an appropriate response. I also try to help them expand their ideas concerning the spiritual, social, and material resources the Black Church has used (and other Christian churches have used).

I initiated discussion with different formats. I may lead off with a question that they answer, filling the blackboard with their answers. I may use the question a student raised in a critical reflection paper. I may draw their attention to a close reading of a specific passage, or invite a student to identify a point of information that was helpful in understanding ministry in the Black church. I admit this is not always done evenhandedly. There are questions that continually get recycled. What have we learned about the contexts of African Americans lives? What has been the historic response to these realities of African Americans lives by the Black Church? How does this analysis of the Black Church inform your own understanding of ministry?

Evaluation

Having taught this course several times now, I offer the following words of assessment. As you may have already encountered in your own teaching, students vary in their level of self-motivation and organizational abilities. Thus, I encountered a mixture of students who had enthusiasm but who had a deficit in skills necessary for field research. Some students will give themselves to the project with vigor and put less energy into their critical reflection papers. I have read some engaging papers about the Black Church's response (including none) to AIDS, the achievement gap, hiphop culture, political apathy, homelessness, and so on. Students seem to like this aspect of the course best. I believe this is due in part to several factors: (1) their selection of the topic; (2) clear requirements for each section of the paper; (3) that they get to work in a geographic location close to where they live or are engaged in field education; and (4) that it helps them integrate their more abstract theological musings with the concrete societal realities.

On the other hand, this part of the course can be the most frightening. Most students are more comfortable with the norms of academe, which require them to read and regurgitate. Many have not done a long research paper in which they have to interpret data they have collected. This work is also a particular challenge for students unfamiliar with the surrounding community. I realize I cannot quell their fears that persons in the African American community will not be open with them. Their reservations, however, are generally less strong than when I require students to focus on just one local congregation and visit it three to five times. For some students this "close up" look at the African American community and engagement with Black Church leaders creates apprehension. I try to mitigate this by pointing them to certain resources I am acquainted with or churches that I know have addressed the concern they are focusing on.

The Black Church comes alive to them. Some gain an appreciation of how much the Black Church does and the ways it has been a compensatory and liberative institution. Black and white students also learn some distinct things. Black students develop their own ways to appreciate and yet critically assess the limited response of the Black Church. They become aware that there is resistance to examining the work of the Black Church with a critical eye. Some learn how the church tries to maintain a balance of responsibility among individuals, church, and society. White students are able to move beyond their views of the Black Church as an emotionally charged preaching venue to a greater understanding of the ministry and community that is sustained by the church. It becomes a real place where lives are reclaimed and anchored by the worship ethos. Both segments of the class have a safer context to talk about the realities of racism and its newest manifestations in the church and the world.

It would be misleading to claim that this course is easy to teach. There have been moments when, against my attempts to do otherwise, I found the black students dominated the discussion section, or I could not seem to frame the appropriate question that would help white students value and contribute their assessment of the readings. This is an important dimension of the class, because I did not merely lecture the texts but expected the students to "think on their feet" about what they read. The age, work, and church and life experiences of the class participants affected this class dynamic. Students who were second-career persons, over forty years old, and active among the laity tended to be less threatened by the class discussions. With our median matriculation age decreasing at the Divinity School, the students had fewer years of experience in church work to inform our class discussions.

I love teaching this class. It developed out of my desire to use African American religion as a point of departure for doing theology and understanding ministry. The course is malleable because the social issues pertinent to the life of a viable church ministry are always in flux. This is not to suggest that the church should respond to every cultural phenomenon or social malaise. It is to suggest that the Black Church has been constituted amid the realities of pernicious social evils and has nevertheless thrived. It has had to interpret Christianity and salvation as a holistic concept and reject those ideas that denied the humanity of Africans and African Americans. The Black Church has exemplified for its constituency how collective faith and action can "make a way out of no way." If I can help my students comprehend this mandate and accrue some of the resources to carve new paths for the church through study of the Black Church, then I will be content with my contribution to forming the next generation of clerical and theological educators.

NOTES

1. My definition of this term relies upon C. Eric Lincoln and Lawrence Mamiya, *The Black Church in the African American Experience* (Durham, N.C.: Duke University Press, 1990), 1. I realize this eclipses the work of black nondenominational churches, as well as churches such as Trinity United Church of Christ in Chicago, Illinois, pastored by Dr. Jeremiah Wright. Wright's congregation would fall under Lincoln and Mamiya's term "greater black church." This term applies to all black congregations that share the cultural heritage and sense of mission of the historically black churches. The implication is that such congregations have more in common with other black congregations than with the white denominations they are part of. The theologian Delores Williams makes a distinction between the sociological manifestation of the church, that is, African American denominational churches, and the "Invisible" Black Church. The latter is the real God force that has sustained African Americans. It cannot be codified or contained by a building or liturgy. It lives within African Americans and their communities. See Delores S. Williams, *Sisters in the Wilderness* (Maryknoll, NY: Orbis Books, 1993), 204–207.

2. The concept of double consciousness was coined by the sociologist W. E. B. Du Bois to describe the struggle for identity and ethnic integrity experienced by African Americans at the beginning of the twentieth century. See W. E. B. Du Bois, *The Souls of Black Folk* (New York: Signet Books, 1982; originally published 1903).

3. C. Eric Lincoln, *Race and the Continuing American Dilemma* (New York: Hill and Wang, 1984), 60.

4. Peter J. Paris, *The Social Teaching of the Black Churches* (Philadelphia: Fortress Press, 1985), 10.

5. Gayraud S. Wilmore, *Black Religion and Black Radicalism*, 3rd ed. (Maryknoll, NY: Orbis Books, 1998), 50.

6. Lincoln, *Race and the Continuing American Dilemma*, 62–63.

7. Olin P. Moyd, *The Sacred Art: Preaching and Theology in the African American Tradition* (Valley Forge, PA: Judson Press, 1995), 34.

8. John Hope Franklin, *From Slavery to Freedom* (New York: Knopf, 1994); Anne H. Pinn and Anthony B. Pinn, *Fortress Introduction to Black Church History* (Minneapolis: Augsburg Fortress Press, 2002).

REFERENCES

Ammerman, Nancy T., Carl S. Dudley, and Jackson W. Carroll, eds., *Studying Congregations: A New Handbook* (Nashville: Abingdon Press, 1998).

Baer, Hans A. "Black Mainstream Churches: Emancipatory or Accommodative Responses to Racism and Social Stratification in American Society?" *Review of Religious Research* 30, 2 (December 1998): 162–176.

Billingsley, Andrew. *Climbing Jacob's Ladder*. New York: Simon and Schuster, 1992.

Carle, Robert D., and Louis A. Decaro, Jr. *Signs of Hope in the City: Ministries of Community Renewal*. Valley Forge, PA: Judson Press, 1990.

Franklin, John Hope. *From Slavery to Freedom*. New York: Knopf, 1994.

Franklin, Robert M. "The Safest Place on Earth: The Culture of Black Congregations." In *American Congregations*, vol. 2, James P. Wind and James W. Lewis, eds., 257–280. Chicago: University of Chicago Press, 1994.

Gilkes, Cheryl Townsend. *If It Wasn't For the Women*. Maryknoll, NY: Orbis Books, 2001.

Hacker, Andrew. *Two Nations*. New York: Scribner's, 1992.

Joyner, Charles. "Believer I Know: The Emergence of African-American Christianity." In *Religion and American Culture: A Reader*, David G. Hackett, ed., 185–228. New York: Routledge, 1995.

Lincoln, C. Eric, *Race and the Continuing American Dilemma*. New York: Hill and Wang, 1984.

Lincoln, C. Eric, and Lawrence H. Mamiya. *The Black Church in the African American Experience*. Durham, NC: Duke University Press, 1990.

McClain, Paula D., and Joseph Stewart, Jr. *Can We All Get Along? Racial and Ethnic Minorities in American Politics*. Denver, CO: Westview Press, 1998.

Milton Sernett, ed. *Afro-American Religious History: A Documentary Witness*. Durham, NC: Duke University Press, 1985.

Moyd, Olin P. *The Sacred Art: Preaching and Theology in the African American Traditions*. Valley Forge, PA: Judson Press, 1995.

Nelson, Timothy J. "The Church and the Street: Race, Class, and Congregation." In *Contemporary American Religion*, Penny E. Becker and Nancy L. Eisland, eds., 169–190. Walnut Creek, CA: Alta Mira Press, 1997.

Odum, John Yancy. *Saving Black America: An Economic Plan for Civil Rights*. Chicago: African American Images, 2001.

Paris, Peter J. *The Social Teachings of the Black Churches*. Philadelphia: Fortress Press, 1985.

Pinn, Anne H., and Anthony B. Pinn. *Fortress Introduction to Black Church History*. Minneapolis: Augsburg Fortress Press, 2002.

Smith, Wallace Charles. *The Church in the Life of the Black Family*. Valley Forge, PA: Judson Press, 1985.

Townes, Emilie. *Breaking the Fine Rain of Death*. New York: Continuum, 1998.

Trulear, Dean Howard. "Black Churches, the Urban Youth Crisis and Youth Socialization." Available online at: www.mountpleasantbaptistchurch.com/morehsldrshp .htm.

West, Cornel. *Race Matters*. Boston: Beacon Press, 1993.

Williams, Delores. *Sisters in the Wilderness*. Maryknoll, NY: Orbis Books, 1993.

Wilmore, Gayraud S. ed. *Black Men in Prison*. Atlanta: ITC Press, 1990.

10

Tribal Talk: African Ancestral Spirituality as a Resource for Wholeness

Will "Esuyemi" Coleman
Transcribed by Elizabeth Tanner

> The following lecture and discussion took place at Augusta State College, Georgia, during the summer semester of 2002. In the context of Dr. Ralph Watkins's sociology of religion class, Dr. Will Coleman offers his book *Tribal Talk: Black Theology, Hermeneutics, and African/American Ways of "Telling the Story"* (University Park: Pennsylvania State University Press, 1999) as an examination of African spirituality. This transcribed and edited text is presented here as an instance of pedagogical engagement in the "contact zone."

I want to thank you all for being here and thank you for inviting me to come and do this presentation on *Tribal Talk*. The commonality between what we've heard in this musical introduction by George Duke entitled "The Ancient Source" and what I am going to talk about is pretty amazing, if you think about it. What is it that is so present within African and African American ways of thinking, being, and knowing that even in what some may call secular—and others sacred—music, you have this, this kind of tempo and beat and rhythm that's not only consistent but also persistent?

"Ashe"

And when you think about the text, *Tribal Talk*, as you have now read, you could say that what I'm talking about is spirit also: the different manifestations of spirit or of, to use a Yoruba term, "ashe" [sounds like "a-shay"]. It's a Yoruba (Nigerian) term that is somewhat similar to "amen." Not exactly. But somewhat. This means kind of "So be it." When we say "ashe," in some ways it is stronger: "It *shall* be so." That's one definition for this word *ashe*. But it also is a term that is an attempt to identify the pervasiveness of the creative spirit in all of life, in every aspect of life, and all aspects of life whether they are considered sacred or secular. So when you hear Yoruba people when they do their libations or their prayers, they say "ashe"; they're also saying "It shall be so." There's a very strong relationship between ideas, the vocalization of those ideas, and the manifestation of those ideas. There's a oneness between thought, intention, vocalization, and manifestation. So, the correspondence with Genesis 1:1 or John 1:1 is what? "In the beginning was the word, the word was with god, the word was god" (John 1:1). That's African. Or, "In the beginning the *elohim* (that's the Hebrew term for the word "god" in Genesis 1:1) . . . "in the beginning the *elohim* created the heavens and the earth." And they did it how? Through the words they spoke. Of course, by the time we get to it in our English translations, it becomes a monotheistic idea: one god, G-O-D. Well, actually in the Hebrew, it is the creative forces, male and female, that bring into being all of creation. And it comes again that there is a relation between thinking, intending, focusing, concentrating energy, speaking, and then manifesting.

Interpretation of "Tribal Talk"

Think about that. When you look at the title of the book, you can begin to interpret what I'm up to just from what the title itself suggests. And in the first handout [appendix 1] I've given you an outline. "Tribal talk": that's exegesis, that's interpretive. *Tribal Talk: Black Theology, Hermeneutics, and African/American Ways of "Telling the Story."* If you read the preface, I've tried to expand upon this. But most specifically, *Tribal Talk* is a book about talking. And it's a book about the pluri-forms of language, the multiforms of speech: my voice as interpreter; the voice of African storytellers, or *griots* (chapter 1); the voices of the characters that they talk about such as Legba, one of my favorites, a *Vodun* or *orisha*, Legba the trickster, the lord of the tricksters, the way-maker, the one who stands at the crossroads between the transcendental and the horizontal. Or the stories about Dambala. Not the serpent in the Garden of Eden. A different mythic system. But here the serpent who represents all of the ancient ancestors that you can't name. But you remember them: from Africa, through the "Middle Passage," through slavery, through Jim Crow-ism. Ancestors who have become, for us, archetypes of different traits—of communication in the case of Legba, of cultivation in the case of someone like Ogun (the *orisha* or *Vodun* of iron)—that you come across in the first chapter. And, as I just gave the example, of Dambala, as representing that connection with eternity because time and space in the African worldview are contemporaneous. There's not past, present, and future as linear. But it's contemporaneous. The ancestors are those who have gone ahead of us. And they connect us with the so-called spirit world. But, so, too, young children and the unborn are a part of that spiritual reality, because they come from that place. And so we live in a densely populated universe that's contemporaneous: past, present, and future.

"Tribal talk." Back to the idea of talking. It has in it the voices of, as you know, former slaves who are telling their stories: their experiences of slavery; their religious experiences; their experiences with ghosts, hanks (I know you want to talk about that some, too), and spirits; their experiences with conjuring and conjurers, with root workers, dust doctors, whatever you want to call them, male and female; their experiences of conversion to Christianity and how they formed their first churches, how they went to church with their masters. But then, how they also create something that they call their own: the "invisible institution."

Then *Tribal Talk* is also about the voice of Will Coleman telling you how he interpreted the narratives and what techniques and strategies he used, what resources he drew from, and how he interpreted those narratives and then how he sees this all as part of the contemporary study of African Americans' religions. So if you look at this outline here [appendix 1], *Tribal Talk* is also a ritual. It is intended to be a process of initiation, so that you as a reader, when you come to the end of the book, have been initiated into a particular way of thinking about—a particular way of interpreting—African American religious genius. A particular way, my way, because I am putting forth this argument! But to make you also think about the density of African American religious genius, of how all ideas, as it were, are transmitted through primarily an oral tradition, one that we just experienced, and even more so how ritual and language and practices have been inscribed in the bodies of persons of African descent, so much so that they have a different epistemology, or a different way of knowing. Not that it's better or worse than "Western" ways of knowing and understanding, but it is as valid. So the oral tradition is also a form of literacy: inscribed, embodied literacy.

Black Theology

That's another subtext to the book, *Tribal Talk*. Black theology has a very specific way of talking about god and interpretations of god based on the experiences of persons of African descent. In the way in which I use the term *Black theology,* it involves both the Christian and non-Christian, because theology simply means "god-talk" or talk about god. As for the way in which I was trained, of course, theology meant talking in a systematic manner: you talk about god, you talk about creation, you talk about redemption, you talk about salvation, you talk about humanity. So these are systematic ways of using language to talk about god. So then you become authorized somehow. "Systematic theology" suggests the work of a theologian with a Ph.D. But the point of *Tribal Talk* is that common folk know how to talk about god. Common folk have a reason behind their talk about god. Common folk have a logic to their way of talking about god. Not necessarily a systematic system, as I was trained. But coherent. Because it creates a worldview. It speaks to the reality of their experiences with god.

"Broken English"

So *Tribal Talk* intentionally uses so-called broken English in the narrative, which some might call bad English. But it's not bad because, as a matter of fact, *Tribal Talk* was inspired by my grandmother, Alice Coleman. I just want to say a word about her. My grandmother, Alice Coleman, is ninety-three years old. We just had her eulogy this past Monday, at ninety-three years old. She is the person who probably inspired me more than anybody else—to listen to, hear, and transmit the stories—because at ninety-three, she still spoke with that bad, broken English. I remember on one occasion when I was interviewing her about family history and about family religion or who was the first person to become a Christian, et cetera, et cetera, I used the expression "Grandmomma, when were you converted to Christianity?" She said, "Conberted?!" She said, "You mean, 'When I come through?' " I said, "Yes ma'am, when did you come through religion?" Now what's going on here is that I, of course, have one semantic structure, "When were you converted to Christianity?" (I was getting my Ph.D. at that point, and I couldn't keep my syntax right. So I was taking copious notes.) And then she said, "through." Of course, she didn't recognize what I was saying my way. "You mean, 'when I come through?' " I said, "yeah." And what she was doing, she was being very precise with her use of language because her generation of African Americans, having been born in 1908—when they went to the "praying ground," when they went to the "mourners' bench"—there was a period or phase through which you underwent this transformation. And the code for that was to "come through 'ligion." And so when you read these narratives, you're reading some of what A. C. is getting at. Our challenge is not "How do we correct it?" but "How do we get initiated?" And, understand, this language system is intended to communicate something in a very precise way.

Hermeneutics

So, again, hermeneutics. That's the second part of the title, of the subtitle here [appendix 1]. Hermeneutics then, is about interpreting a text or something that functions like a text because activities can have a textual quality if they give us meaning. The word, "hermeneutics," as you may know, is derived from the Greek god, Hermes. Hermes is like Legba. You've read about Legba—the go-between. So too, in ancient Greece, Hermes was the one who communicated or symbolized communication between the gods and human beings and among human beings themselves. So it's all about language and communication and the interpretation of language. Hermeneutics. And then the next phrase here, "African [slash] Americas." By African [slash] Americas, what I'm saying is that something is identical. African narratives—chapter 1, "Dahomean West African Narratives"—despite the displacement between Africa and the Americas (U.S., Caribbean, South America), when it comes to preaching, teaching, or rapping, there is continuity. That's what I'm trying to suggest, when I put that slash [/], I'm trying to suggest that there is continuity. But also discontinuity, because there's been a "middle passage" between Africa and the Americas. So, it's about African and African/American, if you will, or African/Americas' ways of telling a story.

"Telling a Story"

And as many of you know, telling a story is what we want the preacher to do. The responsibility of the preacher is to tell the story, the story that we call "the gospel." And we don't believe that a preacher has told the story if he or she cannot "wax" a narrative and cannot move us in the spirit. Right? Exactly right. We say, "Well, it's a bit late today, but they really did tell the story." Or we can take it in another form, especially traditional Baptists and the Pentecostal churches like those I grew up in. We don't believe that the story has been told until you get to who? You get to . . . "Jesus . . . Mary's baby . . . the lily of the valley . . . the bright and morning star . . . the rose of Sharon . . . the hope for tomorrow." There's a certain way in which you recognize the cadence and the catechism, the catechism and the cadence. And what *Tribal Talk* is trying to do is to help us to understand that those categories are much broader than we've ever imagined. That it's all about telling a story.

Tribal Talk Is for Everybody

As you see in chapter 7, that's why I say, "I'm playing a dance here." I'm going back and forth between my voice, the reporter's voice, the narrative collector's voice, the slave's voice, and the ancient African's voice. Because it's all tribal. And there's one other thing I'm doing about *Tribal Talk* in the title. I'm trying to reevaluate and, what we call, transvalue the term "tribal" to say that "tribal" is not a bad thing. "Tribal" is a good thing. These so-called ancient and so-called primitive ways of engaging in language and in using language and in participating in ritual, in fact, give us expressions of the genius of African American survival through slavery to the present. One other note: *Tribal Talk* is also a book that's not just about African American religious history. But it rattles out all of American religious history because African American religious history is part of the fabric of all of American religious history, social history, political history, economic history. So even if you're not an African American, you do yourself a disservice not to know this history and not to become acquainted with it, because it is a part of the American history, the American experience. And it has made a vital and significant contribution to that. Okay?

Ritual of Reading

Let's see here. I've given you a few handouts. Now I want to kind of loosen up and relax even more. And I want to use these four pages [appendices 1, 2, 3 and 4] more for reference than to go through it point by point. So what I've done here is given you the whole view of the text to try to help you understand how this book works as a liturgy or ritual itself. One other comment is that if you look at part 1, what I'm doing primarily is reading the narrative from a variety of perspectives. So, that's the work of reading and telling the stories. Then when you get to part 2, I go into some of that deeper stuff about the sources I draw from, about the different types of theories that I make use of, and about how this contributes to contemporary Black theology. So you've got two parts, but they're interconnected. And yet, they can be read separately and understood, to some extent, separately. It's really through the reading of the whole text, all seven chapters, that you get the full sense of *Tribal Talk*: from pouring libations in chapter 1 to pouring more libations in chapter 7. When you complete that, then you go through the whole ritual.

Dr. Watkins said to me that some of you had questions about the way in which I have parenthesized some of these expressions. I want to respond to that if you have questions about that specifically. What am I up to? For example, in chapter 2, "Root Work," in quotation marks, or "(Re)Configuring the Transatlantic 'Middle Passage': West African Roots of Religious Life in the African Americas." Well, the term "root work" is a double entendre. You know somebody. They know how to work with their hands in the mojo (sympathetic magic). They know how to work with herbs. They've got these, what some people consider, secret techniques. You read about some of these in the book. They have these little secret techniques; manipulating the elements, as it were. That's root work.

But root work is also what I'm doing in the chapter. In other words, I'm digging up some of the commonalities between African ways of thinking and being and African American ways of being. Not only here in the States, but also in the Caribbean and in South America. That's root work: when I present these things that people call the "sacred cosmos" and I try to talk about the different forms of, or interpretations of, spiritual presence in Santeria, in Candomblé, in Vodun. You see how that's connected to root work? And then what I'm also doing with that is I am—and I'm just going to point out one in particular—I'm trying to imitate or represent a journey from a West African source to, in chapter 4, the reconstruction of an African American communal self-identity, a new sense of being as a people.

The other thing that happens throughout that section, chapters 1 through chapter 4, is talk about spirit. That's what the Vodun are, the spiritual presence in chapter 1. That's what the hanks and ghosts and spirits are. But that's also what the Holy Ghost is by the time you get to chapter 4. So what I'm saying in a way is: you can trace the essence. Or to use George Duke's term, "the ancient source" can be traced from West Africa to the church you went to on Sunday, if you know how to look and if you know what it is you are looking for. The clues are there, but how do you make the connection? That's another aspect of what I'm up to in this particular text. Any questions or comments thus far? Is everybody with me? I'm not leaving anybody? All right.

Sacred Cosmos

Let me highlight some points on the second page [appendix 2] about the "sacred cosmos." In most West African traditional religions, contrary to much popular belief, there is the idea that there is one supreme being. In chapter 1 of *Tribal Talk* the supreme being is called Nana Buluku. That's in the Dahomean Vodun tradition. And most of our people, African American people, came from either Dahomey, or what was called Yoruba, or what was called the Congo. There are three regions. The one that I chose to talk about as the supreme being here and all throughout chapter 1 is primarily from Dahomey—where we've got Nana Buluku. But in the Yoruba or modern Nigeria it is Olodumare, which means "owner of heaven." There is this idea that there is one, supreme being who creates or brings into manifestation the universe and then more or less withdraws himself or herself. That being is quite often depicted as androgynous, both male and female. Then there is this (I don't want to say secondary) other layer, if you will, of a being that interacts in a more constant way with human beings and with other spirits. In this case, in *Tribal Talk*, it's Mawu-Lisa. Again, an androgynous being: male/female. And Mawu-Lisa is at the top of the (I don't want to say pyramid) but the top of the list of spirits that include other superhuman beings and, as well as, those who have died long ago, the ancestors, and even spirits that may be present: present in those who are yet unborn! So the world of spirits pervades everything.

Human beings, in the sacred cosmos, include both those who are alive and dead. Not just those of us who are in this room physically, but those who are yet to be born as well as those, like A. C., my grandmother, who have left this particular form. So, all of this constitutes the community of human beings. The sacred cosmos recognizes that animals and plants also have *ashe*, or life force. Before we get to modern physics or microbiology—notions of how everything is contained with atoms—Africans understood this, too. Everything—wood, metal, anything that the human being produces—contains this life force, *ashe* or spirit or, as I was saying in chapter 1, Vodun. So animals and plants also contain life force. And then, finally, as I said, objects that are produced that don't have biological life also have *ashe*.

What does that really mean? In the West African worldview there is really no such thing as a division between sacred and secular. There's no such thing as animate and inanimate. There's no such thing as human life being better than any other form of life. There's no such thing as simply spiritual or physical; instead, all of life is part of a reality that's all-inclusive. Everything vibrates. Everything, in that sense, is alive because it contains this life force, this ancient source, as we've heard in the text. Everything has spirit, and therefore, everything is revered. So when you see an African pouring libations or talking to a tree, he or she is not worshiping that tree. That's not what he or she is up to. They are recognizing the continuity of life and honoring the life force that that tree is going to offer in order to build a hut. Or that that goat is going to offer in order to provide meat.

You hear the difference? It's not worship. It's veneration and respect. There's only one supreme being to worship. But that supreme being has given many different forms for the life force to be recognized in, to be appreciated, and to receive energy from. How many of you . . . when you go to Kentucky Fried Chicken . . . when you do go there, think about the life force that is being transferred from that chicken to you? Or if you're vegetarian, from that carrot to you? How often do we not think about that? "Gi' me a Big Mac . . . hold de onions . . . cheese . . . what you want, man? . . . okay . . . gi' me a Coca-Cola . . . hold up! . . . no . . . gi' me a Sprite." Then you drive on away. See: the irony is that in our modern technological society we so often have divorced ourselves from the recognition that for everything there's always an exchange of energy. But the so-called ancient African or the practitioner of traditional African religions recognize that this hen or that rooster is literally transferring energy from itself to you. And so the prayers of respect and the libation that is poured is an acknowledgement that in order for my *ashe* to be strengthened, it becomes necessary to transfer the *ashe* of this animal or plant from itself to myself. That's at the core of libations or what people call the veneration and respect in the ritual.

African-Derived Religions in the Americas

Now on the second handout [appendix 2] I present a variety of African American religions. And I do that because I want to emphasize, particularly for us in the United States, that African American religions have taken many different forms, whether it is called Voodoo or Hoodoo or Macumba or Candomblé or Lecumi or Santeria or Myal or Obeah—and I'm just going down a list—or Ifa or Islam. Protestant African American Christianity is only one expression, only one expression, of African American spirituality. And we all need to become more familiar with the ways in which Africans or persons of African descent have transmuted and transformed and combined traditional African beliefs with Christianity or with Western religion. Do you hear what I'm saying? The way in which, during slavery, they were able to engage in both the master's religion and create their own. There's a strong similarity—once you stop looking at TV, once you stop that TV from telling you what to think and how to think—between a powerful Haitian Vodun ceremony and an African American Pentecostal one. Very strong. It's amazing. The singing, the invoking of the spirit, the spirit: the spirit possession. Even some of the colors. I mean, some of you go to church on Sunday, you might as well be a devotee of Legba if you're wearing red and black. Or yellow. All you sisters who wear yellow to church: that's Oshun (the *orisha* of sensuality) coming in on Sunday morning. All you brothers with green suits. That's Ogun (the *orisha* of metal) coming in. You don't even know this. It's subconscious [see appendix 4].

A STUDENT   What about the white, what's the white?

COLEMAN   The white is Obatala. White suits are Obatala, who, in a Yoruba tradition, is called "the owner of the white cloth." So if you're wearing all white, that's Obatala. Preachers—white shoes—white everything. That's Obatala standing up there on Sunday morning. The text and how it's described: certain colors for particular expressions of the *orishas*.

The point is that Protestant African American Christianity is just one expression of spirituality. We need to become familiar with the others. And I try to introduce some of the many forms in the book. Euro-American Christianity has also taken many different forms. Protestant denominations, in a certain sense, are different ethnic expressions of Christianity. Some people are Baptist, because in the old country their ancestors were what? Baptist. Presbyterian because at some point in the history of Geneva, Switzerland, a man named John Calvin began to interpret and understand scripture, liturgy, et cetera, and practice things differently. And therefore, the Reformed tradition was born. It's an ancestral tradition that goes from Geneva to Scotland to parts of the Americas. Some people are still Roman Catholic. Why? Their ancestors were Roman

Catholic. So we're talking about ancestral religions, and, in that respect, in the same sense that one speaks of denominations. Roman Catholic, Protestant, Eastern Orthodox: these are different ancestral traditions because they are different interpretations of religion that began in Africa or in what is now called the Middle East but really is Northeast Africa.

African America's Religious History

Now if you look at [appendix 3], you see listed in the first section, the different developments of African American religious history. You can see that I've given you four different periods. Now when we think about American religious history, we begin with the migration of peoples to the Americas. And of course the first people here were Native Americans, out of Asia who migrated here thousands, perhaps millions, of years prior to the Portuguese or the Spanish or the English or the French or the African. So the first thing is to realize that there was already here religious sensibilities, cultural ways of understanding the relation between the divine and the human, and that these indigenous Native American people were encountered by Europeans first. Those same ethnic groups I just told you about: Roman Catholic and Protestant, Baptist, Methodist, different Roman Catholic orders. And they brought with them their interpretations of Christianity. Interpretations, by the way, that had developed over thousands of years. Okay? From the first century, what we call the first century A.D., to 1492. They've had thousands of years to develop and make something their own, which initially had come out of the Mesopotamian basin through Judaism and then Christianity. So the Europeans bring their culture, their religion, their politics, their economics, along with them on the *Mayflower* or whatever other ships they came on. And then the third one. We have Africans who bring with them, as slaves, as indigenous servants—some of them initially free and then as slaves—their religion. And this, too, is pluri-form. It's not that they all came here with one particular belief. Some of them were already Muslim. Some of them were Yoruba. Some of them were Dahomean. Some of them were from the Congo. And they had different tribal expressions, cultural expressions. So you have this confluence between 1492 and about 1620 of Native American, European, and African religious cultures and sensibilities. And out of that comes conflict and assimilation.

Then, the second period is the Great Awakening, when Anglicans, Baptists, Methodists, Presbyterians, and Congregationalists have a revival up and down the eastern coast of the colonies. Very few either Native Americans or African Americans are converted to Christianity at that time. In fact, the debate is whether or not these people really have souls and can be converted to Christianity, because Christianity is understood to be a cultural religion of Europeans and for people who have been born as Christians. So the debate is whether or not they really can be converted. When they resolved that debate, the interesting thing that happened is, they said, "Well all right, Christianity is good for the souls of the slaves, but it doesn't change their economic or political status." So, if you're born a slave, you stay a slave. But you become a Christian. You hear the divide? This is why today, I argue, so much of Christianity is still understood as primarily the business of "saving *souls*," rather than the whole person. This is part of the legacy that we still continue to perpetuate: Christianity is not really for the whole person—political, social, economic being—but is primarily for "saving the soul." When they "save the soul," it doesn't matter so much what the rest of the status of that person is as long as they know the person is "born again" and headed for heaven. I'm doing this as somewhat of a caricature, but you can see the roots of it.

Then comes the Second Great Awakening from the 1800s to the 1830s. This is when most African Americans were converted to the Baptist, Presbyterian, or Methodist denominations. And part of the reason was because this was a revival: there were mass conversions to Christianity. You had a popular preaching style and you had ministers who didn't have to go up to Princeton to get their degrees in order to come back and preach (because some of the Presbyterians required that you be able to get your degree in theology before you become an ordained minister). The Baptists and Methodists, they were more lenient. But they had something else. Their style of preaching and talking and the way they did revivals resonated, at least in part, with the less formal African style—with immersion baptism, a freer style of speaking, and some opportunity to clap your hands, stomp your feet, sway your head, say "amen." Blacks and whites, of course, were doing this, but you began to see that that was a little bit more relaxed than the god's "frozen-chosen" in front of the church. So you could "kick around a little bit"—as I called it in *Tribal Talk.* So this freer style appealed to African Americans and resulted in significant conversions.

And then, finally, from 1865 to the present, you have the emergence of the emancipation or independent African American churches: Baptist, Methodist, and then later on, at the turn of the century, the Pentecostal. And it's really with Pentecostalism that the strong impulse of "African-ness" comes back out: with drums, with extemporaneous singing, with visions, with prayers, with healing. All of those are Africanisms. All of them. Speaking in tongues. All of them. "Falling out." Yes. I talked with a Haitian Mambo recently, and she said, "See, I don't understand why the Pentecostals are so hard on us." She said, "When I go to a Pentecostal church, and they get to shouting and they 'fall out' and somebody puts a white sheet on them, Dambala has arrived." She said, "I recognize that. That's Dambala." Or, she gave me another example. She went to a Pentecostal church and a person began speaking in tongues. And she began to interpret it, because she recognized that some of those were African Congo phrases coming from back here—the back of the head. So she came in and she started interpreting what the woman was saying. And she said, "Oh yeah, she's speaking Congo." Uh-huh. Remember? Ancestral memory.

So the problem is that (I'm saying this because I grew up in that church) so many Pentecostals have adopted a certain closed way of understanding doctrine. And they also reacted to what the dominant structure, at the time, called "foolishness." So in order not to be foolish, you've got to say, "Well this is Christian, and we're talking only about Jesus and The Bible" rather than: "Well, this is an expression of who we are." And so you'll find a kind of conflict, when on the one hand Pentecostalism is probably the most liberating expression of Africanisms but, at the same time, most entrenched in saying, "Well, what we're doing is of God, and what they're doing is of the devil." There's that kind of dualism where they can't, in my opinion, recognize that there's a strong continuity between how they have adopted ways of expressing the spirit: Protestant Pentecostalism, in one form, is a cousin to the ways of expressing Roman Catholic Vodun in another form. If you can open your mind, you begin to see more of what I'm trying to talk about.

There's one other piece here just on the historical development [appendix 3]. And you see I've got it in parentheses, in early 1700s to 1865, that there began to emerge something that was called the "invisible institution." And all that really is intended to suggest (and you read about it in chapter 4 of the book) that African Americans also discover a way to "steal away" and create their own institutions, to create or re-create the extended family, to worship god in their own way. So that alongside with going to church with their masters—in the morning at the same church, or in the afternoon at the same church but a different part of the church, or on the plantation with the overseer supervising the ceremony—they also took opportunities to steal away, steal away, and create the "invisible institution," which then gave birth to the independent Baptist, Methodist, and Pentecostal churches after the emancipation. So it came out of two forms: one, the "invisible institution," and the other form, the many African Americans who left the churches of their masters to form their own churches.

QUESTIONS, COMMENTS?

DR. WATKINS   Valencia has a question. Valencia, you have a question or comment.

VALENCIA   Um . . .

COLEMAN   Oh, put it on out here.

VALENCIA   You put me on the spot.

COLEMAN (LAUGHS)   I don't see you trying to hold back. Go ahead. I know you're workin' with it. Come on, come on. We support you.

VALENCIA   With the "invisible institution": Did they practice pure Christianity or something else?

No Pure Doctrine or Religion Anywhere

In the "invisible institution," we're talking about the Protestant South. Now, the form and the teachings were primarily Christian. But, again: as a reinterpreted Christianity. And what you need to bear in mind is that nobody, absolutely nobody, teaches or lives a pure religion. There is no pure religion. Once we get our hands on it we've got to find some way to make it our own. What the Europeans gave them was not pure Christianity. What the Europeans taught them was the European interpretation of Christianity. And it was a European interpretation of Christianity based on either Baptist doctrine or Methodist doctrine or Presbyterian, et cetera. When the slaves accepted or converted to Christianity they did the same thing any other people do. They already have content. They already have their ways of understanding. They take that information, and they, in one way or another, integrate it with this new information or this new interpretation. So the slaves, when they were converted, understood themselves to have been converted from the state of being a sinner, like their white counterparts would have said, to being now a Christian or a saint. The Africanisms come through though, in the way in which it's expressed. And the way in which it is expressed is through the "call and response" style, through the way in which they preach, through the way in which they use hand-clapping and foot-stomping to accompany or replace the drum, the way in which they talked about their visions.

Hermeneutics of Suspicion

Now remember now, they are not able to read the Bible. Why are they not able to read the Bible? They can't read, number one. And why couldn't they read? Because they were not allowed to read. So if you can't read because you are not allowed to read, what are you going to do? You're going to do a variety of things. You're going to take the catechisms and the sermons that you heard master preach, and you're gonna say, "Well, that don't apply to me because I sure don't believe him or her" or "I'm not gonna do it that way" or "don't tell me to be obedient." And you try to, you know, try to feel a certain kind of way: "Okay, so now I'm not going to listen to those stories about being obedient. Forget about those. I'm only going to listen to the one about Moses. Now I like that one." So then the Exodus story becomes more powerful among African Americans. Why? Because they're trying to get free. Or the story of Daniel in the lion's den. Again, the suggestion of captivity and freedom. So those particular stories become the determinative ones for them instead of the ones about service, obeying your masters, blah, blah, blah. Be obedient. They've still got to do that. Obviously. But in their own consciousness, they begin to frame that differently. That's why they want to steal away to Jesus. They want to steal away to Jesus because they want to leave the plantation and go north. So the song becomes a code. So that's the other thing they do. They create codes.

They're the first rappers. Rappers need to know this. Rappers are the contemporary *griots*, the contemporary storytellers. They come out of a tradition that goes back to gospels, spirituals, blues, jazz, R & B, and now rap. It's all a part of that same "tribal talk." So, I think what I kind of feel behind your question is this: they're just mixing this stuff all up. Well in some cases they did. But they took the best of what they had and tried to make it relevant. And that's what it's always about to some extent. And it was that way with Europeans. They're reading the same Bible aren't they, the same books? Then why do we have so many different denominations? Roman Catholic and Protestant? They're debating over politics. They're debating over land, gold, money, and all these things get inter-meshed. So the religion never is—and sociology knew it—never is pure or pristine. Never the case. Sure, you could argue that some forms are more normative than others. In other words, that even when slaves have a conversion, then they have a very particular understanding of their relationship to Jesus Christ now rather than to Legba. Okay, so that becomes a distinction. Jesus has established within me a very particular relationship where I don't do or believe those things the same way anymore. But part of what I'm arguing, of course, is that it's still there. It takes a different form.

Someone once told me that for many African American Christians, Jesus has become our collective ancestor. Whereas our ancestors may have a variety of spirits—Legba and Oshun and Ogun (and these are all different attributes of Olodumare)—for Protestant Christians Jesus becomes a collective spirit. And you can see how it happens. I just did the example earlier, didn't I? And it works through the "call and response." When I said earlier "Jesus," everybody knew, "Mary's baby." " 'Jesus' . . . the bright and the morning star." How do we get that? It's a catechism that's been communicated across geography and across time among African American Christians. And Jesus, for us, becomes that new—that new *orisha*—who represents a certain type of infusion of power. So it's a combination. Does that help?

> STUDENT   Do you say "tribal talk" is just communication between cultures or storytelling or is it a combination of all?
>
> COLEMAN   What it attempts to do is to represent to you, the reader, the variety of ways in which persons of African descent both create stories and tell stories, in a nutshell, to make the world better for themselves.
>
> STUDENT   Would you say the reason why we have lots of tension, racial

tension and low acceptance of African culture is because people don't hear that?

Misinformation about Voodoo

No, they definitely don't hear it. And I think they partly don't hear because we've been so misinformed, and we've been so misled—I'll use that word— by the dominant messages. I mean, I used chapter 1 intentionally to provoke people, because most of us when we think about voodoo, I mean . . . [Coleman proceeds humorously to act out someone who is "spooked" by "voodoo"]. And, yet, voodoo, or *Vodun*, is a cool spirituality. Vodun is what comes out of the funk of James Brown. Vodun is what Toni Morrison is talking about in her novels. Vodun is what the rappers are tapping into. But, see, the question is, how did you get your contemporary understanding of voodoo, and why is it that you're not questioning how you got that information? Let me give you an example. Why is it that we get more worked up about the idea of someone with a doll and a pin? That's some powerful imagery. Why does that disturb you more than the knowledge that someone can press a button and start a nuclear war? Why is it that you can rationalize the button? How have you been conditioned, how have we been conditioned, to accept the immensity of global power in the hands of certain individuals who can work thermal nuclear "voo-doo," if you want to use that term? [Laughter from the audience.] I'm serious. And you can walk around and continue to eat sandwiches and so forth and say, "I really can't get worked up about that." But the moment voodoo is as-sociated with anything African—and this is important, this is the most re-vealing point—the moment it's associated with anything African, it's totally demonic.

Or let's use another example. Like any other religious tradition, much of Euro-American/European religious history is replete with violence. It is. I mean, they write about it. They've been writing about it for hundreds of years. And yet people find ways to nuance and look at the good and bad aspects of Christianity. Right? Yes. Or someone's gonna say, "Well, *they* weren't really Christians . . ." Well, they were baptized! Sure they were Christians! Christians have behaved atrociously toward each other—we know this—and they con-tinue to do so. But we don't say that all Christians are demonic devils just because there's a brutal and bloody history also associated with Christianity. And, on the other hand, you talk about voodoo: it's totally bad. How does that happen? Do you hear the ideological game that's going on? How does that happen? You watch TV, movies, whatever. That's why. Because of the ways you have received this information; the connotation is that anything African is totally bad. That's really the text. Because it's African, it is bad. It can't be nuanced. It can't be. I mean, certainly there are antisocial characters in *Tribal*

Talk. I don't try to hide them. They're antisocial. But there's also a strong communitarian emphasis in Vodun or Ifa.

The Ongoing Mystery

So you've got to start using the same type of, I would say, discretion or judgment that you have been conditioned to use when you talk about Christianity, Judaism, or Islam: three of the most violent religions on the planet. What's going on in the Middle East right now is an expression of religious orientation. And, as Joseph Campbell once said, the tragedy is they're talking about the same deity. But they're killing each other. They've got the same text. Exclusivism. Intolerance: "I've got it, therefore, you've got to die," rather than a more open tolerance and respect for differences. None of us really knows the mystery of how god reveals god's self, then or now. And none of us has perfect knowledge of how that has happened, is happening, or will happen in the future. God is bigger than all of the stuff we do to try to be right or to promote our particular religious orientation.

APPENDIX I: *TRIBAL TALK: BLACK THEOLOGY, HERMENEUTICS, AND AFRICAN/AMERICAN WAYS OF "TELLING THE STORY"*

Part 1

1. Pouring Ancestral Libations: The Coming of the *Vodun*
2. "Root-Work" or (Re)Configuring the Transatlantic "Middle Passage": West African Roots of Religious Life in the African Americas
3. (Re)Establishing Spirituality within an Oppressive Cult(ure): Mediators, Spirit(s), and "Holy Ghost Power"
4. Emancipation and (Re)Construction into a New Communal Self-Identity: The Work of the Spirit among Communities of the Faithful

Part 2

5. Speaking Out: The Origin and Development of the Slave Narrative Collection
6. Divination and Conjuration: Employing Interpretative Strategies
7. Pouring More Libations: Black Theology as a Resource for Liberation Hermeneutics

APPENDIX 2

The West African Sacred Cosmos

The Supreme Deity: Nana Buluku (Dahomey)
Spirits (both superhuman beings and those who died long ago): Mawu-Lisa and her-his offspring: "Da" and "Yo"

Humans (those alive and unborn): humans, the unborn and the deceased ancestors

Animals and plants (biological and botanical life): Tortoise, Dog, objects used in making a *gbo*

"Phenomena and objects" without biological life: objects used in making a *gbo*; metal and stone that display supernatural properties

African-Derived Religions in the Americas

Vodun/Voodoo: Haiti and New Orleans

Macumba, Candomblé, and Umbanda: Brazil

Lucumi, Santeria: Cuba

Santeria: Puerto Rico, Cuba, New York, and Miami

Myal and Obeah; Rastafarianism: Jamaica and the United States

Ifa: United States, Cuba, and other parts of the Caribbean

Islam: United States

Hoodoo: Southern United States

Protestant African American Christianity: United States, Jamaica, Barbados, and Canada

Roman Catholic African American Christianity: Haiti, Puerto Rica, Cuba, Brazil, and Canada

APPENDIX 3: AFRICAN AMERICAN RELIGIOUS HISTORY

African Americans and the Bible: Religio-historical Context

1492–1620: Migration of people from Europe and Africa to the Americas. Native American Spirituality, Roman Catholic Christianity, Protestant European Christianity, African Islam, and Traditional Religions

1727–1740: The First Great Awakening. Anglicans, Congregationalists, Presbyterians, Baptists, Methodists. Revivalism along the eastern colonies. Few conversions of Africans and Native Americans (debate over the nature versus spiritual state)

1800–1830s: The Second Great Awakening: Presbyterians, Baptist and Methodists. Massive conversions in the southern and western frontiers

(Early 1700s–1865: Euro-American churches versus the "invisible institution." Catechisms versus the Bible as an open book with respect to African Americans and illiterate Euro-Americans)

1865–present: Emergence and establishment of the African American churches: Baptists, Methodists, and Pentecostals

Some Characteristics of African American Protestant Christianity

Presence: God, the preacher, and the congregation

Prayer: talking and struggling with God

Song: spirituals and gospels as catechisms
The Word: Bible and oral tradition
Call-response: God, the preacher, and the congregation in dialogue
Rhythm: Building up the cadence for ecstatic mysticism
The Shout: experiencing the overpowering presence of God
The Invitation/Response: dedicating one's life to God

Some Characteristics of Contemporary Black Biblical Interpretation

Popular versus technical interpretations of the Bible
Evangelical piety versus liberation praxis
Closed (infallible) canon versus canonical criticism
Rhetorical dramatics versus political relevance
Ecumenicity and interfaith dimensions of black biblical exegesis versus
Jesus-only Christianity

APPENDIX 4: SOME DIMENSIONS OF AFRICAN/AMERICAN MYSTICISM

Some Characteristics of West African Worship

Libations (response "Ashe"): invocation to Olodumare and other *orisas*
Invocation of the ancestors
Song: "Omi tutu"
Individual silent prayers to the ancestors
Song: singing to Esu Elegbara
Individual testimony: acclamation to the *orisa* and community response
The voice of Olodumare through the Odu
Offerings (to Esu, the *orisa* of the day, and general offering to the Ile)
Ritual of the day (salt, honey, sugar, Atari)
Drumming, dance, possession
Common meal

Some Characteristics of African American Protestant Christian Worship

Presence: God, the preacher, and the congregation
Prayer: talking and struggling with God
Song: spirituals and gospels as catechisms
The Word: Bible and oral tradition
Call-response: God, the preacher, and the congregation in dialogue
Rhythm: Building up the cadence for ecstatic mysticism
The Shout: experiencing the overpowering presence of God
The Invitation/Response: dedicating one's life to God

PART III

Decoding and Other Modes of Analysis

II

Teaching from the Crossroads: On Religious Healing in African Diaspora Contexts in the Americas

Linda L. Barnes

I write this chapter as an interstitial creature, one who lives at the junctures of a liminal life and who writes from the crossroads of disciplines and institutions. The following work is one expression of such intersections, drawn from my training as a religious studies scholar on the one hand and medical anthropologist on the other. I am a member of the faculty of Boston University School of Medicine (BUSM), at the same time that I also supervise field site placements from Harvard Divinity School (HDS) and serve on the board of the American Academy of Religion (AAR). My students are as likely to come from religious studies and anthropology as they are to be caught up in preparing to be physicians.

My teaching, scholarship, and writing invariably visit and revisit permutations on a consistent set of interwoven themes: culture, race, religious traditions, and healing practices—or, as I often put it, the culturally and religiously grounded approaches to healing of different groups, and their meaning in given contexts. I find it difficult to separate out the "religious" and the "healing" dimensions of different traditions, seeing both, instead, as two aspects of a single phenomenon. I suggest that religious traditions and healing traditions represent a crossroad in their own right, where issues of suffering, affliction, resilience, and resistance converge.

Both religious and healing traditions provide explanations for suffering, not only in its macrocosmic dimensions but also in its more immediate expression in the form of personal or group affliction. Both suggest different concepts of the person and of the parts that comprise a person—an indispensable issue if one is to understand which part has sickened and what must be done to heal it. One must, that is, be able to discern the unit in need of healing, whether it be a part of what Albert Raboteau calls "the body personal" or the "body social."

The healing in question may or may not forestall death. It may require different kinds of specialists, whose particular gifts or expertise derive from culturally recognized and sanctioned forms of authority. The meanings of healing may be multiple, ranging from the cure of a physical ill to the redressing of an emotional rupture between persons. It may extend beyond the bounds of the physical life, thereby becoming Healing. It is no surprise, within this framework, that we find Jesus the Physician or the Medicine Buddha.

There are relatively few courses in religious studies designed to train students in the study of medicine and healing traditions as an intellectual undertaking. Those that do often focus on new age or popular sources by authors like Herbert Benson or Larry Dossey, or on an extremely narrow sample of religious healing like Christian Science. Such courses rarely include theoretical and methodological training; nor do they look at the issue of healing as a theme running through the history of different religious traditions.

In contrast, medical anthropologists focus on the cross-cultural study of medicine and healing traditions, and have done extensive work developing related theoretical tools. They are prone, however, to being tone-deaf when it comes to interpreting such traditions religiously. In addition, relatively little work has been done on local settings in the United States. Medical school courses on "spirituality and medicine" focus either on studies trying to prove that religious practice, or "religiosity" (often represented in primarily Christian terms), contributes to better health outcomes, or on teaching medical students to take "spiritual histories," using models assumed to be generic and universal but that often contain unexamined cultural, religious, and class biases.

In this chapter, I propose two ways in which one can engage in the study of religion and healing. The first grows out of a program I coteach; it involves the urban ethnographic study of culturally/religiously based approaches to healing in the African Diaspora communities of Boston, Massachusetts. The second is related to ways in which the findings of the first kind of course can be incorporated into different levels of medical education, thereby introducing a highly focused aspect of religious studies into the training of biomedical clinicians.

The Boston Healing Landscape Project

During the 1990s, Diana Eck undertook the mapping of the religious land-scape of Boston in order to demonstrate that the city had developed a histori-cally unprecedented degree of religious pluralism and complexity. This work began as an undergraduate seminar at Harvard University, engaging the stu-dents in locating and studying different religious communities in the city. From there, Eck went on to direct similar mapping projects in cities around the United States, under the rubric of the Pluralism Project.

The course I team-teach with Ken Fox and Eugene Adams, the other faculty of the Boston Healing Landscape Project, grew out of the hypothesis that, just as the religious landscape of the country has grown more complex, so has the landscape of culturally and religiously grounded approaches to healing. The question was: how to document it? We decided to establish a seminar through BUSM that would be open to graduate students in departments of religious studies, African American studies, ethnic studies, anthropology, sociology, and public health, from around Boston. Clearly, working across institutional bound-aries would not necessarily be a goal for instructors. However, it would be just as possible to work across departments within a single university setting.

We applied for, and received, funding from the Ford Foundation to support the salaries of the faculty, our office manager, and the costs related to the course. Because we teach the course through a medical school, the securing of such funding is necessary. Faculty who do not bring in clinical income as physicians must generate their own support through grants, and physician faculty must fund their own teaching time. In another kind of institution, the resources to teach such a course would be configured differently.

Recruiting Students

To recruit students, we requested that departments in which we had connec-tions disseminate an announcement of the course through email. We also placed flyers in student mailboxes. To apply and participate, students could come from any graduate program in Boston, but they had to be able to make arrangements for independent study credit through their home institution. We also decided to give preference to students who had taken at least one course in some aspect of African Diaspora cultures and/or religious traditions, so that we could build on that background. Were the course to be offered within a single school, it would be appropriate for upper-level undergraduates or for graduate students with previous coursework of some kind in these traditions.

We deliberately sought out students from different disciplinary back-grounds in order to promote interdisciplinary collaboration. The limitation to this approach lay in differences in methodological preparation and orientation.

However, given that our core orientation involved urban ethnography and qualitative research methods, we figured that we would provide related training—a framework, that is, within which other disciplinary differences could enrich the discussions.

The Structure of the Year

Because our students come from different institutions, we decided to hold the research seminar on one evening a week, to bypass the constraints of institutional differences in calendar and schedule. We arbitrarily arranged our schedule to conform with the academic calendar of one local university, given that no two institutions have identical calendars. So far, this approach has worked. We also select a meeting location that will be most central to the students for a particular year.

The course represents a substantial time commitment on the part of both faculty and students. As we teach it, it runs for a full calendar year, which we divide into three segments: spring semester; summer internship; fall semester. Alternate time frames might involve one full academic year consisting of two semesters, or three quarters, divided into the three components of project design, fieldwork, and analysis and presentation. In addition to gathering research material about traditions and practices, we also understand one of our central goals to be the mentoring of upper-level students through a full cycle of professional work. We hope thereby to produce a cadre of cutting-edge scholars who can enter other settings and continue to promote this kind of work.

THE SPRING SEMESTER. This seminar is the first third of the 2002 Ford Scholars Program with the Boston Healing Landscape Project. The first goal entails the visual mapping of the African Diaspora communities of Boston. The mapping draws its inspiration not only from the Pluralism Project but also from the Newark Project, directed by Karen McCarthy Brown (the well-known author of *Mama Lola: A Voodoo Priestess in Brooklyn*), in which students are assigned to different wards in the city of Newark and are directed to go street by street, photographing everything visibly connected with religion. Building on this idea, we provide our students with point-and-shoot 36-millimeter cameras, slide film, and an electronic log sheet. We purchase Ektachrome film because we can have it developed locally within the same day; we can also have the photographer's name, the year, the roll number, and the slide number all printed on the slide, making cataloguing easier. The course pays for the developing costs, with the understanding that the slides then belong to the project.

We assign each student a specific area within selected sections of Boston, and require them to turn in a minimum of one roll of film a week, shot in their area. They are expected to use the log form to note the address or location where the slide was taken, the content, and any field observations they want to make. Within a week, they must transfer these notes to the electronic version of the log form and send them in to us. The logs then correspond to the sets of slides. A word about log sheets will clarify their importance. Students learn fieldwork methods, including clear ways to notate their observations. (Log sheet instructions with sample entries are included at the end of this essay in appendix 1.) When the slides are developed, we have the photographer's last name, the year, the roll number (in that student's work), and the shot number printed on the slide. We store the slides in plastic sheets with twenty pockets a page, interleafing the log sheets with the slide sheets. Doing so facilitates being able to scan the collection for images, and to tell at a glance what is contained in a given set of slides. It also lays the foundation for building a database of our images—a necessary step as the collection grows.

Every few weeks, we devote half of the seminar session to viewing and analyzing samples of the students' visual work. Early on in our work, we met a local documentary photographer, and we brought him into the project as our photographic consultant and as one of the faculty. He goes out with the students to coach them in street photography and directs the assessment sessions. The point of building a visual collection is twofold. First, it provides us with visual resources for teaching, presentations, and future projects. Second, it encourages our students to develop visual sophistication to parallel the text-based sophistication more common in academic training. In a different teaching context, if a school had a photography program of any kind, one of the faculty might be involved as a member of a teaching team.

The second component of the spring is the designing of the research proposal to be submitted to the Institutional Review Board (IRB). This proposal is required whenever a study is done under the auspices of a medical school and involves human subjects. Its primary purpose is to ensure a review of the ethics of the study. A key piece of what one must submit is the informed consent form one plans to use, to explain to interviewees the purpose of the study and their role in it. The IRB review process reflects the disastrous history of medical research in relation to African Americans in the United States. In projects involving children under the age of eighteen, an informed *assent* form is required for the child, and an informed *consent* form for the parent or caretaker.

Every week, we require students to submit completed sections of the IRB form, based on a template used at BUSM, which we review and return to them. To make this process more straightforward, we provide each student with a course notebook containing copies of IRB proposals from previous years that were approved and that can serve as working models. Thinking through the various aspects of an IRB form proves useful in this process because students are pushed to consider the specifics and details of how they will carry out their research. On the other hand, reviewing IRB components every week adds work to the faculty load. It would not be easy, for example, to do this course with a group beyond the size of a small seminar.

The review process to which these proposals are subjected usually takes anywhere from four to six weeks. In a medical school setting one cannot begin fieldwork without signed approval from the IRB of all the parts of one's proposal. We therefore require the students to have completed their proposals by mid-April, in order to ensure that we will have secured permission to proceed by the beginning of June. These demands have meant that we have had to develop expertise in writing IRB proposals grounded in anthropological methods in a setting where virtually none of the medical school reviewers are trained in such methods. The process has presented interesting challenges as we juggle different components.

Because we are rather unusual, in being based in a department of pediatrics, we require that student projects have something to do with (1) children's health (even if in the form of practices chosen by parents), (2) religion, and (3) an African Diaspora group or practice as found in Boston. There is nothing intrinsic to the course design, however, that requires the inclusion of child health or, for that matter, an exclusive focus on African Diaspora cultures and traditions.

Early in the semester, students must conduct literature searches to determine what has (or has not) been written in relation to the project they hope to do. We review these searches and make additional recommendations. The fine art of the literature search requires the creative ability to second-guess the authors' and cataloguers' use of keywords. The student's task is to try to dig out everything that has been written about the group and phenomenon to be studied. This process will allow the student to say, with some measure of certainty, what has or has not been addressed in the literature.

We also assign the students two mentors and require them to locate a third one. The first is a scholar in the field or tradition that they will be studying. This scholar may or may not be local, so in some cases the consultation happens by email or telephone. The second is a physician who works closely with patients from the group being researched. The reason for having a physician and a scholar as mentors is to begin to introduce our students to future senior colleagues who may help them develop their careers, and to increase the likelihood that the projects will not duplicate existing research. The third must be a mentor from the community being studied. The community mentors are there to make sure that issues are represented as viewed by members of the community, and to train the students to think about being accountable to the communities they study. In all ways possible, we ask students to engage community members in formulating the research problem, designing interview questions, and introducing issues related to indigenous epistemologies. Generally, the students locate the third mentor at some point during the spring or early in the summer. The students are expected to check in with each of their mentors at least once a month to invite advice and comments in the design of their work. We find that we often have to give many reminders to ensure that they do so. Students are instructed in the syllabus that their project design should reflect the input of the mentors (physician, academic, and community). We work to assign appropriate mentors as promptly as possible.

If the mentor is not available for a meeting, students should set up time to talk by phone. If the person turns out to be hard to reach by phone, questions by email facilitate communication. It is the student's responsibility to ensure the interchanges with mentors. If a student finds that one of his or her mentors is simply not working out, we ask that he or she communicate this to us sooner rather than later so that we can determine how to address the situation. Each student must submit a summary of the mentor's input at two different points and should be able to show how it has been factored into his or her research design.

Our grant funding provides for a small stipend for the mentors, but one could also turn to the kindness of one's colleagues around the country. What makes this mentorship different from general advising is that the eventual goal is to produce a publishable piece of work. According to the standards of medical publication, anyone who has participated in a study throughout—whether he or she actually conducts the fieldwork—is to be included as one of the authors. In the articles that emerge, students have first authorship while mentors, when appropriate, are listed as second or third authors. Presumably, scholars around the country may feel greater interest in mentoring a project that may lead to another publication, albeit as a second or third author.

To cultivate student sophistication regarding the interplay between theory and research design, we assign weekly readings that address such issues. We discuss these readings both in relation to general comprehension and to how one might apply these different theories and methods to one's own research design. We also discuss practical issues of how the implementation might actually be done. During the final session, we review the plan for the summer and gather the students' ideas regarding what they feel would be helpful resources during the summer.

THE SUMMER INTERNSHIP: FIELDWORK. The spring session ends at the beginning of May, giving the students a month-long recess. The summer session starts at the beginning of June and continues through the end of August. Because we team-teach the course, we can spell each other if one faculty member is taking vacation time off. We have found that twelve weeks is barely enough time to conduct the level of fieldwork these projects require. Our grant provides the students with a stipend of $3,000 to enable them to spend less time on a summer job. However, they can also carry out the summer component of the program as an internship or summer course, in which case they pay no additional tuition and receive course credit. We work out such arrangements on a case-by-case basis. Other institutions might want to look into whether or not the school has summer research money for which students can apply, or whether they can take the internship as a summer course, receiving credit for doing so.

As in the spring, the research team meets once a week. During that meeting, students check in on what has been happening in their fieldwork and discuss what they have read for the week. The conversation ranges from challenging logistical issues to personal ones that arise while doing one's fieldwork. We assign weekly readings, shifting to a focus on practical fieldwork skills for the first part of the summer and to examples of ethnographic writing during the second. We keep the reading load at approximately twenty pages a week, with the expectation that students will also be reading from their own literature searches and that they will be immersed in their fieldwork.

The readings for June focus on basic fieldwork methods and techniques—interviewing, taking fieldnotes, self-awareness as an ethnographer. The second month presents issues related to publishing qualitative research in medical contexts. Although this is not ordinarily a forum in which religion scholars publish, it is our contention that the kind of student work we promote integrates religious studies with issues that are of growing importance to the medical community. One of our goals is to mentor students so that they are trained to publish across disciplines.

One of the most important lessons we have learned is the need for explicit fieldwork requirements. We now require a minimum of two interviews a week, and that these interviews be transcribed and turned in within two weeks of their recording. One way or another, we require a total of twenty transcribed interviews by the end of the summer. As faculty, we find that we have to keep up with reading the transcripts so that we are better prepared to discuss what students are finding. This approach makes it easier, too, to mentor students in the analysis of their interviews and to make sure they don't distort their findings because of personal bias or inexperience.

Students are prone to thinking that ethnographic fieldnotes function along the lines of a personal journal, which—in their minds—makes such notes more or less optional. As a result, they tend to think they don't have to do them, or that they don't need to do them in the way that we ask. We now require students to submit samples of their fieldnotes every week so that we can get a better sense of what they are writing; and we interject guidance where necessary.

About midsummer, we begin to identify the professional journals to which the students will eventually submit their articles. In the course notebook that we distribute at the beginning of the summer, we include copies of downloaded instructions for authors of selected journals in medicine, medical anthropology, and religion. We try to discuss some of the specific ways in which the nature of the journal they have chosen will influence the structure of all the work they will produce in the fall. To give them examples of such articles, during the final month of the summer program, the readings are chosen from these journals and from ethnographies that illustrate effective the integration of theory, method, and analysis. Students begin to examine styles and structures, and to think their way toward their own writing.

THE FALL SEMESTER: ANALYSIS, PRESENTATION, AND WRITE-UP. A three-week recess precedes the beginning of the fall semester. During the first half of this fall component of the program, the students work on their public presentations; they spend the second half writing their articles. Our role as faculty entails mentoring them in how to translate their data into effective, conference-quality papers written for two different kinds of audience. We require them to give two presentations, the one to the community they have studied, the other to an academic audience. We require the community talk in order to guarantee that the community has the opportunity to hear what is being written about them, and to critique or challenge it. It is one step toward accountability. For example, our students have spoken to such groups as a local organization that uses hiphop music to educate young women of color about sexual behavior; an organization serving gay, lesbian, bisexual, and transgendered youth of color; members of the house of a local Santero; and women at a local Haitian center.

The academic audience could well take the form of an afternoon symposium for the school where the course is taking place. In our case, we bring together the members of the project's executive committee, which consists of scholars, physicians, and persons who direct programs related to religion and healing. Each week, through mid-November, the students must turn in specific pieces of their presentation, reading them to the team and discussing revisions.

Following their presentations, the students spend the balance of the semester writing their articles. We expect them to factor in the comments made during their presentations. Given that they have seen samples of articles from these journals, they have been able to structure their presentations accordingly. Again, we have organized the assignments according to sections that must be submitted at specific times. Finally, students must follow through on the process of formatting and preparing the article to be sent out according to the author guidelines of the particular journal. The faculty members assist in the publication process by including information on how to structure articles for medical journals. (A sample form follows in appendix 2.)

We have found that the faculty subsequently has to do a fair amount of revising, regardless of how closely we have mentored the students' writing over the fall. We do so with the understanding that we are coauthors of the resulting article. The student is generally the lead author, based on our commitment to mentor a group of junior scholars doing cutting-edge work in this field. In only one case did a student's mentor actually develop the project idea and many of the questions in the interview. In that one case, we negotiated first authorship for the mentor and second for the student. Thus, there is a certain amount of room for negotiation. In general, however, we have tried to create a model that opposes faculty appropriation of student work.

This dual role of faculty and collaborator is a complicated one, the ethics of which we have wrestled with from the beginning. One way in which it resolves is that many of the students take the courses under the Pass/Fail or Sat/Unsat category. Given the generally low requirements for both, such students invariably pass. When a student is going to receive a grade, we evaluate his or her work according to the quality of the final article submitted and do not begin the revision process until the fall component of the project has ended. We have had the experience of having to fail one student who did not complete the requirements, and whose final article was not of a quality that could be salvaged for a journal submission. To date, this is the arrangement we have come up with to try to maintain some boundaries between our different roles.

The Project Website

To facilitate the dissemination of our research, we sponsor a website that draws on this work. A local university has a program in which graphic arts and animation students—many of whom have web design skills—are required to do six-month internships. We pay for the services provided by these students, but if a school had a computer-related department, it is conceivable that one could involve an advanced student in developing a site for one's students' work. (The address for our site is www.bmc.org/pediatrics/special/bhlp.)

The purpose of this site is to provide resources of different kinds related to African Diaspora cultures and religious traditions. The site offers:

1. Links to current news sources from local, national, and international Diaspora communities, cultures, and countries (e.g., online newspapers)
2. Online versions of our team's slides, which can be downloaded for teaching purposes
3. Bibliographies, links to sites on Diaspora cultures, religious traditions, countries, and other resources
4. A curriculum section, which we are in the process of developing, that will suggest how to use the resources on the site for different educational levels (e.g., elementary schools, middle and high schools, community colleges, colleges and universities, and medical education programs)

Medical Education

It is beyond the scope of this chapter to describe to the same degree of depth the different ways in which the research that grows out of a course like this can be introduced into medical education. Here I provide a sketch of some of the primary features. The first involves the structure of medical education. Generally speaking, people preparing to become physicians begin by going through four years of medical school. They take two years of classroom courses—often highly structured and not necessarily allowing for any electives. Consequently, one must often look for sympathetic faculty through whom a lecture or two can be introduced. One can also try to develop an elective course, but it is difficult to do so unless a faculty member from the medical school is willing to coteach or to sponsor the course.

During their third year, students go through miniapprenticeships in the different areas of medicine (e.g., surgery, pediatrics, and psychiatry), usually for about six weeks. It is at this point that they really begin to interact with patients and to get an immediate sense of life in a clinical setting. A given rotation will also usually provide brief lectures and seminars on a weekly basis. If one can build a relationship with the director of medical education for a particular rotation, one can sometimes find a way to introduce a lecture in this context as well. Here is where the slides taken by our team have proved extremely useful. We use them to introduce medical students to the communities from which the patients they have been seeing come, and to some of the practices their patients may be using and not discussing in clinical sessions.

Fourth-year students spend part of their time in the clinic and also take month-long intensive electives. Here is a good place to propose a course (again, in tandem with someone on a medical faculty). For example, we have developed a course on culturally based understandings of complementary and alternative healing practices. We plan to introduce fourth-year students to Diaspora traditions through interactive modules on our website, through lectures, and by taking them into the Diaspora communities surrounding our teaching hospital so that they can meet practitioners.

Three years of residency follow medical school. Residency functions something like a graduate program, in which the recently graduated doctor must acquire intensive training in clinical work. Residents are chronically overworked, have little time to read anything, and respond best to training that provides them with hands-on knowledge and skills. Teaching cases that represent cross-cultural dilemmas in clinical contexts have proved extremely effective. We recruit residents to tell us stories from their own experience, and then help them develop them with teaching notes. Such teaching narratives provide a context for clinicians to discuss the more affective, interpersonal, and cross-cultural dimensions of medicine.

After residency, doctors who want to go on and develop further specialized skills, including a research component, go on to do a fellowship, usually lasting two years. This part of a physician's training is roughly equivalent to doing a postdoc. The fellowships usually provide an annual stipend on the order of $25,000–30,000, so fellows frequently also moonlight. Finally, having completed this training, a physician may go on to engage in clinical work exclusively, or to look for a combination of clinical practice and research at a medical school. In our program, we work with medical faculty in our department by directing pertinent resources their way and by acting as consultants to their interest in doing qualitative work of their own—still a relatively rare phenomenon among doctors, but one that is slowly growing in our department. For all of these levels, we search out ways to adapt the website content and specific resources or research data to respond to the needs of each one.

Concluding Thoughts

One of the goals of this course/program is to promote the intersection of religious studies, medical anthropology, and medical education. This kind of interdisciplinary work is a hitherto little explored variation on the anthropology of religion. It introduces students to interdisciplinary methods and trains them in the kinds of skills that should prove invaluable if they want to go on to do any kind of fieldwork-related scholarship.

Equally important, I see a growing need in medical education for scholars who are schooled in working across these particular disciplines. Increasingly, physicians are discussing the need to be prepared to provide what is referred to as "culturally competent care"—care, that is, that takes into account the particular needs of a culturally diverse patient population. Insofar as this cultural diversity includes alternative forms of healing (many of them rooted in religious worldviews), religion scholars stand in a unique position to influence medical training. There is, therefore, a critical applied dimension. Moreover, this role represents an expanded set of job possibilities for religion scholars.

Had I been asked some years ago whether I could have imagined myself teaching on a medical faculty, I would have said no. I fully expected to be a member of a religion department. However, with three years of working in a medical setting behind me, I can only strongly encourage other faculty to consider teaching that lends itself to going beyond the humanities and bridges into different domains of religion and healing. The work, in its own right, is all about just that.

APPENDIX I: THE INS AND OUTS OF LOG SHEETS

Note: These instructions were developed by Olivia Hsin.

The slides that you take can be useful tools for teaching viewers about your assigned neighborhoods. They reflect the distinctive cultural and religious backgrounds of the residents and the diverse forms of local healing and environmental and economic resources available. For your slides to be useful, it is imperative that you keep detailed and informative log sheets. An incomplete or sparse entry on a log sheet can undermine the value of a stunning slide. Slide captions are based on your log sheet entries. Hence it is most helpful for you to write entries with a caption format in mind.

The following are guidelines for how to fill in your log sheets. Slides sometimes fall out of order and are not always printed in order numerically. It should be possible to put slides back in order based on the log sheet and know what each slide is. At the end of this packet, you will find examples of helpful and unhelpful log entries from past years.

Identification: Give the official name of the place if there is one. Avoid writing just "Church" or "Pentecostal Church"—write "Zion Fire Baptized Holiness Church of the Americas." Try to give the slide a name that makes it easily identifiable.

Address/Location: Give a full address whenever possible. If one is unavailable, take down as much information as possible about the location that will help locate the official address later on—e.g., a telephone number from which one can do a reverse-search using the internet, nearby cross-streets, or names of adjacent landmarks and store names that can be found in the telephone book. The more complete you are in writing an address down on the log sheet, the less time needs to be spent searching for an address later on.

Observations/Comments/Reflections: Start each entry with: "[identification of object] at [address] in [city, state]." See examples.

Content: What are you trying to depict in your picture? What do you want your viewer to notice or learn from your slide? What makes this slide different from another in the same roll? Is one slide focused on herbs sold in the store and another focused on the way in which it is packaged? The most important part about this section is INFORMATION INFORMATION INFORMATION. Give as much detail as possible. If you are in doubt of whether to include something, include it. It is always more helpful to err on the side of writing too much than writing too little. It is easy to delete unnecessary information later on; it is harder to fill in missing information retrospectively. Don't take mental notes. Take physical notes. Slides start blending together very quickly. Fill in as much information as possible at the time.

The following is a sampling of the kinds of questions you might answer. Use it as a guide if you are stuck but try to think of your own questions too. What are you curious about? If you were someone accessing the picture on the website, what kind of information would you like to know? If this slide were to be blown up, framed, and on exhibit at a museum or education center, what kind of caption would you find beneath it?

Context: What is nearby? Is this church next to a mosque? Is it next to a homeless shelter? Is it next to a nightclub? Is it in a residential neighborhood or a commercial area? What sticks out about the place? What makes this store different from another? What makes this park different from another? Why did you notice the object of your picture? Put things in perspective. Is this garden in full view? Is it hidden behind alleyways? Is there broken glass nearby and lots of weeds? Is it very well kept?

Religious Places: What kind of church or synagogue or temple, etc., is it? What is unique about it? What populations is the place reaching out to? Is the congregation made up of people from the neighborhood or other cities as well? What languages are the services in? Is your picture focused on congregation members? Posters? A statue? Stained glass? The Star of David? Do two churches share the same building? Does the location provide other services such as community gatherings, food shelter, childcare, legal services, language classes, etc.? What kind of area is the building in? What else is nearby? These are just a few examples of questions you might try to answer—by all means, the more you can think of, the better.

Religious Objects or Statues: What is the object? Where does it originate? What kind of religious traditions does it belong to? Has it been adapted to fit a certain racial or cultural group in any way? (e.g., a statue of Jesus painted in colors that represent the African Diaspora.) How is the object used? In religious services? Everyday life? At dinner? Where is the object? In a store? In a garden? On a windowsill? If in a store, what other kinds of things does the store sell? If in a garden, is there anything else noticeable about the garden? (e.g., a home garden with statues of Buddha and the Virgin Mary placed together).

Public Places and Community Centers: What kind of area is it in? What kind of condition is it in? If it offers any special facilities, what kind of facilities does it have? (e.g., basketball courts, baseball fields, pools, art rooms, playgrounds). Are there advertisements of functions held at the park? (e.g., community barbecues, cultural festivals, self-defense classes, concerts). What other kinds of activities occur? What kind of transportation is there to the area? Is there handicap access? What populations are served—racial, ethnic, age, gender? Is there public access or a membership requirement? Is it covered in trash? Do children play in the area? Is it near stores still operating? Residential areas? What was the previous function of the place?

Stores: What kinds of food or items are sold? Where are most of the items from? Are they mostly Western traditional drugs? Are they sold alongside other forms of healing treatments? What kinds of groceries are sold? What kinds of canned and dried foods are sold? Religious objects? Clothes? Books? What kinds of payment are accepted? (e.g., WIC or food stamps? Credit cards?) Are there interesting religious or moral messages and posters on display? What kinds of advertisements are there? What languages are the advertisements in? Who works in the store? Who shops at the store? Do people know each other?

Schools: Was your picture taken when school was in session? Is it a public, parochial, or private school? What is the context that the school is in? What is nearby—stores? cemeteries? homes? churches?

Murals: What is depicted and what part of the mural is your slide focused on? What kinds of colors are used? What is noteworthy? What kind of condition is it in? Does the mural convey any kind of message or contain any symbols? Who painted it? Who funded it?

Centers of Healing: What kinds of treatments are offered? What is advertised? What kind of location is it in? What is nearby? (E.g., is the physical therapy office located above a shoe store or in a building on its own?) What kinds of languages do the healers speak? What kinds of insurance or payments are accepted? Is there free care available?

Buildings and Agencies: What are the goals of the agency? What is its function? How long has it been around? What population does it serve? What languages are spoken? What services are offered? What kind of building is it? What is located inside? Is it handicap accessible? Is the building new or in repair?

APPENDIX 2: STRUCTURE OF ARTICLES FOR MEDICAL JOURNALS

Note: these instructions are based on discussions with Paul Wise, M.D., and Fred Rivara, M.D.

The articles represent a structured expansion of your presentations. In general, articles for medical journals should be no more than 12 pages (including references), or 3,500 words for the body of the text (not including cover page or references). Organize your article as follows:

- *One-page introduction:* This section sets up the problem—the gap in knowledge that this paper addresses—"This is the question." Unlike social science publications, in which introductions may be much longer, medical journal articles want this part to be short, sharp, and focused.

- *Two pages on methods*: The methods section can be shorter than two pages but must address the "who, what, where, how, and when." It must describe how interviewees were recruited, where they were interviewed, how they were compensated, etc. It must also specify that the study was reviewed and approved by an IRB board. Much of the material for this section can come out of the IRB proposal and field experience.

- *Four pages on the results of the study*: Here you present the themes that emerged in your data, and support each one, in turn, with illustrations. Each theme must, in some way, represent an aspect or answer related to the question/problem you laid out in the introduction. The reader must also see how these themes fit together. You do not discuss the findings in this section. (Here is another way in which a medical journal article differs from one that you might write for a social sciences journal.)

- *Four pages to discuss the findings*: Here is where you say something about what the data means. How does it fit in with previous published research? (Here is where you fold in related and supporting literature.) What is the new information here, or the new spin on the problem? What are the limitations of the study? What are the implications?

- *One page for conclusions and implications*: Here you don't want to make any huge leaps. Be circumspect. "Here are some themes, and we take them to mean . . ." Be succinct.

The key to a strong article lies not only in having a good problem and strong data but also in structuring your article so that all the pieces fit together clearly.

In general, avoid long, complex sentence structure. Medical editors and readers prefer declarative sentences. Avoid beginning your sentences with subordinate clauses. Avoid jargon at all costs. If you absolutely *must* use a jargon-like term, provide a brief explanation, and cite a reference to back up the definition.

Study the articles in the course binder to see how others have written up their qualitative work.

Remember that medical readers will not take the pertinence of cultural and/ or religious factors as a given. You must show how and why these factors are also a medical issue, and in what ways.

SUGGESTED BIBLIOGRAPHY

African Traditions

Appiah-Kubi, Kofi. "Religion and Healing in an African Community: the Akan of Ghana." In *Healing and Restoring: Health and Medicine in the World's Religious Traditions,* Lawrence E. Sullivan, ed., 203–224. New York: Free Press, 1989.

Ayim-Aboagye, Desmond. *The Function of Myth in Akan Healing Experience: A Psychological Inquiry into Two Traditional Akan Healing Communities.* Uppsala: Uppsala University, 1993.

Feierman, Steven, and John M. Janzen, eds. *The Social Basis of Health and Healing in Africa.* Berkeley: University of California Press, 1992.

Green, Edward C. *AIDS and STDs in Africa: Bridging the Gap between Traditional Healing and Modern Medicine.* Boulder, CO: Westview Press, 1994.

Janzen, J. "Health, Religion, and Medicine in Central and Southern African Traditions." In *Healing and Restoring: Health and Medicine in the World's Religious Traditions,* Lawrence E. Sullivan, ed., 225–254. New York: Macmillan, 1989.

Janzen, John, Adrien Ngudiankama, and Melissa Filippi-Franz. "Religious Healing among War-Traumatized African Immigrants." In *Religion and Healing in America,* Linda L. Barnes and Susan S. Sered, eds., 159–172. New York: Oxford University Press, 2004.

Lawuyi, O. B. "Water, Healing, Gender and Space in African Cosmology." *Etnologie* 21, 4 (1998): 185–190.

Owoahene-Acheampong, Stephen. *Inculturation and African Religion: Indigenous and Western Approaches to Medical Practice.* New York: Peter Lang, 1998.

Peek, Philip M., ed. *African Divination Systems: Ways of Knowing.* Bloomington: Indiana University Press, 1991.

Pfeiffer, James. "African Independent Churches in Mozambique: Healing the Afflictions of Inequality." *Medical Anthropology Quarterly* 16, 2 (2002): 176–199.

Sullivan, Lawrence E., ed. *Healing and Restoring: Health and Medicine in the World's Religious Traditions.* New York: Free Press, 1989.

Thomas, Linda E. *Under the Canopy: Ritual Process and Spiritual Resilience in South Africa.* Columbia: University of South Carolina Press, 1999.

African American Traditions

Anderson, Alita, ed. *On the Other Side: African Americans Tell of Healing.* Louisville, KY: Westminster John Knox Press, 2001.

Bair, Barbara, and Susan E. Cayleff, eds. *Wings of Gauze: Women of Color and the Experience of Health and Illness.* Detroit: Wayne State University Press, 1993.

Bankole, Katherine Kemi. *Slavery and Medicine: Enslavement and Medical Practices in Antebellum Louisiana* New York: Garland, 1998.

Byrd, W. Michael. *An American Health Dilemma: The Medical History of African Americans and the Problem of Race.* 2 vols. New York: Routledge, 2000–2002.

Chireau, Yvonne Patricia. *Black Magic: Religion and the African American Conjuring Tradition.* Berkeley: University of California Press, 2003.

McAuley, William, J., Loretta Pecchioni, and Jo Anna Grant. "Personal Accounts of the Role of God in Health and Illness among Older Rural African American and White Residents." *Journal of Cross-Cultural Gerontology* 15, 1 (2000): 13–35.
Townes, Emilie M. *Breaking the Fine Rain of Death: African American Health Issues and a Womanist Ethic of Care.* New York: Continuum, 1998.

12

Teaching African American Religions as Learning to Resist Racism

Peter R. Gathje

What strategies help to facilitate learning about African American religions as resources for resistance to racism? I have taught in two relatively small colleges; each had a small department of religion and few religion majors. Under such conditions, regularly offering a course focused entirely on African American religions is often impractical. Nevertheless, it is appropriate to attend to the importance of African American religions in a variety of courses. Further, as someone who believes that education should be transformative, it is crucial to stress the role African American religions have played and continue to play in resisting racism in American life.

I began to incorporate material about African American religions and racism into a variety of courses while teaching at Kalamazoo College, a small liberal arts college in Kalamazoo, Michigan. I now teach at Christian Brothers University, a small Catholic university in Memphis, Tennessee. In both settings I have taught different courses in which I have developed units that address African American religions (and others) in relation to racism. These courses have included "Modern Christian Thought," "Christian Ethics," "Religion and Prejudice," "Religion and Nonviolent Social Change," and "The Life and Thought of Gandhi and King."

As a white male teaching in these two different settings I have heard many voices, histories, and theologies that emerge from the widely varying experiences of my students.

At Kalamazoo College almost all of the students were white and most came from upper-middle-class families. It was rare to have a black student in a class. My white students were typically not very religious and prided themselves on being racially tolerant. But when affirmative action was discussed they quickly complained of being victims of "reverse discrimination," while sitting in a classroom with no black students. They did not consider themselves racists but remained blind to the dynamics of institutional racism.

At Christian Brothers University I have much more diversity, both racially and economically. About 25 percent of my students are African American, 5 percent Asian American, and 5 percent Hispanic, and the remaining 65 percent are white. Most are first-generation college-goers. Here it is rare to have a class without some black students, and both my black and white students are typically quite religious. However, because race is such a volatile issue, most students prefer not to discuss it in the classroom. The white students are wary of being labeled "racist" and see little connection between themselves and the old days of slavery and segregation. The black students have plenty of experience with both individual racist behavior directed against them and ongoing institutional racism, but, given the history of racial oppression in the South, they are reluctant to share their experiences with a white teacher and white students.

In both settings, therefore, despite significant differences that must be attended to, I have faced a similar set of questions: How may I help to create enough trust, between the students and myself and among the students themselves, to have an honest discussion of our experiences and perspectives? How may we together be moved to understand the ongoing dynamics of racism? And how may we come to see African American religions (among other religions) as a power for transforming the affects of racism within our own lives and the larger society?

Through my experiences with my students in these settings, I have slowly developed two strategies that have proven to be helpful both in terms of building trust and creating a transformative understanding of African American religions in relation to resistance to racism. Both strategies open up conversation in ways that can be challenging but nonthreatening. The first strategy helps students to see diversity within African American religion (and thus also African American experience). The first strategy does this by providing a helpful lens by which to begin analysis of arguments, persons, and events within the history of African American religions. The second strategy helps students see how their own experiences and perspectives on racism are related to the various dimensions of racism in the United States. This strategy, through analyzing the various ways racism may work, allows students to see how, while their experiences shed light on racism, a variety of lights are needed to more fully understand it.

I have used these two strategies together in one course, and I have used them separately in different courses. They are units that can be transported into a variety of courses. Whether used together or separately, both strategies may accomplish two related goals. The first goal is to make possible patterns surface within the variety of voices in order that categories of analysis may be developed. The second goal is to use those categories of analysis to better analyze the dynamics of racism in the United States. The first strategy, in particular, helps to illuminate how resistance to racism is an ongoing dimension of African American religions. When used together, I have found that these strategies can empower students in their analysis of racism and the variety of ways African American religions have resisted racism. This in turn may help students to consider their own relationship to racism and resistance to it.

First Strategy: Understanding African American Religion in Resistance to Racism

I use a strategy developed in *Black Religion and Black Radicalism*, by Gayraud S. Wilmore, as a lens through which to view and discuss the various ways in which African American religions provide resistance to racism.

Wilmore identifies and analyzes two broad approaches within African American religions in the United States that have responded to and resisted racism: separatism and integrationism.[1] Separatism, by Wilmore's account, sees little if any possibility that African Americans will receive or attain freedom and justice in the United States. Separatism thus urges African Americans to seek forms of economic, political, cultural, and religious independence. Integrationism, on the other hand, acknowledges the power of racism in U.S. society, its culture and social institutions, but also remains hopeful that these may be transformed so that African Americans may share in freedom and justice on an equal basis with other citizens in the United States. In identifying these two approaches to racism within African American religions, Wilmore offers a key for analyzing a wide variety of leaders, movements, theologies, and institutional practices as either separatist or integrationist.

These broad categories gain needed refinement and nuance as Wilmore further identifies three elements that may be present in varying degrees within each. Both separatists and integrationists can be analyzed in terms of how they attend to and reflect the three elements of survival, elevation, and liberation. Each of the elements thus provides opportunities for further critical discussion. By considering responses to racism that are either separatist or integrationist in terms of the elements of survival, elevation, or liberation, students may analyze how a variety of dynamics within African American religions offer resistance to racism.

In discussing survival, attention is directed toward concerns in African American religions for nurturing and strengthening African Americans. The survival element is evident whenever African American religions provide comfort and relief from the world so that survival in that world is possible. Discussions may address a variety of related questions. How do the various religious communities help members bear the burdens of life in a racist society by providing a place of refuge and mutual aid? How is survival evident, for example, in forms of worship that give joy and "power in the Spirit," so that worshipers would both experience God's presence and be empowered to survive in a hostile world? Further, how might this survival element serve within an integrationist religious community compared with a separatist community? Discussions of this element in African American religions can be further deepened through womanist critiques that point out the fact that the work of survival has often fallen upon African American women and thus can lead to the perpetuation of inequities.[2]

Elevation seeks through education, self-help groups, and a variety of organizations to raise African Americans' abilities to sustain their own communities and to compete within the larger society. Elevation includes personal moral reform and discipline, intellectual development, acquiring business skills, and gaining political power. Elevation recognizes that it is not enough to pray, one must also work in the spirit of that prayer. Elevation as an element raises question such as: Is the work of elevation—as it empowers persons to engage in society with the skills necessary to succeed personally, professionally, and politically—inherently integrationist? Or may elevation also be evident in efforts to create a separate but economically and politically powerful community? A further important aspect of discussing this element in African American religions is to raise social class issues. For example, has an emphasis upon elevation led to the development of an African American middle class that is willing to deny racial solidarity for the sake of the dominant white society's definition of "success"?

Liberation is the element in African American religions that works to create the cultural and institutional conditions necessary for racial justice in the United States and thus for African American freedom. This element was evident in the struggles against slavery and the civil rights movement of the 1950s and 1960s; it continues in a variety of contemporary efforts to resist racial repression in the United States. Liberation draws strength for the struggle from the element of survival and it draws skills for the struggle from the element of elevation. The element of liberation in African American religions moves from prayer and personal transformation to challenging the cultural and institutional powers of U.S. society. This element too raises many questions. How do various contemporary movements in which African American religions and religious leaders are active reflect this element? For example, how does the reparations movement reflect this liberation element? Further, is liberation best achieved through integrationist or separatist approaches?

Wilmore is careful in his discussion of the two approaches and the three elements to see them as points of emphasis or motifs rather than as mutually exclusive oppositions. In using Wilmore's categories to spark discussion and analysis, it is important to recognize the two approaches as two points on a continuum, to explore how the three elements can be present in either separatist or integrationist approaches, and to recognize critical perspectives on the approaches and the elements.

The helpfulness of Wilmore's lens for studying and discussing African American religions can be demonstrated by briefly considering how it intersects with other analyses of African American religions. To begin, in his landmark study of Malcolm X and Martin Luther King, Jr., *Martin and Malcolm and America: A Dream or a Nightmare,* James Cone reflects Wilmore's two major approaches when he draws and analyzes the contrast between Malcolm X's (separatist) view of U.S. society as a "nightmare" and King's (integrationist) "dream."[3] Likewise, in *African-American Religion in the Twentieth Century: Varieties of Protest and Accommodation,* Hans Baer and Merrill Singer reflect the three elements within African American religion, inasmuch as they seek to

> reveal the social essence of Black religion as a culturally produced structure that simultaneously offers some protection from the elements, provides a sheltered arena for personal development and expression, and allows a controlled level of protest of the external social world.[4]

Indeed, the very title of their book suggests the two approaches: separatist in the form of protest, integrationist in the form of accommodation.

Peter Paris, in *The Social Teachings of the Black Churches,* provides an example of the approaches and elements in his examination of the social ethics expressed in the African Methodist Episcopal Church and the National Baptist Convention, U.S.A., Inc. He sees "no distinctive differences in the social thought of the respective black Baptist and Methodist denominations."[5] Instead he sees both engaged in the ongoing pull between two loyalties, one to the race and the other to the nation.[6] As he describes aspects of the first loyalty—to race—Paris reflects the separatist category described by Wilmore. In describing the second loyalty—to nation—Paris reflects Wilmore's integrationist category. Further, Paris's analysis of the African American churches recognizes the three elements identified by Wilmore. Paris writes that the African American churches have achieved "considerable success" in the areas of "the sanctuary of God and the inner life of the individual," while there has been "very little substantial progress . . . realized in effecting racial justice in the larger society in spite of the various changes that have taken place in it."[7]

The approaches and elements Wilmore has identified may also be helpful in structuring an analysis of the variety of voices and arguments in black, womanist, and Islamic theologies and their critiques of aspects of African American religions. Students may be asked, for example, to consider whether or not a theological or ethical argument is more separatist or integrationist. Or students may be encouraged to analyze how an argument is more concerned with survival, elevation, or liberation or perhaps seeks to integrate the various elements. For example, consider Delores S. Williams's statement that "Womanists not only concern ourselves about the liberation of woman, we also struggle along with Black men and children for the liberation, survival and positive quality of life for our entire oppressed Black community."[8] Students who are alert to Wilmore's categories may analyze how Williams seeks to integrate survival, elevation, and liberation, and how her womanist perspective raises the historic and contemporary roles of African American women in relation to each of those elements.

For those who want to also move beyond the territory of African American religions and consider other important voices within African American thought and history, Wilmore's categories may still be helpful. For example, in *Race Matters*, Cornel West offers an analysis that also can be understood in light of Wilmore's categories. West's discussion of "the nihilistic threat" to black America begins by taking aim at social critics and policy-makers who reflect either a "liberal structuralism" or a "conservative behaviorism." Liberal structuralists emphasize the need for institutional change if African Americans are to flourish in American society, while the conservative behaviorists emphasize the need for behavioral change if that goal is to be accomplished.[9] West draws upon African American history to recall that

> the genius of our black foremothers and forefathers was to create powerful buffers to ward off the nihilistic threat, to equip black folk with cultural armor to beat back the demons of hopelessness, meaninglessness, and lovelessness. These buffers consisted of cultural structures of meaning and feeling that created and sustained communities; this armor constituted ways of life and struggle that embodied values of service and sacrifice, love and care, discipline and excellence. . . . These traditions for black surviving and thriving . . . consist primarily of black religious and civic institutions that sustained familial and communal networks of support.[10]

West sees a loss of these elements of survival and elevation in contemporary African American life largely due to the pressure exerted by "corporate market institutions."[11] He further argues for a "politics of conversion" grounded in a "love ethic" that affirms the self-worth of African Americans.[12] This sounds very much like Wilmore's element of "survival." Reflecting Wilmore's element of "elevation," West argues that this politics of conversion, building upon the love ethic, will proceed "principally on the local level—in those institutions in civil society still vital enough to promote self-worth and self-affirmation."[13] Finally, West moves to institutional change by saying: "the advocates of a politics of conversion never lose sight of the structural conditions that shape the sufferings and lives of people."[14] Reflecting the element of liberation, West contends that the love ethic and the work on the local level will together lead to the social transformation necessary to achieve racial justice.

Finally, perhaps standing behind Wilmore's two approaches and three elements and the analysis of the others, is the African American experience of what W. E. B. Du Bois described as "double consciousness." Du Bois wrote of a feeling of

> twoness—an American, a Negro; two souls, two thoughts, two unreconciled strivings, two warring ideals in one dark body, whose dogged strength alone keeps it from being torn asunder. The history of the American Negro is the history of this strife—this longing to attain a self-conscious manhood, to merge his double self into a better and truer self. In this merging he wishes neither of the older selves to be lost. He would not Africanize America, for America has too much to teach the world and Africa. He would not bleach his Negro soul in a flood of white Americanism, for he knows that Negro blood has a message for the world. He simply wishes to make it possible for a man to be both Negro and an American without being cursed and spit upon by his fellows, without having the doors of Opportunity closed roughly in his face.[15]

Du Bois gets to the heart of the struggle to resist racism as it is engaged by African American religions. This struggle includes what Wilmore has identified as separatism (identity) and integrationism (accommodation) and the three strategies that can be used by both, survival, elevation, and liberation.

In using this lens of analysis drawn from Wilmore to analyze diversity within African American religions in relation to racism, it is also important to reverse the lens so that our discussions take up the dynamics of racism in our society. For example, I have sometimes seen in my students and in myself a tendency to evaluate the tension between separatism and integrationism as a "black problem" or a "black issue" alone. But this ignores a crucial dimension of any exploration of African American religions in relation to resistance to racism, namely, how racism in the United States is also a white problem, that is to say, a problem that is rooted in domination engineered by whites and that benefits whites. Cornel West's insight is a helpful reminder. He writes:

> To engage in a serious discussion of race in America, we must begin not with the problems of black people but with the flaws of American society—flaws rooted in historic inequalities and longstanding cultural stereotypes. How we set up the terms for discussing racial issues shapes our perceptions and response to these issues. As long as black people are viewed as a "them," the burden falls on blacks to do all the "cultural" and "moral" work necessary

for healthy race relations. The implication is that only certain Americans can define what it means to be American—and the rest must simply "fit in."[16]

Thus my first strategy of choosing a lens with which to analyze and understand the varieties of African American religions as they engage in resistance to racism must not be allowed to restrict resistance to racism to African Americans or African American religions. But this raises an important question: how to generate discussions of racism that are inclusive of persons from other races and experiences and open up the possibility of transformation toward racial justice? The second strategy provides one way to address that question.

Second Strategy: Discovering and Discussing Definitions of Racism

Trying to talk about racism in ways that are honest, are civil, and help create an awareness of racism that is transformative toward racial justice rather than destructive is no small task. "Racism" is one of those big words like "love" or "morality" that we frequently use and often argue about. Yet the word carries so many meanings that participants in a discussion can easily argue past each other because they wrongly assume everyone shares the same experiences and understandings when in fact they do not. To build trust, the various experiences of the students need to be validated. But at the same time the students must be invited to see these experiences as limited, as reflecting their individual perspectives. In taking these steps together, classroom discussion may move toward transformation, as students and teacher arrive together at a richer understanding of the dynamics of racism, and thus the need for different responses to different aspects of racism. The strategy I have developed is one way this may be done.

I have learned that if I simply try to impose a definition or understanding of racism at the outset of a class (either my own or one drawn from a particular book or article), then students quickly see that I am imposing a view that tilts discussions in a particular direction. Students rightly resist such defining because they recognize, at least implicitly, how important a definition is in shaping what can then be discussed. On the other hand, if African American religions are to be analyzed in terms of responses to racism (or other racial issues are going to be discussed), then we need some parameters by which to understand racism. How can we arrive at those parameters in a way that respects student knowledge and experience but also leads to consideration of viewpoints beyond those limits?

I begin by asking students to write their own definitions of racism. Depending upon the class, I may also ask them to do further research and find other definitions of racism; or I may simply present to the students some different definitions or understandings of racism. If I take the latter approach, I may begin with a dictionary definition of *racism* such as the one in the *Merriam-Webster Dictionary*: "a belief that some races are by nature superior to others; also: discrimination based on such belief."[17] An initial discussion can analyze the adequacy of this definition. Does it express the realities of racism in the United States? How does this definition compare with their experiences and definitions? Why do they think there are such differences in definitions? After this comparison of definitions the door is opened to bring other definitions into play for further comparison and discussion. I offer the following definitions from different perspectives as a way into an expanded discussion about racism.

Fumitaka Matsuoka: Racism is "a system that promotes domination of the vulnerable by a privileged group in the economic, social, cultural, and intellectual spheres."[18] And: "Racism is sociologically defined as a structural and systemic deprivation of the human rights and dignity of people of color by those who are in positions of dominance. Racism is more than that, however. It is the negation of relation and the absence of direction for a collective human life due to the devaluation of life generated within societal institutions functioning as powers and principalities in our communal life."[19]

Nibs Stroupe and Inez Fleming: Racism refers to "a system of race" which is "a system of classifying people so that some gain access to opportunity and powers while others are denied access. The system of race rewards those called white and penalizes those called black and other people of darker colors."[20] And: "The system of race not only denies the humanity of people of darker color. It also works to assign responsibility for this racism not to whites, who created the system, but to the people of darker color, who suffer from it."[21]

Louise Derman Sparks and Carol Brunson Phillips: "Racism is an institutionalized system of economic, political, social, and cultural relations that ensures that one racial group has and maintains power and privilege over all others in all aspects of life. Individual participation in racism occurs when the objective outcome of behavior reinforces these relations, regardless of the subjective intent. Consequently, an individual may act in a racist manner unintentionally."[22]

Joseph Barndt: "Racism is clearly more than simple prejudice or bigotry. Everyone is prejudiced, but not everyone is racist. To be prejudiced means to have opinions without knowing the facts and to hold onto those opinions, even after contrary facts are known. To be racially prejudiced means to have distorted opinions about people of other races. Racism goes beyond prejudice. It is backed up by power. Racism is the power to enforce one's prejudices. More simply, racism is prejudice plus power."[23] And: "Racism structures a society so that the prejudices of one racial group are taught, perpetuated, and enforced to the benefit of the dominant group."[24]

Paul Kivel: "Racism is the institutionalization of social injustice based on skin color, other physical characteristics, and cultural and religious difference. White racism is the uneven and unfair distribution of power, privilege, land and material goods favoring white people."[25]

U.S. Catholic Bishops: "Racism is a sin that divides the human family, blots out the image of God among specific members of that family, and violates the fundamental dignity of those called to be children of the same Father. Racism is the sin that says some human beings are inherently superior and others essentially inferior because of race. It is the sin that makes racial characteristics the determining factor for the exercise of human rights. . . . The structures of our society are subtly racist, for these structures reflect the values which society upholds. They are geared to the success of the majority and the failure of the minority."[26]

Peter J. Paris: Racism is "a phenomenon that employs race as a proscriptive principle for denying rights and opportunities, that is, a principle of societal exclusion."[27]

George M. Frederickson: "Racism . . . is a matter of conscious belief and ideology, and can be distinguished from prejudice, which is a matter of attitude and feeling, and discrimination, which is a description of behavior."[28] Frederickson goes on to distinguish between an "explicit and rationalized racism" that is ideological, providing a conscious and consistent rationale for the superiority of one race over another, and an "implicit or societal racism." The latter can exist "if one racial groups acts as if another is inherently inferior . . . even if the group may not have developed or preserved a conscious and consistent rationale for its behavior."[29]

Susan E. Davis and Sister Paul Teresa Hennessee: "Race is a social construct. . . . 'Prejudice' results when an individual or group holds that some races are by nature superior to others. Racial discrimination based on the belief of racial superiority is 'bigotry.' 'Racism,' then, is the abuse of power by a 'racial' group that is more powerful than one or more other groups in order to exclude, demean, damage, control, or destroy the less powerful groups. Racism confers benefits upon the dominant group that includes psychological feelings of superiority, social privilege, economic position, or political power."[30]

James Newton Polling: Drawing from the Cornwall Collective and Patricia Collins, Polling uses the term "domination" to get at the dynamics of racism. "The 'matrix of domination' is a system of attitudes, behaviors and assumptions that objectifies human persons on the basis of [socially constructed categories such as race, gender, class, etc.], and that has the power to deny autonomy, access to resources and self-determination to those persons, while maintaining the values of the dominant society as the norm by which all else will be measured."[31]

George Yancy: "True racism is the degradation of others on the basis of race."[32] Yancy goes on to distinguish among different types of racism. (1) "Redneck racism," to begin with, is a system based upon the premise that "whites are superior to other races. Since this is the case, it is fair that whites are given extra privileges in society. Whites dominate society because they have natural abilities to run society while other races lack these abilities. . . . Usually when whites think about racism, they are thinking about redneck racism. This is useful since it allows them to escape the responsibility of dealing with racism in our society." Yancy also calls this "traditional racism."[33] (2) "Modern racism" assumes that "racial discrimination is a thing of the past. In modern America there is an even playing field. Racial minorities can compete in the marketplace as well as whites, and therefore, any measures that aid minorities are seen as unfair since they give racial minorities an unwarranted advantage. . . . Modern racism tends to give explanations for the continuing economic disparity between racial minorities and whites by focusing on factors other than racism."[34] (3) "Aversive racism" is emotionally based. "Like modern racism, aversive racism denies traditional racism. But the aversive racist still has emotional biases against individuals of other races. It is possible that one individual may be both a modern and an aversive racist."[35] (4) "Institutional discrimination" is defined as "the discrimination that is incorporated into the social structures and norms of our society."[36] Yancy writes: "Discrimination is something that the society does to a group of people. . . . Discrimination is not just an isolated incident but it is an entire system that works to the detriment of an entire group of people."[37]

In analyzing these different definitions and understandings of racism, I typically propose a series of questions to stimulate discussion with my students. I have used the following questions to encourage students to become aware of the differences among the definitions and to consider the significance of the differences in terms of both how racism is understood and what difference that makes for considering strategies of resistance to racism.

1. Which of these definitions of racism appear most similar to how you would define racism?
2. What, if any, changes would you make to your definition of racism after reading and discussing these definitions?
3. Which of these definitions do you find the most helpful? Why?
4. Which of these definitions do you find the least helpful? Why?
5. Do you find it helpful or not helpful to recognize different types of racism? Why or why not?
6. Why is it important to have a definition of racism?

Through discussion I also encourage students to identify the different types of racism indicated in the definitions. Typically, the first type of racism we identify is individual racism or personal prejudice. This is when a person holds attitudes, beliefs, or feelings or engages in behaviors that promote one's own racial group as superior to others and thus unfairly discriminates against another racial group or groups. In individual racism or personal prejudice, harmful attitudes and actions are enacted by one person and directed toward another individual or individuals because they belong to a racial group.

A second type of racism we often identify is cultural racism. In cultural racism the culture of one racial group is seen as superior and the culture of another racial group is actively ignored or denigrated. In discussing this type of racism students may be encouraged to consider what types of art, music, and literature dominate a school curriculum, or to consider cultural standards of beauty.

Finally, a third type of racism we eventually identify is institutional racism. This is evident when institutional structures, rules, organizations, laws, social policies, and customs maintain the superior or dominant status of a particular racial group. In institutional racism there is systemic oppression that enforces domination of one racial group over others. Here there is not only individual prejudice but also the power to enforce that prejudice through institutional means (government, economy, education, church, social clubs and organizations, etc.). Given the strength of the mythology of individualism in the United States, this type of racism is often the one most difficult for students of all races to acknowledge, let alone to understand. I have found Peggy McIntosh's checklist of white privilege as a helpful tool for opening the eyes of students to see the sometimes subtle and sometimes not so subtle way in which white dominance is built into our society.[38]

The key in all of these discussions is that the students recognize their own experiences as valid, as revealing some aspect of the realities of racism in our society, while at the same time seeing that their experience is not all-inclusive. White students are much more willing to openly discuss racism when they see how the advantage they accrue from a system of race is related to—but is not the same as—being individually prejudiced against blacks. Black students are much more willing to openly discuss racism when they identify the ongoing power of racism in our society in ways that do not simplistically present all black people as victims or all white people as enemies.

Using the Two Strategies Together

These two strategies facilitate discussions about both African American religions as, among other things, systems of resistance to racism, and to the enduring problem in our culture of racism itself. The first strategy offers a way to read and discuss African American religions as resources for resistance to racism. Wilmore's categories both provide helpful lenses through which to see and discuss patterns within the great variety of African American religions and may also open critical discussions of those very patterns. The second strategy, by examining different attempts to define racism, invites classroom discussion of the multifaceted dimensions of racism in this society. In conjunction with the first strategy, students are able to consider why different elements from African American religions are important in resisting racism. Used together, these strategies help students to use categories of analysis for understanding African American religions in terms of resistance to racism; they may also critically reflect upon their own relationship to African American religions and the racism of this society.

What are student responses to the strategies? In regard to the first strategy for discussing African American religions, student comments indicate recognition of gaining an ability to analyze diversity within African American religions and to see this as related to resistance to racism. One African American student said, "I didn't really understand the conflicts in my church before this class. Now I see them as built upon the way my community has fought for equality in this country." A white student observed, "Seeing the diversity in African American religion has made me think more about how racism runs through American life."

In terms of the unit on racism, student comments indicate appreciation of both recognizing their experiences and being challenged to develop a more inclusive view. One student wrote, "I learned how important it is to listen to others' arguments." Another said, "This class opens the boxes everyone tries to keep shut." A third observed, "The teacher is able to present this controversial information in a way in which he doesn't directly involve his opinion. Very effective!"

NOTES

1. The final chapter of *Black Religion and Black Radicalism* provides a clear overview of Wilmore's categories of analysis. See Gayraud S. Wilmore, *Black Religion and Black Radicalism*, 3rd ed. (Maryknoll, NY: Orbis Books, 1998), 253–281.

2. For an analytical summary of womanist theology see Stephanie Y. Mitchem, *Introducing Womanist Theology* (Maryknoll, NY: Orbis Books, 2002).

3. In particular see James Cone, *Martin and Malcolm and America: A Dream or a Nightmare* (Maryknoll, NY: Orbis Books, 1991), 3–17.

4. Hans A. Baer and Merrill Singer, *African-American Religion in the Twentieth Century: Varieties of Protest and Accommodation* (Knoxville: University of Tennessee Press, 1992), xxii.

5. Peter J. Paris, *The Social Teachings of the Black Churches* (Philadelphia: Fortress Press, 1985), xi.

6. Ibid., 29.

7. Ibid., 86.

8. Delores S. Williams, "Straight Talk, Plain Talk: Womanist Words about Salvation in a Social Context," in *Embracing the Spirit: Womanist Perspectives on Hope, Sal-*

vation, and Transformation, Emilie M. Townes, ed. (Maryknoll, NY: Orbis Books, 1997), 97–121.

9. Cornel West, *Race Matters* (Boston: Beacon Press, 1993), 11–14.

10. Ibid., 15.

11. Ibid., 16.

12. Ibid., 19.

13. Ibid., 19.

14. Ibid., 19.

15. W. E. B. Du Bois, *The Souls of Black Folk,* in *Three Negro Classics* (New York: Avon Books, 1965), 214–215.

16. Cornel West, *Race Matters* (Boston: Beacon Press, 1993), 3.

17. *The Merriam-Webster Dictionary* (New York: Simon and Schuster, 1974), 57.

18. Fumitaka Matsuoka, *The Color of Faith: Building Community in a Multiracial Society* (Cleveland: United Church Press, 1998), 3.

19. Ibid., 58.

20. Nibs Stroupe and Inez Fleming, *While We Run This Race: Confronting the Power of Racism in a Southern Church* (Maryknoll, NY: Orbis Books, 1995), 5.

21. Ibid., 22.

22. Louise Derman-Sparks and Carol Brunson Phillips, *Teaching/Learning Anti-Racism: A Developmental Approach* (New York: Columbia University Teachers College Press, 1997), 2.

23. Joseph Barndt, *Dismantling Racism: The Continuing Challenge to White America* (Minneapolis: Augsburg Press, 1991), 28.

24. Ibid., 29.

25. Paul Kivel, *Uprooting Racism: How White People Can Work for Racial Justice* (Gabriola Island, British Columbia, Canada: New Society, 1996), 2.

26. United States Catholic Bishops, *Brothers and Sisters All, Pastoral Letter on Racism* (Washington, DC: United States National Catholic Conference, 1979), 3.

27. Peter J. Paris, *The Social Teachings of the Black Churches* (Philadelphia: Fortress Press, 1985), 3–4.

28. George M. Frederickson, *The Arrogance of Race: Historical Perspectives on Slavery, Racism, and Social Inequality* (Hanover, NH: Wesleyan University Press, 1988), 189.

29. Ibid., 189.

30. Susan E. Davies and Sister Paul Teresa Hennessee, "What Is Racism?" in *Ending Racism in the Church,* Susan E. Davies and Sister Paul Teresa Hennessee, eds. (Cleveland: United Church Press, 1998), 1.

31. James Newton Poling, *Deliver Us from Evil: Resisting Racial and Gender Oppression* (Minneapolis: Fortress Press, 1996), 8.

32. George A. Yancy, *Beyond Black and White: Reflections on Racial Reconciliation* Grand Rapids, MI: Baker Books, 1996), 22.

33. Ibid., 26–27.

34. Ibid., 27–28, 29.

35. Ibid., 41.

36. Ibid., 43.

37. Ibid., 49.

38. Peggy McIntosh, "White Privilege and Male Privilege: A Personal Account of Coming to See Correspondence through Work in Women's Studies," in *Race, Class, and Gender: An Anthology,* Margaret L. Anderson and Patricia Hill Collins, eds. (Belmont, CA: Wadsworth, 1992).

REFERENCES

Anderson, Margaret L., and Patricia Hill Collins, eds. *Race, Class, and Gender: An Anthology.* Belmont, CA: Wadsworth, 1992.

Baer, Hans A., and Merrill Singer. *African-American Religion in the Twentieth Century: Varieties of Protest and Accommodation.* Knoxville: University of Tennessee Press, 1992.

Barndt, Joseph. *Dismantling Racism: The Continuing Challenge to White America.* Minneapolis: Augsburg Press, 1991.

Cone, James. *Martin and Malcolm and America: A Dream or a Nightmare.* Maryknoll, NY: Orbis Books, 1991.

Davies, Susan E., and Sister Paul Teresa Hennessee, eds. *Ending Racism in the Church.* Cleveland: United Church Press, 1998.

Derman-Sparks, Louise, and Carol Brunson Phillips, *Teaching/Learning Anti-Racism: A Developmental Approach.* New York: Columbia University Teachers College Press, 1997.

Du Bois, W. E. B. *The Souls of Black Folk,* in *Three Negro Classics.* New York: Avon Books, 1965.

Frederickson, George M. *The Arrogance of Race: Historical Perspectives on Slavery, Racism, and Social Inequality.* Hanover, NH: Wesleyan University Press, 1988.

Kivel, Paul. *Uprooting Racism: How White People Can Work for Racial Justice.* Gabriola Island, British Columbia, Canada: New Society, 1996.

Matsuoka, Fumitaka. *The Color of Faith: Building Community in a Multiracial Society.* Cleveland: United Church Press, 1998.

Mitchem, Stephanie Y. *Introducing Womanist Theology.* Maryknoll, NY: Orbis Books, 2002.

Newton Poling, James. *Deliver Us FROM Evil: Resisting Racial and Gender Oppression.* Minneapolis: Fortress Press, 1996.

Paris, Peter J. *The Social Teachings of the Black Churches.* Philadelphia: Fortress Press, 1985.

Stroupe, Nibs, and Inez Fleming. *While We Run This Race: Confronting the Power of Racism in a Southern Church.* Maryknoll, NY: Orbis Books, 1995.

Townes, Emilie M. ed. *Embracing the Spirit: Womanist Perspectives on Hope, Salvation, and Transformation.* Maryknoll, NY: Orbis Books, 1997.

United States Catholic Bishops, *Brothers and Sisters All, Pastoral Letter on Racism.* Washington, DC: United States National Catholic Conference, 1979.

West, Cornel. *Race Matters.* Boston: Beacon Press, 1993.

Wilmore, Gayraud S. *Black Religion and Black Radicalism.* 3rd ed. Maryknoll, NY: Orbis Books, 1998.

Yancy, George A. *Beyond Black and White: Reflections on Racial Reconciliation.* Grand Rapids, MI: Baker Books, 1996.

13

Teaching African Religions at a Traditionally White Institution in the South

Ralph C. Watkins

The goal of knowledge arising from love is the reunification and re-construction of broken selves and worlds. A knowledge born of compassion aims not at exploiting and manipulating creation but at reconciling the world to itself.

—Parker Palmer, *To Know As We Are Known*

Teaching "African American Religions" is an exercise in love. I love Africans and I love teaching. What I find in teaching this course are bruised, battered, and broken members of the African Diaspora looking for missing links in their identity chains. They come looking for something but not knowing quite how to call or label what it is they are in search of. Many have been given simplistic answers to religious questions in their very conservative Christian traditions. Teaching the course calls on the teacher to love the students through the transitions they will make over the next sixteen weeks. This course has to be seen as the beginning of a journey. It must be framed as a process of reunification, reconstruction, and remembering of broken selves. Compassion must fuel this endeavor, as the teacher works in the community reconciling students to their roots as they explore the foundations of African American religiosity. Teaching African American Religions is a love child.

Teaching "African Americans Religions" in the South, specifically, in Augusta, Georgia, presents a unique set of challenges. The challenges are linked to space, place, and the religious history that forms the South. My institution is located in the Bible Belt, the haven of Southern Baptist dominance. I find myself teaching undergraduate students who come to class looking for a Sunday school lesson. They walk into the room expecting me to preach, and they are confronted with the root of African American religion: African traditional religion. From the Vodun to the African American Pentecostal movement, there is a thread of continuity. When the parallels are introduced between Vodun and Pentecostalism, the students' eyes brighten immediately. Much care is needed to keep this spark of interest alive, to make it grow. The contrast between what they believe religion to be and what they are about to experience over the next sixteen weeks creates in them an experience of intense educational dissonance. Because they are about to be shaken, it is important that I remain sensitive to what the students are going through so that I can nurture them through this process, creating a balance of challenge and safety.

Being in a predominantly white institution means that "African American Religions" is one of those "black classes." The students who sign up for the course are 90 percent African American, and the remainder involves primarily white students—often, the Eminems of the campus—who consider themselves liberal or "down" with African Americans. The key difference between the white students and the African American students is simple. The white students come in admitting their lack of knowledge concerning African American religions, while many African Americans students feel like they "know this stuff." One of the first goals of the course is to help African American students see how much they do not know so as to establish their desire to learn. If they are allowed to hold onto the idea that they "know this stuff," they treat the material with disrespect. They have to be impressed immediately with the complexities of the rich African roots of African American religions. Taking them back to Africa early and often tends to establish a common ground of unknowns among the students—an immediate need to read, learn, and grow. We start with what they do not know to establish an impetus to grow in the learning community.

I begin: "This class will not be about your Grandmamma's church Sunday School class. The title of this class is real African American religions!" The plurality of African American religious life must be stressed, with an emphasis on the African root of African American religiosity. For many African Americans, "if it ain't Baptist it ain't religion." The Southern Baptists dominate in both black and white communities in the South; therefore, the students come to the classroom with their defenses up about anything that is not part of their Baptist heritage. When I mention Vodun or ancient Africa, they rise up in protest. Students are quick to condemn African ways of knowing and religious dimensions. They fight to remain closed to this discussion. They try to quote the Bible as a defense against the new subject matter they see coming. This defensive posture has to be broken down if they are to learn and grow. They have to be shaken up in order to be opened up.

To start the class with the intent to shake them out of their shoes is, perhaps, pedagogically debatable—but it works. The Southern setting and the religious orientation they bring to class have to be introduced into the dialogue immediately: as the syllabus is reviewed and as the texts for the course are discussed. It is my goal for them to leave that first class reviewing that syllabus and those texts and asking if I am crazy. It is important for them to ponder whether they should drop the class. It is important for them to buy into this journey. Indeed, I introduce the class as journey, playing on a familiar religious trope. Students must accept that they are starting on a journey to learn about the African American religious experience—a journey, probably, unlike any they have undertaken before. Key values and beliefs they bring to the class will be examined. African roots to their religious practice will be identified. This class will challenge, as does no other.

Challenge is balanced by support. I reassure them that I will be the guide on this journey. My promise is this: "I will never leave you out there, and I will always be available to talk to you about the class and what you are learning." They have to know that we are going on an adventure together, and they must know that I will be their loving and challenging guide. Therefore, I want them to leave that first class with a question: "Do I want to go?"

The first class period becomes a key point of orientation. Upsetting expectations, as I will do throughout the course, I take my time in that first class. We do not get out early. I want them to be fully informed about the trip I am inviting them to take. I do not want the work of the class to sneak up on them in six or eight weeks. That would be unfair. Students who take this course in this setting must at least be willing to be disturbed.

The dissonance continues as the work of the course begins. I take them back to Africa. It is important for them to take the journey back across the Middle Passage to realize that African religious life did not begin in the Americas. To convince them that Africans had a past prior to coming to the Americas is the start of this journey. As simple as that sounds, it is one of the most disturbing, profound, and key lessons on this journey. They must go back to Africa!

Students in the Bible Belt know little African history and have virtually no African religious historical framework from which to enter and with which to center critical discussion of African American religiosity. An assumption that must be challenged is that Africans were completely robbed of their cultural and religious history upon coming to America. The common assumption held by students is that the African past was wiped out. It is important to correct this assumption and to make this discussion personal and relevant. African American students tend to come to class questioning the use of the term *African American*. They are quick to say, "I ain't never been to Africa. I don't know nothin' about Africa. I'm just black." My response is, "Do you know your great-great-great-great-great-grandmother?" Their response is "No." I say, "Well, just because you don't know her, does that mean that some of her is not in you? The fact that you don't know her, does that mean she is not your great-grandmother?" In this discussion, I want to emphasize the social fact that African Americans can claim Africa as their Motherland. This is a process I call, utilizing W. E. B. Du Bois's idea of double consciousness, "double acculturation." To engage the students in this process prepares them to understand the doubleness of culture in slaveholding society.

During this first phase, I start each class with George Dukes's song "The Ancient Source." This song takes them back to Africa as they are led in discussion about what the "ancient source" is and who has access to the ancient source. The song claims that the ancients are calling us and that they are inside of us. This part of the course is experiential: students have to feel. The teaching must speak to the heart, not just the head, and this takes on the form of a ministry. The joy and pain the students are experiencing must be touched and honored. They are in a recovery phase, and they must be treated almost as if they are in therapy. During this period classroom discussions are intense. I am careful to take time at the beginning of each class to get them focused and settled to enter into the learning moment. Care must also be taken to provide closure for each class: a reflective song also works at this point. I prefer to use the Stevie Wonder cut off of the *Bamboozled* soundtrack called "Some Years Ago." Students have to sit and listen to the song with hands on the table—no packing book bags, no preparing papers to be turned in. They sit still and listen. These reflective moments are necessary as they digest what they have experienced in this intense learning session and transition back to their ordinary worlds.

Students have to be nurtured in this early process. Their religious foundations are being challenged. All they thought was true about God and the church is being reexamined. This course goes to the heart of their value systems. They are asking all kinds of questions about identity, their religion, their God, and their faith. The first few weeks of the course cannot be taken lightly. They must be ushered into the process of remembering.

A book like *Africanisms in American Culture*, edited by Joseph Holloway, helps to facilitate the opening weeks of the course. African American and white students must be educated about what Africanisms are and about their existence in American culture. The process of double acculturation, as I suggested earlier, is the centerpiece of phase 1 of the course. I confront students with the sociological fact that Africans did not come to America as passive agents to be acted upon. Rather, Africans were forcefully brought to America, and they fought to hold onto their G(g)od(s), their culture, and their history and to carve out an identity in this strange land.

The point must be made that one thing Africans had were their memories. They fought hard to hold onto these memories, and they appealed to ritual and religion to exercise and keep fit that memory. Moreover, they shared their values and cultural heritage with the whites they encountered. Whites were not immune to learning from African Americans. Whites were as affected, culturally, by Africans as Africans were by them. This process of double acculturation appears obvious on the surface, but it is a point that few students have pondered. They have acquired the view that Africans were almost brainwashed and that they left Africa in Africa. This myth has to be challenged, and it has to be made personal for the students so that they can hold onto this finding throughout the course.

To make this happen, I again use an experiential exercise. I ask the students to do an assignment in which they reflect on being stolen from Augusta. As they enter the parking lot to go home today, a slave trader is going to capture them to fly them to a foreign land to be held in slavery. They must write a paper answering the following questions.

1. When you get on the plane what physical things will you have with you?
2. What beliefs about God will you take with you?
3. What religious ways would you take with you?
4. What church songs or other songs would you remember?
5. Who would you pray to?
6. What would your faith be (Christian, Muslim, Seventh Day-Adventist, etc.) when you got off the plane?
7. What language would you speak?
8. What would you remember most about your homeland?
9. What would your name be when you get off the plane?
10. How would you try to remember of Augusta?

This assignment helps them work through the first phase of the course in a more personal way. They see how it makes sense that Africans did not forget. Even going through the seasoning islands and in slavery itself, Africans, dismembered from their homelands, still remembered.

This assignment is very practical and very powerful. We spend the next class period talking about this assignment in light of what they have read thus far on Africanism in America. The power of remembering is brought full circle in this discussion. I ask the class to look in their wallets, purses, and book bags and find those things they would look at on the plane to help them remember. For this class there are no reading assignments. The students share each other's papers and talk about the power of remembering.

I pay special attention, in this assignment, to religious memory and the construction of gods and religion. The walk here has to be delicate because the territory is treacherous. Even though students are learning how Africans remembered, in the back of students' minds is still the idea that, at some point, Africans become "fully Christianized." They are looking forward to the end of the fairy tale in which everybody lives happily ever after in "Christian America." Therefore the tension of double acculturation must be woven in throughout the discussion in the course.

Location plays a significant role in this problem. Remember: we are in the South, at a traditionally white conservative institution. There is no African American studies department, no African American studies major or minor. Most students who sign up for the course admit that they want to know more about the African American church. When pushed by what they mean by "the African American church," they respond that they are talking about Christian denominations. They come looking for information about "the church" and not an exploration of African American religions from a sociological perspective.

The history and identity of my student population also has an influence. Even though this classroom, historically, has been racially mixed and even though the African American students outnumber the white students ten to one, the African American students are defensive. They want to defend their ancestors and elders from the accusation of being "heathen." They come to this class to find out what good Christians their people have been. On the other hand, the white students are even more perplexed than the African American students because they do not understand the struggle I am having with my African American students in convincing them of the worth of African roots to their identity and faith.

My identity is also a factor. Being an African American, male professor who is a known Baptist preacher creates a set of unique dynamics in my courses. Many of my African American students see this as a safe class. They come expecting me to be Reverend Watkins. When we start the journey back to Africa and trace the beliefs of Africa as forming a basis for African American religious belief and practice, African American students have two reactions. The first reaction is to deny the reality they are reading about and talking about. The second is to react negatively; they are almost hostile. They come to class unsettled about what they have read in, for example, the Holloway book. The class discussion is helpful, but on their faces is this shame that this is taking place in front of white students. It is as if they wished they did not know.

This shame is linked to the shame of Africa and the shame of slavery. The majority of African American students have yet to embrace the African Continent. They have yet to learn about and, thereby, take pride in Africa's values and religious history. They have yet to see the beauty of a people who survived and flourished under terrible conditions. Therefore, they resist what they are learning because it is so new, forcing them to rethink positions they and many of their family members have held for years. Even with creative assignments, this resistance tends to live throughout the course. I whittle away at it, but I must always recognize its existence.

A key to making this class work is realizing how important the class discussions are for the processing of the material. Attendance and some type of required participation is essential for students to successfully negotiate this journey. How can I guide them if they do not come to class? One-on-one conversation is also key. I think that it is important for them to visit me during office hours to talk about the course. I schedule, for each student, a fifteen-to thirty-minute meeting that is a part of the course requirements. Each student must come by and sit with me by himself or herself. No friends are allowed to accompany the student in the meeting. It is important that they have a safe place to talk with me about what they are experiencing in the class. I want to know what students are feeling and experiencing. In these meetings, I can acknowledge to each person that I am pushing them to learn about and to see African American religion in a way many have never explored before and reassert that this class is not like their other classes. This class does not speak only to the head; I want them to acknowledge and to deal with the emotive side of the class. I therefore take a week before the midpoint of the semester to meet with the students. It is time-consuming but necessary. I then take one class period at midterm to talk to the class as a whole about how the course is going.

As we enter the second half of the course, I begin to see a greater divergence between African American and white students. African American students and white students have very distinctly different views about what they are learning in the class and how they are approaching the material. White students struggle with what to do with what they are learning. They take two stances. On the one side are the papers, written during the second half of the course, reflecting the attitude "I always knew something was different about black folk." And on the other side are the white students who approach the class like a neat archaeological dig. They see Africans and Africanisms as exotic, something to be gazed at. They are detached from the class and sit in as non-involved observers. They do not enter discussion with passion. It is "all academic" to them. Both stances are, partly, self-protective. When they see the emotion flying around the room among their African American colleagues, they feel ill-equipped to contribute or get involved. But this holding back may also involve negative judgment. Their minds are made up, "I told you these folk weren't really Christians: pagans, pagans, pagans."

I have to work hard to get these students involved and to arouse their passion about African American religions. It is important to let them feel what they feel but to get them to experience the course. They are quick to suggest that because they are not African American they cannot contribute to the discussion. On the one hand, they see this as an academic exercise; on the other, they see being a member of the African American Diaspora as a requirement to speak authentically on the topic. I point out this contradiction and that this is packed with serious implications concerning epistemology. It is packed with suggestions that only African Americans can know this stuff, which could imply that only whites know the other stuff. You know: stuff like sociological theory. Whites feel like they can't speak in this class, but they never hesitate to speak in classes like sociology of religion. Why? If they speak freely in sociology of religion but not in African American religions, what does this say about their view of African American students and teachers who speak in other classes? Do they not know like whites know? I have to make sure the students know that I am not teaching as an ordained minister, that this class is founded on the experiences of the students in the class—particularly as they interact with the scholarship pertaining to our subject—and that all are invited to experience the class as equals.

As the course progresses and as we move through the second phase of the course looking to the third and final phase, we have to look more carefully at African American religion. Students now have an empathy as well as a new set of analytical lenses, and I ask them to use this new set of lenses, set with African bifocals, to see what of Africa remains in African American worship and religious practice. We start by reading Will Coleman's *Tribal Talk*; we move from there to Anthony Pinn's *Varieties of African American Religion*; up ahead, the womanists Cheryl Townsend Gilkes and Kelly Brown-Douglas are waiting to talk to us through the final weeks of the course. Much of what Coleman does in his book returns us to the South. So we go out to see what we can see as we visit authentic worshiping communities looking for African roots. I also use Will Coleman's *Cross Currents* article, "'Amen' and 'Ashe,'" which charts the roots of African American worship in the Christian context back to Vodun. This disturbs them, but I challenge them to see if it has any truth in it as we move to our field study.

Now, they are at a turning point. It is time now for the first of two church visits to prove our points and to get the white students to feel the religion. We visit the largest and loudest Pentecostal-type church in the city. I need them to see people being ridden by Shango and Damballah. They need to witness spirit possession, shouting, dancing, laying on of hands, and prayer in the spirit. We then come back and watch the film *Sankofa*, and they are at a turning point. Prior to the visits, I do a lecture based on *Old Ship of Zion: The Afro-Baptist Ritual in the African Diaspora*, by Walter F. Pitts, Jr. This is a nonthreatening way to bring them to terms with the African influences present in African American worship. They enter the churches with new lenses, and they see things they have never recognized before. They are excited about what they see, and this is a high point in the course. During the worship experience, we sit together, and immediately after the experience, we remain at that site, and they complete a one-page reflection. After the reflection, they are dismissed.

We find that the next class is a class of connections. The students have made a major turn. Their frowns and discomfort have turned to smiles of joy. They are seeing the connection in a real-life way. They see what has survived, and they celebrate what appears to be Africanism. What started out as disturbing is now healing, as the African American students in particular are being put back together again. The church visits are critical to this process.

As we leave the churches and come back to the classroom, we move to looking at the role of gender and sexism in the construction of African American religions. This is a perfect time to broach this discussion of sexism in the church, so we start reading Cheryl Townsend Gilkes's book *If It Wasn't for the Women*. We use the church visits as the basis for this discussion. The final phase is tough, but it is important for students to experience it. I save it for last because I want them to leave with this issue in the front of their minds. Gilkes's work is read in concert with Kelly Brown-Douglas's book *The Black Church and Sexuality*. These two books help students think about the role of sex, gender, and sexism in the construction of African American religion. The powerful role of women in leading the Black Church from the pew is the biggest revelation students have. By this time in the course, students have regained an African comfort with their religious traditions. They have identified the Africanism in African American religiosity, and now they have to confront the sexism in the church.

The initial response is to fall back on outdated, sexist interpretations of the Bible. After carefully challenging this construct, students move. The class discussions are filled with sexist constructs that are as rooted in Southern culture as racism. Unsettling as the discussions are, students tend to respond in a healthy way. I stick to the text in these discussions and do very little inserting of myself. I make them fight with Gilkes and Douglas. This forces them to engage the text and take the arguments seriously. As they progress through these readings, these authors become their favorites. We end the class with students writing a letter to the favorite author they read in the class. Cheryl Townsend Gilkes always gets the most letters. Students praise her work. A work they initially fought they now embrace. The key here for students is that I let them know up front that it is hard for them to hear the voices of African American females because they have not been taught to listen to their voices. Most of what they read is written by white males, and as a result their ears are tuned to a different frequency. I force them to tune in, and once they tune in, they hear what the sisters are saying and they can't help but say "Amen!"

The final project in the course is a paper charting the students' journeys. I ask them to go back to that first day in class and to walk through the semester. I reissue a copy of the syllabus, annotated to show how we actually traversed the reading, including changes, canceled classes, and all else that impeded the initial plan of the course. I ask them to review every class session, go back and touch the readings, review the Power Point presentations, reexperience the songs we listened to, the movies we watched, the clips we talked about, the assignments that were graded and returned, and the two field trips. In this journey of remembrance, there must be an entry for every week, an entry that both charts the course and tells me what they remember. They have to answer the following questions for each week.

1. What stood out?
2. What touched you?
3. What will stay with you?
4. What will you share with others?

These four questions can be answered directly or in paragraph form. The final pages of the paper are dedicated to one question: How will you continue this journey? This is the most powerful part of the paper. Students show how they have bought into the journey. They talk about their quest for truth and gaining more knowledge about the African Diaspora. They talk about the project of remembering. It is a perfect closure to the course.

The final presentation is a two-minute reflection. Upon entering the classroom, as they bring their final papers to class, each student receives one 3 × 5 index card. Students are asked to write one thing from their paper that they want to share with the class. This is called our final offering. For this class, the lights are turned down low. Candles are burning, and soft music is playing. I call on the first student; then, each student calls on the next student. At the end of the class, I come and share my offering, and we stand and listen to "The Ancient Source." Class is dismissed, but it never ends. This closing ritual is sometimes teary but always touching. The class has spoken to the head and the heart, and I believe students are forever changed.

REFERENCES

Brown-Douglas, Kelly. *Sexuality and the Black Church: A Womanist Perspective.* Maryknoll, NY: Orbis Books, 1999.
Coleman, Will. *Tribal Talk: Black Theology, Hermeneutics, and African/American Ways of "Telling the Story."* University Park: Pennsylvania State University Press, 1999.
———. "'Amen' and 'Ashe': African American Protestant Worship and Its Western Ancestor." *Cross Currents* 52, 2 (2002): 158–164.
Duke, George. "The Ancient Source." *Cool.* Warner Brothers Records, 2000.
Gerina, Haile, dir. *Sankofa.* Mypheduh Films, 1993.
Gilkes, Cheryl Townsend. *If It Wasn't for the Women.* Maryknoll, NY: Orbis Books, 2000.
Holloway, Joseph, ed. *Africanisms in American Culture.* Bloomington: Indiana University Press, 1991.
Palmer, Parker. *To Know As We Are Known.* San Francisco: HarperSanFrancisco, 1983.
Pinn, Anthony. *Varieties of African Amercan Religious Experience.* Minneapolis: Fortress, 1998.
Pitts, Jr., Walter F. *Old Ship of Zion: The Afro-Baptist Ritual in the African Diaspora.* New York: Oxford, 1996.
Wonder, Stevie. "Some Years Ago." *Bamboozled* soundtrack. Polygram Records, 2000.

14

Watching for Religion and Race at the Movies

Theodore Louis Trost

Twenty-first-century women and men are watchers. We are *homo spectator*. Generally speaking, we connect most immediately to our world and to other worlds through images, particularly those that appear on movie and television screens. All sorts of people appear in American households through the medium of television and its various accessories—videos, DVDs, computer games—and we invite friends and family members into our homes to watch these images with us. Consequently, the contemporary American student comes to college particularly well prepared to watch. This is not the same thing as "watchfulness," mind you, but it is a start.

The main purpose of religious studies as an academic discipline, it is frequently asserted, is to make "the strange familiar and the familiar strange."[1] This is what I try to do in my course, "Introduction to Religion in America: Religion Observed in Popular Film"— with particular emphasis on making the familiar strange. The class has three clusters of concern: religion, movies, and America. All of these initially impress students as familiar topics. The fact that movie-watching is a central feature of the class suggests to many students that the class will be not only fun but, perhaps more significantly, easy (and there are certain pedagogical advantages to this presumed familiarity). However, during the course of the semester I endeavor to complicate the conversations about these interrelated topics so that, by the end of the semester, in the words of T. S. Eliot, we "arrive where we started / And know the place for the first time." Or, to invoke Joni Mitchell, we recognize that we "really don't know [the place] at all."[2]

Race is not the main focus of this course, at least not initially. But inevitably where normative claims are made—in valorizing what constitutes religion, what conventions connote the popular, and what narrative trajectories count as key ingredients of the American story—students come to understand that race matters. In this chapter, after a review of the issues at stake in the introduction to religious studies course and a description of the operative method, I focus on race as a crucial concern in the interpretation of three movies: *Being There*, *The Color Purple*, and *Daughters of the Dust*.

Peculiarities of the Introductory "Religion and" Class

A casual perusal of any introductory religious studies textbook gives the reader a sense of the difficulties involved in defining the term "religion." Definitions that displace the burden of clarification onto explanatorily empty concepts like "the sacred," "spirituality," or "the duty we owe to our creator and the manner for discharging it" do not resolve the problem. It is sufficient to note for the purposes of this chapter that the contested nature of the concept of religion is a fact I introduce to my students from the outset of this course.[3] I do not attempt to resolve the contest in this class; rather, the problem accompanies religious studies majors, in particular, throughout their undergraduate careers. We begin, then, with assumptions that students bring to the concept of religion and the operative hypothesis (given the subject matter of the class) that, whatever else religion might be, it has to do with watching; more important, religion includes a certain kind of watchfulness that involves—but is not limited to—the physical act of seeing.

Many traditional stories and practices emphasize watchfulness; I mention two in this regard. First, consider the story of Jesus in the Garden of Gethsemane as developed by the gospel writer Mark (14:32–52). After a satisfying, if somewhat ominous, dinner in an upper room, Jesus and his disciples retire to Gethsemane. Jesus separates himself from the group and tells three of his followers to "keep watch" or to "be watchful." The verb here is *gregoreo*, which the Revised Standard Version translates as "watch" and the New Revised Standard Version as "keep awake." The issue is not so much the difference between keeping awake and watching as it is the quality of the activity in which one is engaged. To apply this remark first of all to the existential situation of students in my class, it is not enough to simply be awake when a particular film is shown in class (though for some scholars who work twenty or more hours a week at part-time jobs, staying awake for two hours in a darkened room is a kind of accomplishment); the key is to be fully awake to the possibilities of the film as text (that is, to be "watchful"). As a biblical theme, the concern is for a quality of discernment that enables one to be watchful, to be discerning in the interpretation of a variety of signs so that one can perform a reading of the entire text—can "actualize the semantic [or semiotic] potential" of the narrative—in order to offer up a testimony of what one has heard or "seen."[4]

A second kind of watchfulness is *darshan*, an activity that figures prominently in Hinduism. According to Diana Eck, *darshan* is the single most common and significant element of Hindu worship. It is a kind of communication in which one sees and is seen by the deity. It is an exchange, therefore: a dialogue between the god and humanity. As the term has developed over time, *darshan* has also come to refer to the various systems of philosophy in the Indian tradition. However, according to Eck, it is misleading to think of these as "systems" or "schools" of philosophical thought. Rather, they are "points of view" that represent "the varied phases of truth viewed from different angles of vision."[5] Eck points out the relationship between seeing and knowing, noting that in the Hindu tradition, as in the "West," one who knows all (or at least a great deal) is called a "seer."

Central to this course are six or seven visual texts, most of which have proved quite successful at the box office during the last twenty-five years. The films are selected for their portrayals of certain kinds of characteristically American heroes and the variety of ways "religion" is incorporated into the narratives. Consider, for example, the famous testimonial made by Annie Savoy (played by Susan Sarandon) in the opening sequence of *Bull Durham*, during which Annie announces that she worships at the "church of baseball." In addition to the films I will discuss directly here, other films viewed in this course in the past have included *Atlantic City, Beloved, The Big Chill, Blade Runner, Bull Durham, Crimes and Misdemeanors, Dogma, Eve's Bayou, Grand Canyon, Magnolias, The Matrix, Tender Mercies,* and the *Wizard of Oz.* About half of the class time is spent watching and discussing the films. The other half is spent interrogating a variety of theoretical texts that frame the matter of interpretation in relation to religion and film. Students are expected to incorporate these theoretical works into their essays.[6]

While seeing clearly, or watchfulness, is a quality associated with various religious traditions, the ability to carefully interpret texts is also a classic liberal arts skill, one that most undergraduate colleges deem desirable. Naturally, this is the case at my university, where a number of courses in the religious studies department function as "service courses"; these courses help students to develop certain desirable skills (critical thinking and writing) or they address concerns (multiculturalism, tolerance) with which it is thought that an educated person in the twenty-first century should be familiar. My course on religion and film in America falls into this category. It attracts students from across the university who might not otherwise set foot in a religious studies classroom, thereby providing service to the college of arts and sciences, as majors from other departments gain skills and insights that will help them in their other academic pursuits.

But the course is also often an introduction to the discipline of religious studies for a number of students who could become religious studies majors. There is pressure at my university at the moment to produce more religious studies majors. Indeed, a commission of educators (or business people—the distinction is not always apparent) in the state has determined that in order for a department to be "viable," it must produce 7.5 graduating majors per year. My purpose here is not to debate the merits of the system but to note that there are material reasons why we feel encouraged to attract the attention of students and keep them interested. The approach my department has taken, in general, has been to nurture a "learning community." As opposed to offering an introductory course to hundreds of students (though, importantly, we do offer a few high-enrollment courses), we try to keep class size below thirty-five and preferably closer to twenty, emphasizing student participation in seminar-style courses with a great deal of give-and-take among students and with the professor. This, we have determined, is the best way to establish a "niche" inside a university system that can, at times, seem impersonal.

Like Chauncey Gardener in the film *Being There*, students "like to watch." And so the interpretation of movies becomes an effective way to introduce them to the "contest of meanings" that is at the heart of the study of religion. The goals of the course include giving students tools to explore the ways in which religious rhetoric and imagery are used in popular media; to enable students to critically evaluate these uses and see how they are incorporated into master narratives that affirm cultural and religious values while, at the same time (which may also be the same thing), advancing nationalistic, racial, gender, and class interests; and to question the extent to which these narratives are simply misappropriations of religion, or if religion—far from being able to be separated off into the realms of secular and sacred—is inevitably implicated in these activities for better or for worse.

Narratives: Myth, Parable, and the American Adam

In *The American Adam* (1955), his classic work of intellectual history, R. W. B. Lewis points to a particular narrative paradigm, or myth, that arises in the nineteenth century and informs the cultural debate, or the debate about culture, in America thereafter. Building on essays by Ralph Waldo Emerson, Lewis acknowledges the parties of memory and hope as contesting partners in this debate and adds a third party to the mix, the party of irony, which he also calls the party of tragedy. Lewis's categories are still exceedingly useful for analyzing contemporary films, and we spend some time dissecting Lewis's allusive and elusive work during the early weeks of the course.[7] These debates about interpretation become the focus of our classroom discussions for the rest of the semester.

The central figure in Lewis's narrative paradigm is the so-called "American

Adam." In a multitude of manifestations (Lewis points to Melville's "Billy Budd," Hawthorne's "Hester Prynn," and Ellison's "Invisible Man," among others; but characters like Dorothy in the *Wizard of Oz*, Celie in *The Color Purple*, or "Neo" in the *Matrix* trilogy fit the paradigm just as easily), the Adamic character undertakes what Lewis considers a particularly American adventure. This hero is the embodiment of America's self-understanding and "new habits"; he or she is "an individual emancipated from history, happily bereft of ancestry, untouched and undefiled by the usual inheritances of family and race; an individual standing alone, self-reliant and self-propelling, ready to confront whatever await[s] with the aid of [one's] own inherent resources."[8]

Obviously this is not an inclusive definition of the American hero. A cruel irony tinges the phrase "emancipated from history"; then again, this master narrative happily skips over the problematic phrase "the usual inheritances of family and race" as if these were settled and insignificant matters in the construction of the myth of America. Still, precisely because we are dealing specifically with myth-making here, the pattern enunciated by Lewis is both useful and provocative. To resort to popular music for a moment by way of illustration, the pattern can support a diverse cast of characters. Consider Chuck Berry's "Johnny B. Goode" (a "country boy" who leaves the back woods of Louisiana to gain fame and fortune as a rock-and-roll star); or the young man in Stevie Wonder's "Living for the City" (who leaves "small-town Mississippi" in search of fame and fortune in New York); or Joni Mitchell's autobiographical song cycle *Hejira* (with its Kerouacian homage to the road and incessant quest for home); or, more recently, Steve Earle's provocative "John Walker's Blues" (in which the protagonist undergoes a typical, individualistic, wholly American quest for meaning even as he joins the partisans fighting for the Taliban in Afghanistan).[9] This pattern also underlies the conception of the hero in the stories that Hollywood produces. Just as Lewis leaves out certain nonparadigmatic stories from consideration as part of American myth-making, so does Hollywood. In particular, movies deal in a kind of shorthand directed toward mass audiences that either excludes minority stories or reduces minority characters to stereotypes in the service of an "American monomyth."[10] This course looks at what *is* there: in particular, the religious rhetoric and imagery that is marshaled to construct the Adamic hero who, more often than not, metamorphoses into a Jesus-like hero (Lewis's term for the process is "apotheosis"). The course is also on the lookout, as it were, for what is *not* there: what stories are left out, sublimated, or domesticated as myth is made and remade.

The license to pursue what is not (obviously) there comes from the critical possibilities of the parabolic. In his insightful study *The Dark Interval*, the biblical scholar John Dominic Crossan locates parable along a continuum that begins with myth and ends in parable. For Crossan, myth is both a paradigmatic narrative (resonating here with Eliade and R. W. B. Lewis) and, perhaps more significantly, a story that mediates or obfuscates the contradictions of experience (drawing specifically on the work of Levi-Strauss). As a narrative construct, parable has a parasitic relation to myth. A parable, as Crossan describes it, is not simply an illustration or a fable with a concluding moral. Its primary function is to subvert myth. The parabolic, then, is one step beyond satire. Whereas myth, as it were, "builds world," satire ridicules—and parable destroys—myth. Some parables merely destroy—as in the parables of Kafka and, to a lesser extent, Borges. Others (Crossan would signal some of Jesus' parables in this regard) begin to offer an alternative worldview—a different way of being in and seeing (perhaps a way of "seeing through") the world.[11]

Entire films can be interpreted along these lines. To anticipate a later discussion, it could be argued that *Being There* functions as satire, *The Color Purple* as myth, and *Daughters of the Dust* as parable. This is not to say that *Being There* is only a satire; it also contains the parabolic. And *The Color Purple*, at times, promotes what bell hooks might call "a counterhegemonic narrative challenging the conventional structures of domination that uphold and maintain white supremacist capitalist patriarchy."[12] Significantly, hooks goes on to explain that multiple standpoints are often expressed in the same story. Beyond genre considerations, the parabolic can also be viewed as a mode of interpretation. Here the focus is on the ways religious rhetoric, concepts, and imagery are used to reinforce myth or authorize the majority culture's social values.[13] A penchant for the parabolic refuses to accept—but rather, submits to radical interrogation—the conventions of mythical practice.

Three Types of Criticism: Theological, Mythological, and Ideological

Myth, parable, and satire are story genres. I also suggested earlier that parable might be adopted as a mode of interpretation or what I would prefer to call in the following discussion a type of criticism. As with bell hooks's observation that multiple standpoints can be found in the same film, multiple critical perspectives can be brought to bear upon a single work. This is, after all, the quality of "watching" suggested by Eck in her discussion of *darshan* as a tradition of truth-seeking that honors multiple angles of vision. In making this assertion, I am applying the work of Eck and hooks to the critical approaches developed in the popular textbook *Screening the Sacred: Religion, Myth, and Ideology in Popular American Film*, edited by Joel W. Martin and Conrad E. Ostwald, Jr. (1995). Although recourse to the word "sacred" might suggest a discrete realm of "the religious," a sui generis preserve at a remove from the rest of life (i.e., the secular), this is not what Martin and Ostwald have in mind when they use the term. Instead, they conceive of religion as "a semiautonomous domain of culture deserving serious academic study." Citing Daniel Pals, they contend that scholars should "press for religious explanations when presented with religious data." Religious data in film, by this reckoning, include such things as "traditional religious teaching or values," "common forms of expression normally associated with religion," "religious symbols," and so forth.[14]

The three types of criticism Martin and Ostwald develop are theological, mythological, and ideological. Theological criticism assumes that certain films are best understood as "an elaboration on or the questioning of a particular religious tradition, text, or theme."[15] In the American context the religious tradition tends to be Christianity. While theological criticism can degenerate into a game of "find the Christ figure," I am interested in, for example, how the Christ figure might be appropriated to advance or critique larger arguments about American culture.

Unlike theological criticism, mythological criticism is not necessarily anchored in a particular religious tradition. Instead, it identifies narratives of purportedly enduring, cross-cultural, even archetypal significance. The mythic realm is one of "terrifying or awe inspiring or enchanting otherness" into which the hero ventures at great personal risk, not so much for personal gain as for the benefit of others. While this definition of myth is limited and leans heavily on the work of Joseph Campbell, for instance, it has the merit of allowing another set of questions to be asked of the film text, for example: what adventure is undertaken and for whose benefit? More often than not, mythical criticism deals with films that take place, in the words of Star Wars, "a long, long time ago in a galaxy far away"; in mythical time, in other words: a realm of purported eternal verities. In the American context, to return to R. W. B. Lewis's somewhat different understanding of myth, mythical and theological elements often conspire to undergird a "secular myth" and advance a particular brand of "civil religion," which amounts to an argument concerning what is eternally true, right, good, and even "holy" about America.[16] This convergence is particularly acute in the films under scrutiny.

Ideological criticism, in contrast, is anchored in the social and political realities of the present. It functions as a parabolic critique of (or attack upon) myth, asking questions about the way race, gender, and class, for example, are represented or erased in a particular film. Thus in his examination of the first *Rocky* movie, Joel Martin downplays the ways in which Rocky appears Christlike (theological), or as a Horatio Alger-type working-class hero (mythical), and focuses on the portrayal of race tensions as they play out in the Philadelphia neighborhood where Rocky lives and as they are finally "resolved" in physical combat when Rocky meets Apollo Creed in the arena.[17]

In my course I initially keep these types of criticism apart in order to pursue the logic of each approach. But as we get deeper into a given film we inevitably discover how these various ways of approaching film complement and often contradict each other, leaving open the question of the work's final meaning. This does not mean that meaning is purely subjective. Rather, to anticipate a conversation with cultural studies, the student "links together those elements of a text which constitute not so much a unity as a configuration of meaning. Such a configuration is not absolute for all time, but it has to suggest some form of coherence or closure that can make sense to a reader in a specific historical context."[18]

The Movies Viewed from a Variety of Perspectives

The following discussion considers three films from various perspectives or angles of vision, exploring some interpretative possibilities via mythical, theological, and ideological approaches.[19] Generally speaking, mythical criticism as outlined by Martin and Ostwald allows for an interpretation that brackets the question of race altogether (at least from a dominant-culture point of view), focusing on an individual character who represents all of humanity's heroic qualities. In the American context—following especially the work of R. W. B. Lewis—this character comes to represent particularly American ideals. Theological criticism takes over the mythical story, essentially Christianizes it, and often further Americanizes it. Only with the inclusion of ideological criticism do the crucial matters of race, class, and gender force themselves into the discussion; and only after these are included can the problem of constructing a coherent configuration of meaning be addressed fully. The examples I offer here assume some familiarity with the films involved. This discussion does not pretend to offer comprehensive critiques of the films. Rather, it suggests the kinds of issues that arise in the classroom when approaching these films from multiple viewpoints with the question of religion in mind.

Purple Reign: Matriarchy and the Reconstituted Realm of God in The Color Purple

MYTHOLOGICAL PERSPECTIVE. As myth *The Color Purple* might be considered a classic hero's journey. Celie, a character "straight out of Dickens" (indeed, she learns to read with the help of *Oliver Twist*), is essentially orphaned by her ostensible father shortly after she delivers to him her second child.[20] Her encounter with the forces of evil continues and intensifies as she is handed over to Mister, a violent and unkempt man. Like Cinderella, she cleans up around the house; Mister, meanwhile, makes advances toward her more attractive sister, Nettie, or eagerly anticipates the next visit from his longtime lover, the blues singer Shug Avery. Eventually Celie discovers her true beauty through her own relationship with Shug. Self-confidence leads Celie to other discoveries, the most important of which is that her long-lost family (her children and her sister) are alive and living in Africa. This knowledge, acquired through great hardship, gives Celie the power to confront her tormentor. She ultimately returns to her ancestral home to live in a household liberated of aggressors. From the mythical point of view, then, *The Color Purple* is the story of one individual's victory over adversity and the endurance of human will. Celie is a latter-day Ulysses, in the tradition of Joyce's Leopold Bloom, who returns home at the end of the journey to reconstitute family relations and to restore domestic tranquility.

Between myth and theology stands an interpretation of this story that Paul Nathanson would call "secular myth." Following this line of interpretation, Celie resembles Dorothy in the *Wizard of Oz*. The tale takes place between the departure from, and the return to, home. In the beginning Celie, like Dorothy, is an alien in her own home; after trials and tribulations, Celie returns to an abode of bliss, having grown up in the process and become a fully actualized human being. Her heroic tale becomes a type of American success narrative, demonstrating the unlimited possibility available to all who take advantage of the freedom offered them in America through a combination of pluck and luck. In this regard the return of Celie's family at the film's end represents a new journey out of Africa, this one undertaken by choice. Ultimately America is affirmed as "home sweet home."

THEOLOGICAL PERSPECTIVE. Incorporating the insights of R. W. B. Lewis, a theological interpretation of this film views Celie as an "Adamic" hero. Her name suggests an orientation to the heavens (from *ciel*, in French: a "celestial" being). Meanwhile the names of her children invoke Eden: Adam and Olivia ("O-*live*-ia," the preacher's wife helpfully articulates, suggesting parallels to Eve, meaning "life," according to Genesis 3:20). Her theological orientation moves from other-worldly (or transcendent) to this-worldly (imminent). When we first meet her she looks up to the heavens as the voice-over intones "Dear God." A notable conversation with Shug in a field of purple flowers reorients Celie's theology to earth, so that by the end of the film a reconstituted community is gathered together in a new Eden that incorporates male and female in a radically altered social construction. In Celie's household (perhaps a prefiguration of the eschatological kingdom of God) the would-be domineering Harpo is now servant, bearing a pitcher of lemonade. This paradigm shift is achieved through a sacrifice of Christian proportions. Celie's suffering brings about this new possibility. An insider to theological debates about the doctrine of atonement can, of course, question the usefulness of specifically African American suffering for constructive theological work—as does Anthony Pinn in his notable work *Why Lord?*[21] Nevertheless, the point to be made here is that a familiar—indeed a foundational—narrative structure is in place. Thus *The Color Purple* offers an American Eve who, through the process of apotheosis as described by Lewis, becomes an American Christ—a savior, by the end, even of the wicked Mister, who repents of his evil ways and helps Adam, Olivia, and Nettie return home. Significantly, the turning point of the story occurs on Easter, when the letters of a virtually dead sister are recovered and a new spirit is resurrected in Celie.

Theological criticism might also take into account the explicit references to religion in this film. Notable here are the preacher (Shug Avery's father), Celie's conversation with Shug about God, and the general role the church plays throughout the story. Ambivalences inevitably arise. As the theological theme develops during the course of the narrative, it seems as if the institutional church is abandoned in favor of a sisterly and earthly spirituality. The story moves from Shug's observation that God gets "pissed off" when people don't notice the color purple in a field to the resurrection of family and the reconstitution of community at film's end: a reunion that takes place, significantly, in a field of purple flowers, suggesting (in accord with Shug's doctrine of God) God's presence. The church, on the other hand, seems to be a place of male power and mock weddings where overbearing males institutionalize their domination over women. Nevertheless, the story line inaugurated by Shug's relationship with her preacher father (a narrative not present in the book) undoes this critique. Her retreat from the juke joint to the church is a deferral of the blues to the gospel tune, a surrender of sisterhood, as suggested in the song "Miss Celie's Blues," to the patriarchy of "Maybe God Is Trying to Tell You Something." The return of the prodigal daughter suggests that the sinner who has soul still needs to submit to male authority after all—or the higher authority from whom he derives his authority. Thus the film presents a conflict of theologies.

IDEOLOGICAL PERSPECTIVE. In complete contrast to the prodigal daughter theme as suggested in one version of a theological interpretation, this film is, from an ideological point of view, a critique of male oppression.[22] The rape of Celie by her (step)father and her virtual enslavement by Mister form the nucleus around which a story of male cruelty is built. The oppressive system is insidious, indoctrinating its victims into a cult of violence. Thus when Harpo asks Celie how to manage his relationship with his strong-willed wife, Sophia, Celie advises him (in perhaps the most chilling moment of the entire film): "Beat her."

This virtually automatic resort to violence signals the brutality underlying the whole narrative. In typical Hollywood fashion this violence is softened, no doubt to qualify for the PG rating characteristic of a Spielberg blockbuster production. While this commercial concession shelters children from scenes of vicious brutality, it also hides real violence or even turns it into a laughing matter. After Celie advises Harpo to beat Sophia, for example, a domestic dispute occurs off-screen, followed by jokes about whether the bruises that subsequently appear upon Harpo's face were delivered by a mule or a person. Later a fight breaks out in Harpo's juke joint that resembles nothing so much as a brawl in which Popeye and Bluto might participate. Most problematic of all is the scene in which Sophia punches out the mayor after his wife harasses Sophia's children.

There are at least two ways to assess this portrait of seething violence. On the one hand, Miss Millie, the mayor's wife, is so ridiculous that she is easily dismissed as a creature of comic relief. Since the horror attributable to Miss Millie happens out of sight—namely, the lengthy imprisonment of Sophia—a disconnect occurs. The narrative, at any rate, does not seem to hold Miss Millie responsible for Sophia's sad fate, and Miss Millie seems too silly and unaware of her own actions to hold herself responsible. On the other hand, precisely because she appears ridiculous, self-centered, and inept, she is also dangerous. Indeed, even the silliest among the white folk has power over African American women of strong character and great wisdom. Meanwhile, the system that perpetuates this absurd imbalance, like Sophia's jail term, lurks in the background but forms an ever-present reality of oppression.

All That You Can't Leave Behind: Bringing and Coming Home in Daughters of the Dust

MYTHOLOGICAL PERSPECTIVE. At the center of this film is a myth of origin: the tale of how African slaves came to Ibo Landing and eventually established a home for the Peazant family. This originary myth, however, is represented in at least two different narratives. According to Nana's version, the Ibo saw the situation of slavery for all of its inhumanity as they disembarked from the slave ships, so they turned around in their chains and walked back over the water to Africa. But according to the version told by the Muslim, Bilal Muhammed, the Ibo disembarked from the ship, assessed the situation, and walked into the sea, their chains dragging them down to their deaths. In either case, both of these stories subvert the American myth, which portrays this new land as a land of infinite hope and possibility. In turning their backs on the "new land," the Ibo reject as a lie the notion that America represents the land of the free and the home of the brave; instead, they return—or die trying to return—to Africa: an alternative homeland where, according to the foundational stories, the ancestors rule.

In the circular movement of the mythical imagination, the challenge that presents itself to the Peazant family now is the same one that confronted their ancestors, the Ibo, long ago. In the words of the Clash: "should I stay or should I go?" Does the journey to the industrialized North offer a "new hope," or is the idea of the "new," so central to American mythmaking, flawed? Here one encounters the complicated (from a "Western" point of view) cosmology of West African religion. The "Unborn Child" who is about to be born to Eula and Eli comes from the ancestors. She is an "old soul" engaged in an eternal return. Contrary to American mythology (where a break from the past is made, where the past is left behind and the community ventures forth "to boldly go where no one has gone before"), the key here is to embrace, to embody, in short, to honor, the past. And so *Daughters of the Dust* both attacks the underlying assumptions of America's secular myth and offers an alternative mythology. It is a parable.

THEOLOGICAL PERSPECTIVE. Many theological concepts are presented in this film. While they are not necessarily Christian in origin (as Martin and Ostwald suggest they ought to be were this a typical Hollywood film—which, after all, it is not), their relationship to Christian modes of thought may be a useful way to investigate the deep conflict with Christianity that is at the heart of this movie. I mention here three: theodicy, the relationship to the ancestors, and syncretism.

Theodicy asks: "Why does evil happen?" This is Eli's question as he agonizes over the rape of his wife. How could the ancestors allow this to take place? And how can he, by implication, cherish the child who is to be born to them? How can he continue to live with his wife Eula after this knowledge? While theological and ideological interpretations inevitably intersect here (and the ideological contours of the situation will be discussed hereafter), the theological argument that Nana Peazant constructs is that children are gifts from the ancestors. They don't come from a specific male "seed" as it were. Eli's smashing of the bottle tree is a heretical act in this regard. He rejects the gifts and the presence (or at least, the memory) of the ancestors; it becomes his specific calling, therefore, to reconcile himself with the ancestors before leaving Ibo Island. This reconciliation does indeed occur when Eli honors the ancient carving of an African deity and, like the ancient Ibo, he too walks on water (giving credence to the originary myth of resistance as told by Nana Peazant). Perhaps on account of this scene, too, Eli, like the Ibo, rejects the "joys of the new" and chooses to stay on Ibo Landing.

The omnipresence of the ancestors is particularly pointed in the character of the Unborn Child, who wears both the indigo ribbon (sharing in the slavery past as also symbolized in Nana's clothing) and the white dress of the contemporary community. The viewers see her, as does Mr. Snead on one occasion—though she does not appear in the family photograph he subsequently takes. Nana Peazant senses her presence: for her the Unborn Child is part of the community that is alive and remembered in bottle trees and the many relics Nana carries with her in her little tin box. This notion of the presence of the ancestors (while related to some understandings of the "communion of saints" in some versions of Christianity) challenges evangelical Christian Viola's belief that people are supposed to die and go to heaven. Fully embracing the modern world and atheism, meanwhile, Hagar says that this kind of hoodoo and superstition will not be necessary in the new place to which they are traveling.

Syncretism as an intentional blending of religious traditions is represented in the "hand" that Nana Peazant makes as her final blessing to her family before they leave. It brings together elements of Africa religion and the Christian Bible and also recalls the pluralism of the island itself, with Islamic and Native American traditions represented. Surprisingly, it is not the evangelical Christian who refuses to kiss the hand and by implication acknowledge multiple religious possibilities; it is the modernist who refuses the blessing, rejecting all religions.

IDEOLOGICAL PERSPECTIVE. As the title suggests, this film is about women; indeed, unusual for Hollywood (though in common with *The Color Purple*), the film's strongest characters are almost all women. Also contrary to typical expectations, there is no particular "heroic individual" as the main character; instead this is a story about a community, indeed, an African American community. While these factors are obvious, it is important to mention them in relation to what is, perhaps, not so obvious—at least, in my experience, not so obvious to white students in particular. As in the discussion hereafter about *Being There* and the previous discussion about *The Color Purple*, I am particularly interested in the underlying presuppositions that shape what occurs onscreen. This story is shaped by violence. At the heart of it lies a tale of resistance to the system of slavery. The memory of slavery is retained throughout the film in the person of Nana Peazant. Visually it is reproduced in flashbacks to the slave times and the making of indigo dyes. Indigo then leaves its mark on Nana Peazant's hands and is dyed into her clothing. That the legacy of slavery cannot be escaped is made clear in the dress of the Unborn Child, who retains a sash of purple in her ostensibly white dress. Thus a discussion about color, about race, is displaced onto the color purple (as also in the case of the Spielberg film). But the question of color remains.

If this is a community that was formed in slavery and the need to maintain community against incredible odds (the violence that takes children away from their parents and the effort involved in naming and keeping track of those children are two examples mentioned in the film), the struggle has not ended. As already mentioned, the central dilemma facing Eli is the rape of his wife. Here violence against African American women continues to be perpetrated by men—especially, it is implied, by white men. And so Eula refuses to tell Eli who raped her because such knowledge would result in the lynching of Eli. At the beginning of the twentieth century, the commonplace of slavery is replaced by the commonplace of the lynch mob.

This reality is a challenge to the whole project of going North. This so-called "Progressive Era" is not so progressive, after all, as it applies to the lot of people of color. This truth is represented in the story of Yellow Mary. She went off in search of a better life beyond Ibo Landing, but she found only a world of white oppression and white male aggression. Significantly, then, Eli and Eula ultimately do not buy into the promise of a new life beyond Ibo

Landing; rather, they reject that promise as a lie and remain on the island when the others decide to go. This rejection is both a rejection of the American dream as told in the white history books and an embracing of African and African American traditions that provide a counter-narrative to the whole story. From the ideological point of view, *Daughters of the Dust* is a highly subversive narrative, one that forces a reconsideration of the American dream as constructed in the Hollywood dream factories and the rhetoric of politicians. Hope lies in a return to—or the retention of—the old ways. "The new" is a lie, a system of violence, an order of power *over* African Americans; it changed shape with the abolition of slavery, but it remained institutionalized in a system that privileges white power, what Gil Scott Heron, speaking politically and theologically in the late 1960s, called the white man's "God complex."

"America Ain't Shit Because the White Man's Got a God Complex": Ways of Being There

MYTHICAL PERSPECTIVE. At one level *Being There* is a typical succession narrative as described by James Frazier in his classic study of magic and religion, *The Golden Bough*.[23] The king is impotent or dying, and a new king must be found. Chauncey Gardener emerges as the one to succeed both the faltering president (references to the president's political and sexual impotence recur throughout the movie: "This never happened when you were a senator," his wife tells him on one particularly unsatisfactory evening) and the business mogul Benjamin Rand—who designates Chauncey as heir to his great fortune and surrogate to his wife, Eve. This is also a classic Horatio Alger success story, except that Chauncey's ascendancy is attributable to chance merely; in other words, this is a story about pure luck in the absence of pluck. From this point of view, a person of humble origins leaves his home in the ghetto and ultimately actualizes the American dream to become (it is implied) president of the United States. This story echoes the one told about Abe Lincoln's early years in a log cabin and anticipates the one told by Hollywood filmmakers at the Democratic Party convention in 1996 about Bill Clinton, the boy from Hope, Arkansas.

In the mode of R. W. B. Lewis, many of the elements of the story fit the American Adam pattern. The primordial gardener finds his mythical (and literal) Eve. His innocence or ignorance is perceived as a special gift or blessing (much like Billy Budd). He simply moves from one garden to another, a man without a past whose future, after a "fortunate fall" (he sprains his ankle in a chance encounter with Eve Rand's limousine) is so bright he ought to wear shades.

THEOLOGICAL PERSPECTIVE. Following Lewis's lead into a theological consideration of the film, the American Adam tends toward apotheosis, that is, he takes on God-like characteristics as the narrative progresses. In the case of Chauncey Gardener, the parallels to Jesus Christ are fairly obvious. Chauncey, a man of constant sorrow (after the Old Man died his "house" was closed down, and Chauncey was left to wander the earth alone), speaks in parables, performs miracles, appeals to persons of all classes and sexual orientations—despite, or on account of, his virginal purity—and offers salvation (indeed resurrection, that is, new life) to both the widow Eve and the dying political party that recognizes Chauncey Gardener as its one and only chance for viability. By the end of the film Chauncey's divinity seems to be confirmed: he walks on water as the president, reciting the words of Benjamin Rand, announces: "when I heard that man was created in God's image I decided to manufacture mirrors."

According to one trajectory of this theological interpretation, Chauncey Gardner is a representative of the kind of childlike innocence that opens a person to the possibility of grace. In one memorable scene, after informing Eve that he "likes to watch," Chauncey initiates Eve into the finer art of self-fulfillment. As he fiddles with the TV remote control, then moves away from her to stand on his head in the middle of the bed, Eve writhes on the bearskin rug on the floor, confirming, eventually, the adage that the kingdom of God is within you. Chauncey's walk on the water at film's end suggests both his Christ-like divinity and innocence: like Peter's initial foray onto the waters of Galilee (Matthew 14:29), Chauncey knows no fear and therefore succeeds. According to an opposing theological trajectory, Chauncey is merely a simpleton. His parables are not profound riddles or insightful metaphors; indeed, he does not use language figuratively at all but only literally, as befits a person who converses at the fourth-grade level. Accordingly, the story of Being There is really about how gullible people are in their quest for a savior (something along the lines of The Life of Brian, perhaps) or how ridiculous religious heroes are, or both.

IDEOLOGICAL PERSPECTIVE. When Chance leaves his garden home and begins his odyssey to Capitol Hill, the axis mundi of American power, he passes a wall emblazoned with graffiti that proclaims: "America ain't shit because the white man's got a God complex." The explanatory segment of the larger slogan is derived from a song by 1970s protorap artists the Last Poets. The ideological criticism I wish to pursue here (as always, there are other possible avenues of exploration) takes its cue from this theological declaration and pursues it in relation to another protorap song of the era, one that also is directly related to the nature and purposes of this film, namely: Gil Scott-Heron's "The Revolution Will Not Be Televised."[24]

The apparition of graffiti from the the Last Poets' song lasts for fewer than two seconds, suggesting, in its hasty erasure from the screen, that race is an obscured presence in the film. None of the "major" characters in the film is black, for instance. Still, the more one pursues it, the more one becomes aware of race's subtle yet significant presence throughout the film. Chauncey's only real face-to-face contact with a black person appears to be with his colleague and the Old Man's maid, Louise. Beyond this, what he knows about race he has learned by watching TV—a dubious guide at best when it comes to race relations. And so, as he bids farewell to Louise during her departure from the Old Man's house, Chauncey tips his hat and exclaims, "Yowsa"—a gesture he had recently seen performed by a black coach driver in a Shirley Temple movie on television. Chauncey repeats this gesture to a group of African American men as he wanders his neighborhood shortly after his own departure from the Old Man's home. Moments later, Chauncey sees an African American woman and, assuming she is a maid, asks her to make him a meal. Then he encounters a gang of African American youths whose manner toward him is overtly hostile. They assume he has been sent by the leader of another gang, a certain Raphael. They tell Chauncey to deliver a message to Raphael and, after his effort fails to make the boys disappear with a push of the button on his TV remote control, Chauncey agrees to deliver the message. Later in the film Chauncey meets Dr. Robert's medical assistant; since the man is black, Chauncey suspects that he must know "Raphael" and endeavors to deliver the message that has been entrusted to him. Finally, on another occasion, as he rides into the Rand estate grounds, Chauncey watches a music video (if the term is not anachronistic) on the limousine's television. Chauncey smiles as an African American cartoon character leads a rousing chorus of "Basketball Jones," the 1972 hit song written and performed by Cheech and Chong and featuring a scathing blues solo by Eric Clapton.[25]

Without venturing into a discussion about whether a white man can play the blues, it is worth noting that neither what Chauncey assumes from experience nor what he sees on television ventures beyond stereotype. "Basketball Jones" may serve as the typical example of the kinds of images of black people available to Chauncey in his media-framed existence. In this regard, I'd simply note that all the characters in this video are cartoon characters and all the major voices are the imitations of African Americans as performed by non–African Americans.

Since Chauncey Gardener's reality is almost exclusively shaped by what he sees on TV, Chauncey becomes the perfect hero in a world defined and mediated by whiteness. And so, when Louise sees Chauncey on television, repeating what she recognizes to be gobbledy-gook, she declares: "All you gotta do is be white in America and you can get whatever you want." In this case a man who is white, dresses well, says nothing to offend, and has no tainted past (indeed, as the quintessential American Adam, has no documented past at all) becomes an overnight sensation and a household name. Louise, in contrast, has disappeared into obscurity and has taken up residency in a group home. This rapid ascendancy to the halls of power is precisely what the Last Poets called the "God Complex." Indeed, it doesn't even matter if Chauncey really is a "moron" (as one subsequently dismissed advisor to the Canadian prime minister, Jean Chretien, recently called U.S. president George W. Bush) because the white men who lurk behind the scenes (the unnamed corporate leaders who carry the corpse of Rand at the film's end, for example, and Rand himself) really run the show.

As should be evident, *Being There* is an extremely ironic story about power in America. The "God complex," omnipotence—that is, overwhelming potency or power—is possessed by white males. If one pursues the angle of vision represented by the characters Robert and Louise, one perceives that Chauncey is simply a gardener and a boy. That "little thing of his," as Louise calls it, is not worth much. Robert, the doctor, understands that Chauncey really is "just a gardener." But in the imagination of his audience, who, on account of his whiteness—which is the same as his TV presence—attributes great power (not to mention intelligence) to him, Chauncey is both seducer and statesman.

From an ideological point of view, this film is all about representation. The character Chauncey Gardener represents what he sees on television. He is both a mirror reflecting back what TV offers (in this regard, Rand's comment about manufacturing mirrors is significant) and he is also the offspring of television (it apparently raised him and gave him words to speak). "The revolution will not be televised," according to Gil Scott-Heron, because television is the preserve of advertisers and other liars; it's the dominion of "[the] white tornado, white lightening and white people." In contrast to television's lies, the revolution will be real. Chauncey, TV's offspring, is not real. He should not be taken seriously.[26]

And so the film concludes with an internal critique of the media's role in manufacturing reality. It certainly appears as if Chauncey walks on water in the end, confirming his apotheosis. But as if to subvert itself, the film does not really end with this ending. Instead, there is a meta–final scene—the precursor to the hidden CD track and the precedent from which emanates all those outtakes that go on underneath the credits of subsequent TV shows and movies (compare, for irony and comic relief, *Toy Story*). Here what "really" happened is on display as Peter Sellers, the actor, attempts to deliver his lines and can't keep from laughing at the absurdity of the message for Raphael. Of course, the deeply cynical (or from another point of view, the properly educated) viewer can question whether this scene too "really" happened this way (if this footage was rescued from the cutting floor as an afterthought) or if the exchange itself was also rehearsed and intended as the ending from the start. In any case, the film bears with it a critique of the medium. It invites viewers to question what they see on-screen and to reject (or accept) manipulation.

Conclusion

"Watching" and "watchfulness" are not the same thing. As Hollywood comes more and more to define what matters in American culture and to demarcate the horizon of what can be hoped for (one thinks of the recent political success of Arnold Schwarzenegger as a case in point), it is crucial that citizens know how to think critically about the movies that provide text and texture to their lives. In this chapter I have focused on ways in which race and religion are resorted to in the storytelling and, indeed the myth-making, of three significant films. The interpretive trajectories I have outlined here are neither exhaustive nor definitive. They are indicative of the kinds of interpretations that arise in the classroom when a variety of perspectives are brought to bear on a common text. An awareness of these multiple possibilities opens students up to the contest of meaning that takes place in relation to sacred texts (among other kinds of texts) and the various religious communities that cherish those texts and derive their systems of value from them, often in very different ways. If, as Jonathan Z. Smith has argued, liberal education is *"training in argument about interpretations,"* the introduction to religious studies class as I have outlined it here offers an important first step in this training.[27]

NOTES

I am grateful for the kind assistance of many friends and colleagues in the preparation of this essay. In particular, I wish to thank the members of the "Mining the Motherlode" teaching workshop sponsored by the Lilly Endowment and later the Wabash Center, especially Will Coleman and Carolyn M. Jones—who helped me to understand *Daughters of the Dust*; the members of the Interdisciplinary Research and Writing Group at the University of Alabama; Russell T. McCutcheon and James Hall, both of whom critiqued this work at an early stage of writing; and three additional "Canadians": Catherine Roach, Paul Nathanson, and Angus Cleghorn.

   1. Mark W. Muesse, "Religious Studies and 'Heaven's Gate': Making the Strange Familiar and the Familiar Strange," *Chronicle of Higher Education* 43, 33 (April 25, 1997); B6; reprinted in *The Insider/Outsider Problem in the Study of Religion*, Russell T. McCutcheon, ed. (New York: Cassell, 1999), 390.

   2. T. S. Eliot, "Little Gidding," in *Four Quartets*, in *The Complete Poems and Plays* (New York: Harcourt and Brace, 1971), 145; Joni Mitchell, "Both Sides Now," *Clouds*, Reprise Records, 1969.

   3. The latter definition has been promulgated recently by the former Alabama Supreme Court Chief Justice Roy S. Moore in his editorial "In God I Trust," *Wall Street Journal*, August 25, 2003, A10. I introduce students to the issue of definition by presenting them with selections from a variety of introduction to religion texts, including, for example, Gary E. Kessler, *Studying Religion* (Boston: McGraw-Hill, 2003); James C. Livingston, *Anatomy of the Sacred*, 3rd ed. (Upper Saddle River, NJ: Prentice

Hall, 1998); and Roger Schmidt, *Exploring Religion*, 2nd ed. (Belmont, CA: Wadsworth, 1988).

4. The phrase is taken from Herman C. Waetjen, *A Reordering of Power: A Socio-Political Reading of Mark's Gospel* (Minneapolis: Fortress, 1988), 63. Waetjen develops his hermeneutic in part with reference to Wolfgang Iser, *The Act of Reading: A Theory of Aesthetic Response* (Baltimore: Johns Hopkins University Press, 1980).

5. Diana L. Eck, *Darshan: Seeing the Divine Image in India*, 2nd ed. (Chambersburg, PA: Anima, 1985) 10, quoting Jan Gonda, *The Vision of the Vedic Poets* (The Hague: Mouton, 1963), 25. See also the helpful introduction to Eck's text with particular emphasis upon the relation between *darshan* and visual culture in S. Brent Plate, ed., *Religion, Art, and Visual Culture* (New York: Palgrave, 2002), 161–170.

6. In addition to the works discussed hereafter, students read David Chidester, "The Church of Baseball, the Fetish of Coca-Cola, and the Potlach of Rock 'n' Roll: Theoretical Models for the Study of Religion in American Popular Culture, *Journal of the American Academy of Religion* 64, 4 (fall 1996): 743–765, and Michele Wallace, "Negative Images: Toward a Black Feminist Cultural Criticism," in Lawrence Grossberg, ed., *Cultural Studies* (New York: Routledge, 1991), 654–671.

7. R. W. B. Lewis, *The American Adam: Innocence, Tragedy, and Tradition in the Nineteenth Century* (Chicago: University of Chicago Press, 1955). Without specific reference to Lewis, Burton Mack pursues a similar theme in his study of the Gospel of Mark. For his discussion of the "myth of innocence" and its particular relevance in relation to American national identity see Burton L. Mack, *A Myth of Innocence: Mark on Christian Origins* (Minneapolis: Fortress, 1991), especially 370–376.

8. Lewis, *American Adam*, 5.

9. Chuck Berry, "Johnny B. Goode," Chess Records, 1957; Stevie Wonder, "Living for the City," *Innervisions*, Motown, 1973; Joni Mitchell, *Hejira*, Asylum Records, 1976; and Steve Earle, "John Walker's Blues," *Jerusalem*, Artemis Records, 2002.

10. The concept, derived from Joseph Campbell's "classical monomyth" in *The Hero with a Thousand Faces* (New York: Meridian, 1930), is developed by Robert Jewett and John Shelton Lawrence, *The American Monomyth*, 2nd ed. (New York: University Press of America, 1988; originally published 1977); see also John Shelton Lawrence and Robert Jewett, *The Myth of the American Superhero* (Grand Rapids, MI: Eerdmans, 2002) and Robert Jewett and John Shelton Lawrence, *Captain America and the Crusade against Evil* (Grand Rapids, MI: Eerdmans, 2003).

11. John Dominic Crossan, *The Dark Interval: Toward a Theology of Story* (Sonoma, CA: Polebridge, 1988; originally published 1975), 32–45. A recent adaptation of Crossan's method is offered in Walter T. Davis, Jr., *Watching What We Watch: Prime Time Television Through the Lens of Faith* (Louisville, KY: Geneva, 2001), xv–xvi.

12. bell hooks, *Reel to Real: Race, Sex, and Class at the Movies* (New York: Routledge, 1996), 3.

13. Along this line, see "Redescribing 'Religion and . . . ' Film: Teaching the Insider/Outsider Problem," in Russell T. McCutcheon, *Critics Not Caretakers: Redescribing the Public Study of Religion* (New York: State University of New York Press, 2001), 179–199, especially 187.

14. Joel W. Martin and Conrad E. Ostwald Jr., eds., *Screening the Sacred: Religion, Myth, and Ideology in Popular American Film* (Boulder, CO: Westview, 1995), 5. See

also Daniel L. Pals, "Is Religion a Sui Generis Phenomenon?" *Journal of the American Academy of Religion* 55, 2 (spring 1987): 278. While there is a circular quality to this definition of religion, it does have the merit of anchoring religious activity in culture.

15. Martin and Ostwald, *Screening the Sacred,* 14.

16. The "secular myth of America" is examined with great acuity in Paul Nathanson, *Over the Rainbow: The Wizard of Oz as a Secular Myth of America* (New York: State University of New York Press, 1991). For recent developments indebted to Nathanson's groundbreaking work see Conrad Ostwald, Jr., *Secular Steeples: Popular Culture and the Religious Imagination* (Harrisburg, PA: Trinity, 2003).

17. See Joel W. Martin, "Redeeming America: *Rocky* as Ritual Racial Drama," in Martin and Ostwald, *Screening the Sacred,* 125–133.

18. Patrick McGee, *Cinema, Theory, and Political Responsibility in Contemporary Culture,* (Cambridge, England: Cambridge University Press, 1997), 24.

19. This approach resembles the "lenses of interpretation" advanced by Davis in *Watching What We Watch.* Davis's ultimate purpose, appropriate for the seminary context, is theological and is summarized in the book's subtitle: "prime-time television through the lens of faith." In the context of a publicly funded liberal arts college, I do not advance this particular approach over others.

20. Fleeber, the film professor in *The Freshman,* mocks the Hollywood convention of the orphaned, diminutive hero in his conversation with that film's youthful hero: "Oh, this is straight out of Dickens: street urchin, wicked stepfather." Dorothy, in the *Wizard of Oz,* participates in the same typology. In other words, myth as type becomes (lucrative commercial) stereotype.

21. Anthony B. Pinn, *Why Lord? Suffering and Evil in Black Theology* (New York: Continuum, 1999).

22. Paul Nathanson and Katherine K. Young describe *The Color Purple* as the prototype of "misandry"—that is, hatred of things male—in American cinema. I would point to the negative portrayal of Miss Millie and the changed character of Harpo and Mister in contrast to their hardened dualistic reading of the film, but certainly they offer a careful and nuanced reading. See *Spreading Misandry: The Teaching of Contempt for Men in Popular Culture* (Montreal: McGill-Queens University, 2001), 13–17.

23. See chapter 24, "The Killing of the Divine King," especially sec. 2, "Kings Killed When Their Strength Fails," in James George Frazer, *The Golden Bough,* abr. ed. (New York: Simon and Schuster, 1996; originally published 1922), 309–318.

24. Alafia Pudim, "White Man's Got a God Complex," the Last Poets, *This Is Madness,* Douglas Records, 1971, and Gil Scott Heron, "The Revolution Will Not Be Televised," *Pieces of a Man,* Flying Dutchman Records, 1971.

25. Cheech Martin and Tommy Chong, "Basketball Jones," *Los Cochinos,* Warner Brothers Records, 1973.

26. As a skillful critique of the media and especially television, *Being There* stands in a noble tradition that includes both Sidney Lumet's *Network* (1976) and Spike Lee's *Bamboozled* (2000).

27. Jonathan Z. Smith, "The Introductory Course: Less Is Better," in *Teaching the Introductory Course in Religious Studies: A Sourcebook,* Mark Juergensmeyer, ed. (Atlanta: Scholars Press, 1991), 188. Italics in original.

REFERENCES

Asby, Hal, dir. *Being There*. Perf. Peter Sellers and Shirley MacLaine. Warner Brothers, 1979.

Bergman, Andrew, dir. *The Freshman*. Perf. Marlon Brando and Matthew Broderick. Columbia/TriStar, 1990.

Berry, Chuck. "Johnny B. Goode." Chess Records, 1957.

Chidester, David. "The Church of Baseball, the Fetish of Coca-Cola, and the Potlach of Rock 'n' Roll: Theoretical Models for the Study of Religion in American Popular Culture. *Journal of the American Academy of Religion* 64, 4 (1996): 743–765.

Crossan, John Dominic. *The Dark Interval: Toward a Theology of Story*. Sonoma, CA: Polebridge, 1988.

Dash, Julie, dir. *Daughters of the Dust*. Perf. Cora Lee Day and Alva Rogers. Kino Studio, 1991.

Davis, Walter T., Jr., Teresa Blythe, Gary Dreibelbis, Mark Scalese, S.J., Elizabeth Winans Winslea, and Donald L. Ashburn. *Watching What We Watch: Prime Time Television through the Lens of Faith*. Louisville, KY: Geneva, 2001.

Doty, William. *Mythography: The Study of Myths and Rituals*. 2nd ed. Tuscaloosa: University of Alabama Press, 2002.

Eck, Diana L. Darsan: *Seeing the Divine Image in India*, 2nd ed. Chambersburg, PA: Anima, 1985.

Earle, Steve. "John Walker's Blues." *Jerusalem*. Artemis Records, 2002.

Eliot, T. S. *The Complete Poems and Plays*. New York: Harcourt Brace, 1971.

Frazer, James George. *The Golden Bough*. Abr. ed. New York: Simon and Schuster, 1996.

Heron, Gil Scott. "The Revolution Will Not Be Televised." *Pieces of a Man*. Flying Dutchman Records, 1971.

hooks, bell. *Reel to Real: Race, Sex, and Class at the Movies*. New York: Routledge, 1996.

Iser, Wolfgang. *The Act of Reading: A Theory of Aesthetic Response*. Baltimore: Johns Hopkins University Press, 1980.

Jewett, Robert, and John Shelton Lawrence. *The American Monomyth*. 2nd ed. New York: University Press of America, 1988.

———. *Captain America and the Crusade against Evil*. Grand Rapids, MI: Eerdmans, 2003.

Juergensmeyer, Mark, ed. *Teaching the Introductory Course in Religious Studies: A Sourcebook*. Atlanta: Scholars Press, 1991.

Lawrence, John Shelton, and Robert Jewett. *The Myth of the American Superhero*. Grand Rapids, MI: Eerdmans, 2002.

Lee, Spike, dir. *Bamboozled*. Perf. Damon Wayans and Savion Glover. New Line Cinema, 2000.

Lewis, R. W. B. *The American Adam*. Chicago: University of Chicago Press, 1955.

Lumet, Sidney, dir. *Network*. Perf. William Holden and Faye Dunaway. Warner Studios, 1976.

Lyden, John C. *Film as Religion: Myths, Morals, and Religion*. New York: New York University Press, 2003.

Mack, Burton L. *A Myth of Innocence: Mark on Christian Origins*. Minneapolis: Fortress, 1991.

Martin, Cheech, and Tommy Chong. "Basketball Jones." *Los Cochinos*. Warner Brothers Records, 1973.

Martin, Joel W., and Conrad E. Ostwald Jr., eds. *Screening the Sacred: Religion, Myth, and Ideology in Popular American Film*. Boulder, CO: Westview Press, 1995.

McCutcheon, Russell T., ed. *The Insider/Outsider Problem in the Study of Religion*. New York: Cassell, 1999.

McCutcheon, Russell T. *Critics Not Caretakers: Redescribing the Public Study of Religion*. New York: State University of New York Press, 2001.

McGee, Patrick. *Cinema, Theory, and Political Responsibility in Contemporary Culture*. Cambridge, England: Cambridge University Press, 1997.

Mitchell, Joni. "Both Sides Now." *Clouds*. Reprise Records, 1969.

———. *Hejira*. Asylum Records, 1976.

Moore, Roy S. "In God I Trust." *Wall Street Journal*, August 25, 2003: A10.

Muesse, Mark W. "Religious Studies and 'Heaven's Gate': Making the Strange Familiar and the Familiar Strange." *Chronicle of Higher Education* 43, 33 (April 25, 1997): B6.

Nathanson, Paul. *Over the Rainbow: The Wizard of Oz as a Secular Myth of America*. New York: State University of New York Press, 1991.

Nathanson, Paul, and Katherine K. Young. *Spreading Misandry: The Teaching of Contempt for Men in Popular Culture*. Montreal: McGill-Queens University Press, 2001.

Ostwald, Conrad, Jr. *Secular Steeples: Popular Culture and the Religious Imagination*. Harrisburg, PA: Trinity Press International, 2003.

Pals, Daniel L. "Is Religion a Sui Generis Phenomenon?" *Journal of the American Academy of Religion* 55, 2 (1978): 274–286.

Pinn, Anthony B. *Why Lord? Suffering and Evil in Black Theology*. New York: Continuum, 1999.

Plate, S. Brent, ed. *Religion, Art, and Visual Culture*. New York: Palgrave, 2002.

Pudim, Alafia. "White Man's Got a God Complex." The Last Poets, *This Is Madness*. Douglas Records, 1971.

Smith, Jonathan Z. "The Introductory Course: Less Is Better." In *Teaching the Introductory Course in Religious Studies: A Sourcebook*, Mark Juergensmeyer, ed., 185–192. Atlanta: Scholars Press, 1991.

Spielberg, Stephen, dir. *The Color Purple*. Perf. Whoopi Goldberg, Oprah Winfrey, and Danny Glover. Paramount, 1985.

Waetjen, Herman C. *A Reordering of Power: A Socio-Political Reading of Mark's Gospel*. Minneapolis: Fortress, 1988.

Wallace, Michele. "Negative Images: Toward a Black Feminist Cultural Criticism." In *Cultural Studies*, Lawrence Grossberg, Cary Nelson, and Paula Treichler, eds., 654–671. New York: Routledge, 1991.

Wonder, Stevie. "Living for the City." *Innervisions*. Motown, 1973.

Afterword: Teaching the Religion behind the Veil

Emilie M. Townes

How does one teach the religious worlds of darker-skinned people behind the veil within the United States? This reference to "the veil" is drawn from the work of W. E. B. Du Bois in his flawed but brilliant masterpiece *The Souls of Black Folk* (1903). The veil is a metaphor for the hegemonic forces of White oppressive ideology, scholarship, and practices that force a bordered world for the darker-skinned people who live their lives behind it. This two-way barrier obscures on the one hand and seeks to establish respite on the other hand. The quality of this contest—a power dance—has within it the religious lives of Black folk in North America. It is a life that is one of pathos and ecstasy, trial and triumph, sacred and profane. These, however, are not antagonistic dualisms. No, the religious traditions of Black peoples in the United States are worlds that embrace such dialectical relationships as natural and, if done and lived well, they are healthy hermeneutical probatives concerning the religious traditions of Blacks in the United States.

This presents a peculiar set of challenges for those who would teach (and seek to learn about) the nature of the religious in U.S. blackface. For as Du Bois reminds us, the relationship is not solely located in the United States. This is a relationship that, in his words, is "of the darker to the lighter races of men in Asia and Africa, in American and islands of the sea."[1] In what Du Bois describes as his "sketch, in vague, uncertain outline, the spiritual world in which ten thousand Americans live and strive," he is clear that Asia, Africa, and the Caribbean are key in understanding the worlds of Black folks in the United States—material *and* spiritual.[2] Hence, considering how to learn and teach African American religious traditions is an exercise that requires one to develop skills in decoding a mammoth cultural world, a world that *is* behind a veil drawn by a shared history of wearying oppression as well as moments of justice.

The year-long workshop that birthed this collection was a multilayered dance among issues of pedagogy, self-critical learning, and consciousness-raising, as the participants and the staff sought to explore dimensions of the world behind the veil. This was not always an easy workshop experience, as the reader will be able to judge from the breadth of the essays in this collection and the careful attention each person has given to his or her own learning as well as thinking through how students learn. The material, on one level, is relatively simple: an examination of the ways in which Black folk in the United States experience the religious. It was also extremely complex: *how* Black folk experience the religious in the United States.

The latter emphasis demanded that *each* participant make an ongoing commitment to take and maintain a personal inventory of the ways he or she is or is not aware of how African Americans have been and remain a critical sylph within U.S. history and life and the peculiar ways in which this awareness (or the lack thereof) plays itself out within the nature of the religious. One sees glimpses of this arduous, but necessary, scholarly task throughout the essays, as each participant is also very concerned with how to engage African American students, in particular, and all students, in general, in the study of African American religious traditions.

The study of the nature of the religious as it weaves in and out of various cultures has never been a neutral thing. We always bring our baggage with us, no matter how scholarly and rigorous our "methods," as we endeavor to gain access to, and understanding of, what this thing "religion" is. Appropriately, the authors have narrowed their task to look at religious traditions. Some will (rightly, in my opinion!) argue that this is trading one gigantic playfield for another equally large one. However, I find that this focusing exercise helps the authors point to the many ways in which tradition and traditions live; they are not embalmed. Moreover, in doing so, they help teachers and students understand that the study of religion will always be a dynamic and reflexive enterprise as much as it is reflective. Here, we have focused on how this manifests itself within Black lives in the United States.

What should become immediately apparent as one surveys the essays in this book is the fact that Black religious life is a rich and complex mosaic in which no one faith tradition or group can capture what it means when we use the term "African American religion." Although the list is long of texts that examine areas of African American religions—a much-needed project of retrieval that is ongoing to be sure—this is the first time that a multiracial and ethnic group of teachers and scholars have struggled to understand how it is that we teach this vast body of knowledge and experience.

This books steps squarely into recent debates as to whether there is such a thing as African American religious studies, responding with a decided "yes" to the query. Mining the motherlode of Black religious traditions requires a penchant for the interdisciplinary, however. True enough, each author has her or his own area of expertise within the religious disciplines—including anthropology, education, ethics, history, popular culture, religion and literature, theology, and sociology. However the reader will note that the writers are drawn to other disciplines to open up just how, through the lens of their primary discipline, Black folk are doing, thinking, feeling, performing, and making "the religious": attesting to, and transforming, the traditions in their lives.

The study of African American religious traditions is often compromised by stereotypes that abound in our popular culture (and in what passes, for some, as scholarship). Students (and often their professors) are flummoxed by the study of these traditions because the scope of the material is considerably more complex and wide-ranging than the stereotypes allow. Rather than dumbing down African American religious experience to a set of practices that are confined by the "smallnesses" of our imaginations, the authors help us see how profoundly beautiful rigorous considerations of the religious traditions can be as they spring from and are played out on Black bodies. This volume, then, serves as a model for how to unfold the stories of any group with profound cultural and aesthetic markers; the emphasis need not be on the racial or ethnic, but rather on situating a people distinctively in the social and religious worlds found within the United States—and elsewhere.

The authors offer both theoretical musings and practical pedagogical methods to assist teachers who seek to engage students in the complexities of how to teach what one does not know, thinks one knows, or hopes one knows how to know. In short, there are no assumptions about "expertness" based on existential or essential realities and the hard side of living. Rather, the study of African American religious traditions means that all who engage it and then seek to teach it must remember that there is *always* much more to be known under the sun—the ever-presence of the veil assures us of this. I count myself privileged to have been a leader and a learner in this project. The authors here taught me more than they will ever know, as we each picked up our pickaxes looking for yet another rich vein of knowledge about how the numinous presents itself where it will.

NOTES

1. W. E. B. Du Bois, *The Souls of Black Folk*, Henry Louis Gates, Jr., and Terri Hume Oliver, eds., Norton Critical Edition (New York: Norton, 1999; originally published 1903), 17.

2. Ibid., 5.

Index